Michael Carroll was born in England but spent much of his early life in India. He is the author of *From a Persian Tea House* and *An Island in Greece* (both Tauris Parke Paperbacks). He is married with four children and divides his time between Sussex and the Greek islands.

Greece

A LITERARY GUIDE FOR TRAVELLERS

Michael Carroll

I.B. TAURIS

LONDON · NEW YORK

Published in 2017 by
I.B.Tauris & Co. Ltd
London • New York
www.ibtauris.com

ISBN: 978 1 78453 380 9
eISBN: 978 1 78672 288 1
ePDF: 978 1 78673 288 0

A full CIP record for this book is available from the British Library
A full CIP record is available from the Library of Congress

Library of Congress Catalog Card Number: available

Typeset by JCS Publishing Services Ltd
Printed and bound in Sweden by ScandBook AB

MIX
Paper from
responsible sources
FSC   FSC® C007584
www.fsc.org

CONTENTS

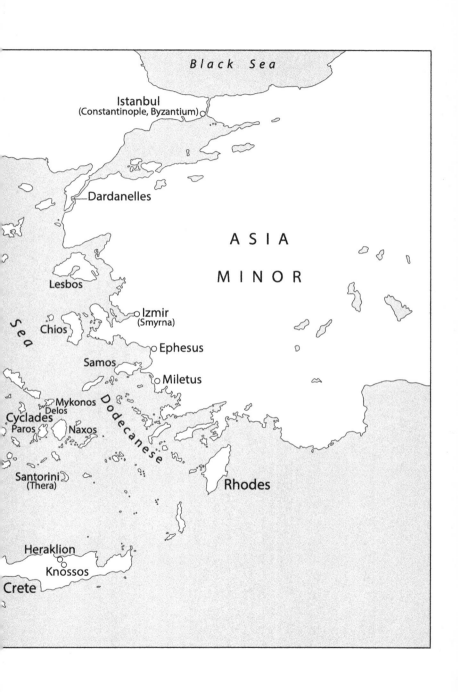

Black Sea

Istanbul
(Constantinople, Byzantium)

Dardanelles

ASIA

MINOR

Lesbos

Sea

Chios

Izmir
(Smyrna)

Ephesus

Samos

Miletus

Mykonos
Delos
Cyclades
Paros
Naxos

Dodecanese

Santorini
(Thera)

Rhodes

Heraklion
Knossos
Crete

INTRODUCTION

A principal source of Western culture and the origin of much of its literature, art, science and philosophy is a small, mountainous sea-girt country in south-eastern Europe. Myths and legends of Greece remain embedded in the unconscious of Western peoples and it is extraordinary that so many of the names of Greek gods, goddesses and heroes, and the sacred places where they were worshipped long ago, still resonate today.

Greece has been called the land of lost gods, and one of the reasons that many of us go there, besides the expectation of sunshine and blue sea, is to make contact with a past we have inherited, that we feel belongs to us. This book aims to help the visitor do just that, by drawing on a wide variety of writers, from ancient times to the present, alike only in their powerful engagement with Greece and their fascination with all things Greek.

Physically, Greece has changed little over the centuries. The rocky, herb-scented mountains still look down on valleys silver-green with olive groves, their slopes scattered with white-walled villages. Thanks to the care and patience of archaeologists, we can walk among the ruins of places famous from long ago; Homer's 'wine-dark' sea can still be admired from the shores of numerous islands, from the deck of a ferryboat, yacht or simple caique, or from behind the curtained glass of a speeding hydrofoil.

Greece has the longest written history of any country in Europe. After the classic periods of Athens and Sparta, the famous wars against Persia, the victories of Alexander the Great, came gradual decline. The city-states of Greece became subject to the Roman

Empire (which in turn surrendered to Greek culture). Invasions by Slavic tribes were followed by Franks, Venetians and Ottoman Turks; the last two centuries have seen independence from the Ottoman Empire, wars in the Balkans, disaster in Asia Minor, occupation in World War II followed by years of bitter civil strife; the Colonels; and the country's present economic woes ... I hope that the voices of the writers quoted in these pages will help to bridge the centuries and make for a better understanding of Greece's sensational and often tragic past.

Many of those who came in the last few centuries did so in pursuit of the ideals of artistic perfection achieved in the sculpture, architecture and art of ancient Greece or, inspired by its famous past as the fountainhead of democracy, to help the Greeks fight for freedom from the Ottoman Turks. More recently they came to escape the suffocation of convention, or the eroding tide of materialism, many to learn from Greek ideals of simplicity and moderation, and to acquire that condition of Delphic wisdom – the ability to know yourself; some came simply to capture the sense of freedom and exhilaration that being in Greece, like a fever, can bring on.

On this literary journey through Greece most of our companions are British and American, from Lugless Willie of Lanarkshire describing his 'painefull' adventures in the seventeenth century – wrecked once again in the Aegean – to Mark Twain breaking Greek quarantine laws in his nocturnal bid to visit the Acropolis; from Lawrence Durrell and his brother Gerald and family in Corfu to Edward Lear and Osbert Lancaster as they sketch and paint across mountain and sea; Patrick Leigh Fermor as he dines waist-deep off the beach at Kalamata or captures a German general as a resistance fighter in Crete; Mary Renault making notes at Delphi as *The Mask of Apollo* forms in her imagination, and Lord Byron as he jokes about dying 'martially' in Missolonghi just before he catches the marsh fever that kills him; and Rupert Brooke, who finds his foreign field on the island of Skyros.

And always, powerful in the background, the great poets of old Greece – the blind bard Homer, and Archilochus and Sappho; the first historians Herodotus and Thucydides, and the playwrights Aeschylus and Euripides: their voices come clear across the centuries; to all of them we owe so much.

I hope this book will accompany a visitor on his travels, but will equally be enjoyed from an armchair at home. Its aim is to enrich the reader's experience of Greece present and past, by seeing the country, temples, towns, seas and mountains through the eyes of writers and travellers whose views from earlier times and in different circumstances can be sometimes provocative and always entertaining.

I am greatly indebted to the many distinguished writers – poets, biographers, classicists, art critics – whose books I have drawn on so extensively: their names are listed in the Bibliography. I can strongly recommend their works for further reading. I owe Charles Seltman, classicist and art historian, Fellow of Queen's College, Cambridge, a special debt for introducing me to Greece. He did this not by taking me there, but simply by talking with such enthusiasm about this country and its people that he loved so much. I was privileged to be one of the undergraduates always welcome to drop in at any time of day at his cottage in Little St Mary's Lane. A bottle of retsina was regularly uncorked soon after breakfast, and a tray with little glasses indicated to visitors as soon as they entered. Charles would be sitting in his customary place, upright in an armchair strong enough to take his weight, white-haired and with a goatee beard jutting out from his impressively Silenian features. In a university founded on the teaching of Classics, there was no shortage of dons who admired Greece – but their devotion was mainly to Classical Greece and its citizens of two thousand years ago, not modern Greeks, whom many considered inconsequential interlopers whose connections with that distant and sacred past were obscure or non-existent. Charles was different: he liked and admired the Greeks of today.

At the time I knew him he was the world authority on ancient Greek coins and had several scholarly publications to his name. But he wanted to draw the attention of a much wider public to Greece and its past and had begun to write non-academic books for a more general readership: *The Twelve Olympians* (1952), *Women in Antiquity* (1956), *Wine in the Ancient World* (1957). To the surprise of some of his peers, these works were successful and, further shock, were brought out in paperback and translated into many languages. Some of his books were controversial; all were witty and entertaining and achieved what their author intended.

To undergraduates making their first journey to Greece, his advice was electric and inspiring. 'Delphi! Climb Parnassus, of course! I'll write you a note for Manoli, he'll take you up to the Corycian Cave, then to the top … he's getting on a bit, like I am … but he'll look after you.' Scribbled notes to old colleagues at the British School at Athens, names of tavernas, hints on wine (under lowered brows, 'I see you've learned to like retsina already …').

Terence Spencer in *Fair Greece Sad Relic* (1954) points out that while ancient Greece has always been respected for its dramatic cultural achievements, 'modern' Greeks have usually been disparaged by Western Europeans, an attitude initiated by the Romans and carried on through St Paul to Christian times, into the seventeenth century and beyond:

> It is difficult to think of any other people who, having fallen so low, rose again to achieve liberty and a respected place in civilization. They were despised by their nearest Latin neighbours as schismatics. They were degraded, humiliated, and inhumanly oppressed (by the Turks); and they were victims of a hateful tax on their children. It is not for any nation, which has not endured long centuries of foreign and non-Christian oppression, to condemn the Grecian nation, in a past century or in the present. They remained

faithful to their religion, to their language, and to the memory of their ancestors, although civilized Europe felt no responsibility on their behalf.

Those sentiments are relevant today.

One of many English men and women who found Greece and the Greeks a revelation was Patrick Leigh Fermor, who wrote in *Roumeli* (1966) that as a young man he identified 'a direct and immediate link, friendly and equal on either side, between human beings, something that melts barriers of hierarchy and background and money'. For Greeks, he discovered:

> existence [...] is a torment, an enemy, an adventure and a joke which we are in league to undergo, outwit, exploit and enjoy on equal terms as accomplices, fellow-hedonists and fellow-victims. A stranger begins to realize that the armour which has been irking him and the arsenal he has been lugging about for half a life-time are no longer needed. Miraculous lightness takes their place.

Richard Stoneman ends his *Land of Lost Gods* (1994) reflecting on the conundrum of why Greece is still so important to us:

> The ideal of Greece no longer holds sway, yet Greece, somehow, for better or for worse, will not go away. It is the seeking for our own roots, our own reflection, in that landscape of spectacular beauty and fierce nakedness, that draws us back [...] The totality of landscape that gave birth to the Greek gods, to Western art, philosophy and politics, to our dreams and passions and our incurable nostalgia, will always lure us on to discovery and reflection.

He goes on to quote from Edmund Keeley and Philip Sherrard's translation of *Mythistorema* (1935) by Nobel Prize-winner George Seferis:

> We who set out on this pilgrimage
> looked at the broken statues
> we became distracted and said life is not so easily lost
> that death has unexplored paths
> and its own particular justice;
>
> that while we, still upright on are feet, are dying,
> become brothers in stone
> united in hardness and weakness,
> the ancient dead have escaped the circle and risen again
> and smile in a strange silence.

Edmund Keeley in his *Inventing Paradise* (2002) wrote that Greek poets have 'the advantage of a landscape and a history in which mortals and immortals once appeared to have lived naturally side by side for generations'. Thanks to the writers and poets of the past, we too can become, for a moment, part of that fabled landscape and dramatic past.

1

IONIAN ISLANDS
AND EPIRUS

A Greekish isle, and the most pleasant place that ever our eyes beheld for
the exercise of a solitary and contemplative life [...] In our travels many
times, falling into dangers and unpleasant places, this only island would
be the place where we would wish to end our lives.

(Anthony Sherley, *His Persian Adventure*, 1601)

Approaching Greece from the west, across the sea to Corfu from
Italy, was the old way, and still to me the best. From the late 1950s
and for the next 30 summers or so a growing flood of young people,
many of them students, travelled south by train down to the heel of
Italy, boarded a ferryboat at the port of Brindisi, paid deck-class fare
and took the overnight voyage to another world.

Those romantic or impecunious enough to have travelled to
Greece this way will remember something of that night, may
recall leaning over a varnished wooden taff-rail crusty with salt,
face stroked by the warm flow of air, staring down at the dark
sea foaming past, the moon's reflection trailed in silver across
the waves. Later, lying on deck, dozing fitfully to the drum and
judder of ship's engines, who can forget the sour perfume of paint
and diesel, the brilliance of stars so many and so close? Or being
woken later by an almost imperceptible change in the star-fading
sky, stumbling forward over recumbent bodies, hearing the hiss
of bow wave cutting through a magically calm sea, peering ahead
into the dimness. There they were, at first only shadows, misty

shapes, gathering before one's eyes and forming into grey outlines:
the mountains of Albania and Epirus, Corfu and the islands, their
dark profiles slowly hardening against the rose-pink dawn. And
perhaps, if you were lucky, you made your way back across the
deck to kneel beside her, lips brushing dew-damp, tousled hair:
'Come and see *this!*'

Lawrence Durrell felt the magic of approaching Greece from the
west. He wrote in *Prospero's Cell* (1945):

> Somewhere between Calabria and Corfu the blue really begins...
> you are aware of a change in the heart of things: aware of the
> horizon beginning to stain at the rim of the world: aware of *islands*
> coming out of the darkness to meet you [...] You are aware not so
> much of a landscape coming to meet you across those blue miles of
> water as of a climate. You enter Greece as one might enter a dark
> crystal; the form of things becomes irregular, refracted. Mirages
> suddenly swallow islands, and wherever you look the trembling
> curtain of the atmosphere deceives.

Durrell was 23 when he first stepped ashore at Corfu, a poet and
writer on course to finding his own voice. 'Other countries', he
wrote, 'may offer you discoveries in manners or lore or landscape;
Greece offers you something harder – the discovery of yourself.'

Since the end of the Napoleonic wars, Britain had occupied Corfu
and the other Ionian Islands, ceding them to the new Greek nation
in 1864. Lawrence Durrell chose to ignore the benefits 50 years
of British rule gave to the islands. For him, besides road-building
and provision of a water supply to the town of Corfu, few traces of
British rule remained. Except of course for cricket – 'a mysterious
and satisfying ritual which the islanders have refused to relinquish'.
Today the game is still played enthusiastically by the Corfiots
among themselves and against visiting teams from England. And
yet Durrell enjoyed calling up ghosts of the past:

The discreet picnics among the olive groves, the memoranda, the protocols, the bustles, side-whiskers, long top-boots, tea-cosies, mittens, rock-cakes, chutney, bolus, dignity, incompetence, book-keeping, virtue, church bazaars; you will find traces of all of them if you look deeply enough. The flash of red hunting coats through the olive groves as the officers galloped over the island on their dangerous paper-chases; the declarations of love among the cypresses, the red-faced sportsmen setting off for Albania.

The Durrell family of mother, Louisa, whose husband had died recently in India, and their four children – Lawrence, Leslie, Margot and Gerald, the youngest, aged ten – arrived on the island of Corfu in 1935, mainly at the instigation of Lawrence, who had already determined to be a writer, but also because all of them, after years in India, found the gloom and grey of the English climate deeply depressing and felt inhibited by the formality and social reserve of their fellow countrymen. The money left by the father seemed enough for the family to move to Corfu, a place much praised by a writer friend of Lawrence and where living was inexpensive.

Their life on the island is best described by Gerald Durrell in *My Family and Other Animals* (1956). Although written many years later, it remains a convincing story from a boy's point of view, full of humour, expressive portraits of people and animals, and loving descriptions of the scenery of the island as it was before World War II.

Gerald had been interested – his family would say obsessed – with animals and all small living creatures since a young child. For a ten-year old, the garden of the house the family rented:

was a magic land, a forest of flowers through which roamed creatures I had never seen before. Among the thick, silky petals of each rose bloom lived tiny, crablike spiders that scuttled sideways when disturbed. Their small, translucent bodies were coloured to match the flowers they inhabited: pink, ivory, wine-red or buttery

> yellow. On the rose stems, encrusted with green flies, lady-birds moved like newly painted toys [...] Carpenter bees like furry electric-blue bears, zigzagged among the flowers, growling flatly and busily. Humming bird hawk-moths, sleek and neat, whipped up and down the paths with a fussy efficiency, pausing occasionally on speed-misty wings to lower a long, slender proboscis into a bloom. Among the white cobbles large black ants staggered and gesticulated in groups round strange trophies: a dead caterpillar, or piece of rose petal or a dried grass-head fat with seeds. As an accompaniment to all this activity there came from the olive groves outside the fuchsia hedge the incessant shimmering cries of the cicadas.

Running free with his dog in the hills and olive groves sloping down to the shore, he wandered with his collection boxes, observing with growing fascination the myriad life forms that flourished in the vegetation, under stones, in the earth and in the pools and shallows of the sea. He brought home the living treasures he had found – the family moved twice during their five years on Corfu – storing them in boxes, on shelves and in cupboards in his room and when space ran out in other places he could find round the house. His interest was always in living animals: 'Live with living things, don't just peer at them in a pool of alcohol.' He was to follow this principle from the very beginning, and as Douglas Botting in his biography *Gerald Durrell* (1999) remarks, his family were to find this out soon enough. The discovery by unsuspecting family members of snakes in the bath and toads under the bed resulted in disasters and confusion, stories lightheartedly told in *My Family and Other Animals* of life on the island for this eccentric but delightful family.

Gerald's passionate interest in all creatures great and small was allowed full expression in this paradise of an island, and provided the foundation for the rest of his life as zoologist, writer, collector of endangered species and conservationist. He was fortunate in having, among the unusual characters eventually called upon to give him some kind of schooling, Theodore Stephanides, himself a naturalist and writer, who became a close friend of the family. That Gerald never had a formal education or passed any kind of exam makes his successful career in a field that then, as now, demanded a high level of scholarship all the more remarkable.

Lawrence passed on to his younger brother his love of words and language, took seriously his first efforts at poetry and encouraged him to develop his undoubted talents as a writer.

Those who know Greece in the spring will recognise Gerald Durrell's description:

With March came the spring, and the island was flower-filled, scented, and aflutter with new leaves. The cypress trees that had tossed and hissed during the winds of winter now stood straight and sleek against the sky, covered with a misty coat of greenish-white cones. Waxy yellow crocuses appeared in great clusters, bubbling out among the tree roots and tumbling down the banks. Under the myrtles, the grape-hyacinths lifted buds like magenta sugar-drops, and the gloom of the oak thickets was filled with the dim smoke of a thousand blue day-irises. Anemones, delicate and easily wind-bruised, lifted ivory flowers the petals of which seemed to have been dipped in wine [...] Even the ancient olives, bent and hollowed by a thousand springs, decked themselves in clusters of minute creamy flowers [...] It was no half-hearted spring, this: the whole island vibrated with it as though a great, ringing chord had been struck.

His brother wrote of another season:

You wake one morning in the late autumn and notice that the tone of everything has changed; the sky shines more deeply pearl, and the sun rises like a ball of blood – for the peaks of the Albanian hills are touched with snow. The sea has become leaden and sluggish and the olives a deep platinum grey. Fires smoke in the villages, and the breath of Maria as she passes with her sheep to the headland, is faintly white upon the air […] Golden eagles hover in the grey. The cypresses hang above their own reflections like puffs of frozen grey smoke. Far out in the straits the black shape of a boat sits motionless – or dragging slowly and uncouthly with the flash of oars – like an insect upon a leaf. Now is the time to break logs for the great fireplace we have built ourselves, and smell the warm enriching odour of cypress wood, tar, varnish and linseed oil. It is time to prepare for the first gale of tears and sunsets from Albania and the East.

The biographer Douglas Botting in *Gerald Durrell* tells us that the conservationist was always dismissive of his own writing, especially when comparing it with his brother's. 'The subtle difference between us is that he loves writing and I don't. To me it's simply a way to make money which enables me to do my animal work, nothing more.' In this he was eventually successful, and his ability to express a passionate interest in the creatures of this world ensured him a growing and eventually worldwide readership. Over the years his 38 books and countless articles – beside the feature films and TV series of his many wildlife expeditions, and the lectures he gave in Britain and America – earned large sums of money which helped finance the zoo he set up on Jersey, today the Durrell Wildlife Conservation Trust, with a training centre for conservationists from all over the world. 'Many people believe that conservation is about saving fluffy animals –what they don't realize is that we're trying to prevent the human race from committing suicide.'

Gerald Durrell believed deeply that humans had no moral right to exploit the natural world endlessly, and that all species had an equal right to exist. That this view is today shared by so many is thanks largely to his lifelong efforts, from ideas that germinated in his early years on a Greek island.

Joanna Hodgkin, daughter of Lawrence Durrell's first wife Nancy by a later husband, wrote in *Amateurs in Eden* (2012):

I can't think of any other place in the world which has been so closely identified with two brothers, which is all the more remarkable considering how young they were when they went, and how comparatively brief their stay was [...] By September 1939 the outbreak of war had brought their island idyll to an end. Yet during those four years Larry and his youngest brother absorbed images and experience that fed into both *Prospero's Cell* in 1945 and *My Family and Other Animals* ten years later, books that could not be more different except that both are as readable and brilliant today as they were when they first electrified a war-weary, colour-hungry British public with their description of a vanished paradise.

For Gerald, Greece was Corfu. While Lawrence's Greek world included Athens and the Peloponnese, the Aegean Islands and Cyprus, places to which after the war he was drawn by work and his own inclinations, Corfu was for him, too, seminal.

He had started a correspondence with the American writer Henry Miller, through his admiration of Miller's *Tropic of Cancer*, a book so frank in its depictions of sex that it was swiftly banned wherever attempt was made to publish it, with the result that it immediately became sought after by most young people who bought and read smuggled-in copies with delighted and sometimes shocked astonishment. (How the literary world has caught up!) The Durrells had met Miller during brief visits to London and Paris, and invited him to stay with them in Corfu.

In his Greek books, Gerald Durrell gives the impression that the whole family lived together while on the island. In fact, Lawrence and his wife Nancy wanted to live independently and soon moved to what they called the White House, at Kalami, a bay under Mount Pantocrator in the north-east of the island. This was partly so that Lawrence could concentrate on his writing, away from the family chaos and unexpected and unpleasant encounters with creatures that Gerald brought back to the house – scorpions in matchboxes and leeches in his bed. It was at Kalami that Henry Miller came to

stay in May 1939. Years after the death of both Lawrence Durrell
and Nancy, Joanna Hodgkin stayed at the house:

> As it happened the top floor section that was let out to tourists was
> the top floor that Nancy and Larry, after staying there a while, had
> paid to have built. The lower part of the house was where the family
> lived – the same family that had lived there since the 1930s – as
> well as housing the bar and tavern. The White House in Kalami
> is a beacon for tour boats and so every morning [...] we watched
> the little boats as they puttered into the bay and paused beneath
> the balcony, loud-speaker systems belting out a glorious medley
> of misinformation. 'This is the famous house where Lawrence
> Durrell wrote *My Family and Other Animals*.' 'This is the famous
> house where Gerald Durrell lived with his father Lawrence.' 'This
> is where Justine Durrell wrote *The Alexandrian Quartet*.'

In *Prospero's Cell* Lawrence Durrell wrote fondly of the taverna
where he and Nancy and their friends often met to talk and share
their thoughts and even their mail:

> When Zarian gets a letter from Unamuno or Celine it is read out
> and passed round the table, and when I get one of Henry Miller's
> rambling exuberant letters from Paris the company is delighted.
> This is the real island flavour; our existence here in this delectable
> landscape, remote from the responsibilities of an active life in
> Europe, have given us this sense of detachment from the real world.

> ... Prodigals of leisure and brown skins,
> Wine mixed with kisses and the old
> Dreamless summer sleeps they once enjoyed
> In Adam's Eden long before the Fall.

As 1939 brought the rumours and rumblings of war ever closer,
the island idyll came to an end. Most of the Durrell family left

Corfu for England, leaving Lawrence and Nancy, who, with Henry Miller, soon moved to Athens. There Lawrence introduced Miller to the poet-diplomat George Seferis and the critic and writer Katsimbalis. Gordon Bowker, in his biography of Lawrence Durrell, *Through the Dark Labyrinth* (1997), describes the 'evenings of poetry and powerful retsina at Katsimbalis's house [...] and meeting in the Plaka with others such as the poet Sikelianos, the novelist Kazantzakis, the painter Ghika'. With extraordinary timing, on 28 September, *New English Weekly* ran Durrell's and Stephanides' translation of Cavafy's 'Waiting for Them', that is, waiting for the barbarians.

Miller formed a poor opinion of the English he met in Athens, especially those of the diplomatic corps, whom he considered arrogant and effete, and returned to Corfu for a time to meditate nude on the beach at Kalami. In November 1939, before leaving for America, he toured the Peloponnese and Crete with Katsimbalis, a journey which formed the basis for *The Colossus of Maroussi* (1941). The book made Katsimbalis – the 'colossus' in Miller's book – famous. It was Durrell who contributed the story of how Katsimbalis had stood one night on the steps of the Parthenon and with his great voice began crowing like a cock. A long moment's silence and then, far below him, a cock began to crow in answer, followed by another and another, until every cock within miles of the Acropolis had taken up the chorus …

'Out of the sea, as if Homer himself had arranged it for me, the islands bobbed up, lonely, deserted, mysterious in the fading light.' Henry Miller fell in love with Greece and the Greeks. He found a 'world of light such as I had never dreamed of and never hoped to see'. He had a romantic admiration for the simplicity of Greek country life and the dignity and generosity of the country people. He felt free and self-fulfilled in Greece and happier than he had ever been before. In Greece 'God's magic is still at work and, no matter what the race of man may do or try to do, Greece is still a sacred precinct.'

In June Nancy Durrell gave birth to a daughter, Penelope. Lawrence had seriously considered defending his adopted home country by fighting in the Greek army, but now he applied to join the Royal Navy. In the meantime he got a job with the British Council teaching English at Kalamata on the southern shore of the Peloponnese. The success of the Greek army in repelling the Italians that winter was short-lived. In April 1941 the Germans invaded, driving the British and Greek armies before them. As the British evacuated, Lawrence, Nancy and the baby found an ageing caique whose skipper was ready to brave the dangers of Stuka dive-bombers and German submarines.

Lying 'on the pitch-dark deck of a caique nosing past Matapan towards Crete', he remembered those magic years on Corfu.

> Seen through the transforming lens of memory the past seemed so enchanted that even thought would be unworthy of it. We never speak of it, having escaped: the house in ruins, the little black cutter smashed. I think only that the shrine with the three black cypresses and the tiny rock pool where we bathed must still be left. Visited by the lowland summer mists the trembling landscape must still lie throughout the long afternoons, glowing and altering like a Chinese water-colour where the light of the sky leaks in. But can these hastily written pages recapture more than a fraction of it?

So ends *Prospero's Cell*.

After a harrowing voyage lasting several days they reached Canea, from where, just in time before the German airborne invasion, they took the last steamer out of Crete to Alexandria. The war years in Egypt saw the final breakdown of their marriage; they also marked the development of Durrell's ideas as a novelist that eventually flowered in *Justine* (1957) and the other novels of the Alexandria Quartet. But that was later.

Durrell's first years in Greece, and his friendship with Miller, shaped him as a writer. *The Black Book* had been inspired by and

would not have been written without Miller's *Tropic of Cancer*.
Gordon Bowker in his biography of Durrell, *Through the Dark
Labyrinth,* writes that Miller was more than just an influence on
him, 'he was for some forty-five years his confidant and unfailing
supporter, and helped him, with his publishing contracts, to
enhance his reputation.' Henry Miller died in June 1980; their long
and remarkable correspondence came to an end with his last letter
to Durrell only a month before his death.

After the war Durrell returned to Greece, where government
postings to Rhodes and Cyprus provided the material for some
of his best poetry and two successful travel books – on Rhodes,
Reflections on a Marine Venus, and Cyprus, *Bitter Lemons.* These
were the years of *enosis* and the Cyprus 'troubles'. As a British official,
Durrell found himself on the wrong side of the conflict, a subject
he hardly mentions in either of these books but which affected him
deeply. Having turned down an OBE in 1962, he claimed to have
also refused the more prestigious CMG on the grounds that he
could not be honoured by a country which still retained possession
of Greek treasures such as the Elgin Marbles.

Durrell moved to France. Among the many books he wrote
from his house in Languedoc were *Tunc, Nunquam* and the novels
known as the The Avignon Quintet, as well as poetry, drama
and humour. Though some his books received important literary
prizes, none was as successful as *Justine.* He married four times.
Lawrence Durrell died of a stroke in France in November 1990.
In their later years drinking too much became a serious problem
for both brothers. Five years after Lawrence, Gerald died from a
failed liver transplant in a hospital in Jersey, the island where he
had created his Wildlife Park.

Talking of his house at Kalami on Corfu, Lawrence Durrell is
quoted by Joanna Hodgkin: 'That house with its remoteness and
the islands going down like soft gongs all the time into the amazing
blue, and I shall never, never forget a youth spent there, discovered
by accident, it was pure gold. But then of course – youth does

mean happiness, it does mean love, and that's something you can't get over.' The lives and careers of the two brothers, so different in many ways, were founded in those years, when both were so young, in Greece.

Many writers who knew Greece during or soon after World War II have been shocked at the damage inflicted on the countryside, most of it during and since the time of the Colonels.

Jim Potts (*The Ionian Islands and Epirus,* 2013) notes that Gerald Durrell was one who became increasingly disappointed with the changes wrought by the passing years to the paradise island of his youth:

> Corfu is its coastline, that's all. The visitors don't spend tuppence. They eat in their hotels, they flake and redden on the beach all day, they patronize the town by buying a couple of postcards. That's their contribution to the economics of the island, otherwise it all goes to tour operators and hotel managers. So Corfu is still poor. And it's ruined. Do you wonder that I am a conservationist?

On his return to Corfu on 1968, he was shocked at the spreading cancer of unplanned concrete choking some of the most delightful areas of the island: 'We are like a set of idiot children let loose in a complex and beautiful garden that we are turning into a barren and infertile desert.' At the same time he felt guilty that the popularity of his own books and especially *My Family and Other Animals* had encouraged tourism to the island and helped bring about much of the destruction he so detested.

Philip Sherrard wrote in his *Edward Lear: The Corfu Years* (1988) that much of the Corfu coastline had been:

> desolated beneath the ferro-concrete hideosity of hotel and boarding-house, discotheque, bar, cafeteria and chop-house, and

the wave after wave of pink-faced, white-bodied neo-Visigoths that summer-long blotch and bespatter its beaches, with the accompanying raucousness of motorcar, motorscooter, transistor radio, motorboat, and the other gimcrackery and detritus (plastic and mineral) of mass tourism, that one searches in vain, across the wreckage of this dishallowed world, for the virginal loveliness that confronted Lear at virtually every footstep.

In *The Hill of Kronos* (1981) Peter Levi, who visited the island around 1970, complained, 'There are certainly unspoiled corners even in Corfu, but they are mostly owned by the rich or the eccentric or the very lucky.' Worse was to come with the opening of Corfu's airport to international visitors in 1972: since then, 'development' and tourist numbers have increased exponentially.

Patricia Storace, in *Dinner with Persephone* (1996), visited Corfu at Easter some time in the 1990s:

> We take the ugly road out of Corfu town, past rows of cheap beach hotels and supermarkets flanked by white plastic versions of classical sculpture and billboard cut-outs of slim-waisted men from Minoan frescoes. Next to a half-finished building, amid a pile of iron and concrete rubble, a man turns a lamb on a spit. A wall near him is covered with sprawling graffiti [...] After fifteen or twenty minutes, the coast becomes the recognizable jewel-like coast whose beauty was perhaps, in the end, a fatal gift to the island. The bays curve like a beautiful woman's cleavage, and are watched by hideous concrete hotels that hover over them like voyeurs.

I sympathise with these and other writers, and have my own memories of the 'golden' years in the late 1950s and 1960s when Greece seemed to offer a simplicity and honesty so refreshing after the dull materialism of the north – the freedom of warm summer seas, dramatic sunlit landscapes scattered with fragments of the ancient past, and the everyday, everywhere friendliness and hospitality of the people. These things have not changed, and I believe they never will. But details have altered and sometimes the details are overwhelming, especially to those who remember an earlier time.

John Freely in *Ionian Islands* (2008) regretfully admits that 'mass tourism, particularly development of beach resorts with their bars and discos, has to some extent spoiled the charm of the islands', and describes (for example) the coast south of Mount Pantocrator as 'completely taken over by tourism, with hotels, holiday villas, restaurants and shops lining every swimmable stretch of the shore'. And yet, he adds:

> the old island life is still there, and one can find it by leaving the tourist centres behind and hiking up to remote mountain hamlets along goat tracks over thyme-scented hills, passing only the occasional farmer on his mule, who will bid you the time of day and welcome you to his village, just as I remember from our first visits to the Ionian isles half a lifetime ago.

Of course those idyllic times – idyllic, that is, to visiting foreigners – when beaches were empty, towns and villages 'unspoilt', when it was easy to find oneself in the spectacular ruins of a temple alone or with hardly another visitor in sight, were largely the consequence of wide-scale poverty as Greece slowly recovered from the depredations of wartime occupation and the civil war that immediately followed. All European countries have become dramatically richer over the last 50 years, but the increase in materialistic wealth is particularly striking in the south – Portugal, Spain, Italy, Greece – where always to be seriously poor was the fate of the majority of their peoples. Thankfully, poverty on such a scale, despite recent economic crises, is a thing of the past. The Mediterranean has been transformed, to the huge benefit of its peoples; inevitably, however, many of the most beautiful places have been choked and smothered by badly planned and ugly building, their charm and beauty destroyed forever.

Yet writers lamenting the past should also remember that much of this development has been specifically to meet the demands of tourism. Those who wrote lovingly about these places (I confess to being one) must bear part of the responsibility for attracting other foreigners who have come to Greece in increasing numbers, demanding inexpensive rooms and hotels to stay in, some even adding to the problem of over-development by building holiday homes of their own.

Passengers on the deck of a ferryboat heading south from Corfu to Kefalonia and Patras are likely to have a striking view of the towering white cliffs of Cape Leucatas, the southernmost point of the island of Lefkas. There is no compelling evidence that the Lesbian poet Sappho, rejected by her lover Phaon, in desperation committed suicide by throwing herself off the cliff, yet the story has appealed to every generation since it was first told by the Athenian playwright Menander in about 300 BCE. (Menander is the author of several maxims, two of which are well known even today: 'Those whom the gods love die young', and 'Let the die (dice) be cast!' quoted by Julius Caesar as he gave the order for his army to cross the Rubicon).

Strabo, who wrote in the reign of the Roman emperor Tiberius, mentions in his *Geography*, translated by H. L. Jones (1924), that it was an ancient custom of the Leucadians:

> every year at the sacrifice in honour of Apollo, for some criminal to be flung from this rocky lookout for the sake of averting evil, wings and birds of all kind being attached to him, since by their fluttering they would lighten the leap, and also for a number of men, stationed all round below the rock in small fishing-boats, to take the victim in, and, when he had been taken on board, to do all in their powers to get him safely outside of their borders.

▦

There is a magic in the name of Ithaka, bringing to mind perhaps the world's oldest and best-known hero – Odysseus to the Greeks, Ulysses to the Romans – whose travels and adventures sung by Homer some 3,000 years ago have inspired countless poets and writers ever since.

In Book 13 of the *Odyssey,* translated by Robert Fagles, the hero embarks on a Phaeacian ship on the final stage of his journey, and as the rowers:

> swung back and the blades tossed up the spray,
> an irresistible sleep fell deeply on his eyes, the sweetest,
> soundest oblivion, still as the sleep of death itself [...]

> Nothing could waken Odysseus as the ship sped forward,
> [...] so the stern hove high and plunged into the seething rollers,
> crashing dark in her wake as on she surged, unwavering,
> never flagging, no, not even a darting hawk,
> the quickest thing on wings, could keep her pace
> as on she ran, cutting the swells at top speed,
> bearing a man endowed with the gods' own wisdom,
> one who had suffered twenty years of torment, sick at heart,
> cleaving his way through wars of men and pounding waves at sea
> but now he slept at peace, the memory of his struggles
> laid to rest.
>   And then, that hour the star rose up,
> the clearest, brightest star, that always heralds
> the newborn light of day, the deep-sea-going ship
> made landfall on the island [...] Ithaka at last.

In his *Divine Comedy* (*Inferno,* Canto xxvi) Dante is led by Virgil to find Ulysses burning in a great wavering flame in hell, condemned for his guile and deceit in the taking of Troy (and for abandoning wife and family in irresponsible pursuit of adventure) and yet it is clear that Dante secretly admires Ulysses. Through Virgil he asks how he died. Dante listens with awe as Ulysses, his voice as if flung from the flame, recounts how he set sail with a few loyal companions towards the westward limits of the Mediterranean, determined to continue to explore the unknown. There, in the narrows where Hercules had set up his landmarks so that men should not pass beyond, he addresses his friends: 'We have come so far,' he says, 'overcome so many dangers, and now surely, in the brief time left to us we must go on.'

> Considerate la vostra semenza:
> fatti non foste viver come bruti
> ma per seguir virtute e canoscenza.

> Think of your origins, where you came from!
> You were not born to live like brutes,
> but to follow virtue and knowledge.

United in purpose they sail and row onwards through the Straits of Gibraltar into the unknown ocean beyond. Rowing day and night always westwards 'in the track of the sun', they see ahead a mountain rising out of the sea, the tallest they had ever seen; but instead of the welcome they had hoped for, a storm came down from the mountain, churning up huge waves that struck the ship, whirled her round three times and plunged her into the deep: 'infin che 'l mar fu sopra noi richiuso' ('and finally the sea closed over us').

Dante's dramatic description inspired Tennyson, who in his poem 'Ulysses', 'a name for always roaming with a hungry heart', imagines the hero in his kingdom of Ithaka, long after his return from Troy. Now deeply discontented with his dull and sedentary life, he gathers around him his former companions, like-minded friends who years ago had rowed with him from the 'ringing plains of windy Troy', and inspires them to join him in one last adventure:

... for my purpose holds
To sail beyond the sunset, and the baths
Of all the western stars, until I die.
It maybe that the gulfs will wash us down:
It maybe we shall touch the Happy Isles,
And see the great Achilles, whom we knew [...]
Though much is taken, much abides; and tho'
We are not now that strength which in old days
Moved earth and heaven, that which we are, we are:
One equal temper of heroic hearts,
    Made weak by time and fate, but strong in will
    To strive, to seek, to find, and not to yield.

Tennyson has no need to tell us whether the old adventurer and his friends in fact left their comfortable lives and indeed pushed their craft off into the western seas, 'to follow knowledge, like a sinking star'. Those words from the mouth of Ulysses remain a trumpet call to all who know that time is running out and feel they yet have passion and energy enough to search again for a meaning to their lives, to take up a final challenge, embark on one last adventure.

In Trieste, 500 miles up the Adriatic coast from Ithaka, James Joyce was engaged on his great novel *Ulysses:* 'I find the subject of Ulysses the most human in world literature.' As Robert Fagles writes in the Postscript to his translation of the *Odyssey* (1999), 'Odysseus is forever outward bound, off to another country [...] changing in the centuries as he goes, a man of many incarnations, with as many destinations.' Joyce's Bloom is equally on the move, 'toward the new Bloomusalem, until he settles for dear dirty Dublin and the moly that is Molly'.

None of these writers ever visited Greece, nor did most of the poets and writers who over the centuries have invoked Homer's *Odyssey*. Can there be many places in the world, especially such a small island, whose single most famous inhabitant has inspired so much great literature for so long?

The island itself has been the inspiration of many poems, an old favourite being Constantine Cavafy's 'Ithaka', where (in John Mavrocordato's 1951 translation) he advises us that in setting out for the island:

> You must pray that the voyage be long;
> Many be the summer mornings
> When with what pleasure, with what delight
> You enter harbours never seen before [...]

> [...] do not hurry the journey at all.
> Better it should last many years,
> Be quite old when you anchor at the island,
> Rich with all you have gained on the way,
> Not expecting Ithaka to give you riches [...]

> Poor though you find it, Ithaka has not cheated you.
> Wise as you have become, with all your experience,
> You will have understood the meaning of an Ithaka.

Homer never tells us how Odysseus ended his days, in fact one supposes he grew old in the arms of his wife Penelope. Except that would never do: we need a Ulysses, he is part of every one of us – rebel? romantic? adventurer? Some of us would dearly love to have at least a few (even one!) of his attributes: daring, resourcefulness, endurance – besides of course intelligence, charm and good looks ...

And yet the identification of Ithaka as the island of Odysseus/Ulysses is by no means certain, and doubts arising from the many landmarks described by Homer in the *Odyssey* have troubled writers, historians and archaeologists for centuries – and none of the competing theories has been found convincing. Present-day visitors whose eyes may glaze over at the thought of deciding in which bay Odysseus, after being wrecked, swam ashore and met Nausicaa ...

or whether the island of Lefkas was Ithaka, or Zakinthos ... may take comfort that Lord Byron in 1823 felt much the same way.

Edward Trelawny, in his *Records of Shelly, Byron and the Author* (1878), tells how when landing on Ithaka:

> it was proposed to Byron to visit some of the localities that antiquaries have dubbed with the title of Homer's school, – Ulysses' stronghold etc. he turned peevishly away, saying to me, '*Do I look like one of those emasculated fogies? Let's have a swim. I detest antiquarian twaddle* [...]' After a long swim, Byron climbed up the rocks, and, exhausted after the day's work, fell asleep under the shade of a wild fig-tree at the mouth of a cavern. Gamba, having nothing to do, hunted him out, and awakened him from a pleasant dream, for which the Poet cursed him. We fed off figs and olives, and passed our night at a goatherd's cottage.

Douglas Botting in his biography *Gerald Durrell* quotes the conservationist as he looks eastwards from the shores of Corfu:

> The sea was smooth, warm and as dark as black velvet, not a ripple disturbing the surface. The distant coastline on Albania was dimly outlined by a faint reddish glow in the sky. Gradually, minute by minute, this glow deepened and grew brighter, spreading across the sky. Then suddenly the moon, enormous, wine-red, edged herself over the fretted battlement of mountains, and threw a straight, blood-red path across the dark sea. The owls appeared now, drifting from tree to tree as silently as flakes of soot, hooting in astonishment as the moon rose higher and higher, turning to pink, then gold, and finally riding in a nest of stars, like a silver bubble.

Sailing south from Corfu, with the mountainous coast of western Greece on your left hand, it is easy to miss the entrance to the Ambracian Gulf, guarded by the promontory of Actium. Here, on

2 September 31 BCE, took place a sea battle that marked the end of the Roman Republic and the beginning of imperial rule. In the sea off Actium two fleets engaged, Octavian's and Mark Antony's. The main warships closing in on each other were huge armoured galleys, sails stowed away for battle, crammed with soldiers, their broad decks weighed down with massive ballistas sprung to launch rocks and missiles, and overlooked by towers manned with archers.

Antony's love affair with Cleopatra, queen of Egypt, was a principal cause of this war between Romans. Cleopatra was with Antony at Actium and he had placed the Egyptian fleet in reserve at the rear; now, as Cleopatra watched the battle continue into the afternoon, her anxiety grew. A gap had appeared in the mass of fighting ships. She made the fatal decision: her ships rowed forwards and as the north wind came up they raised sail and headed south. Antony saw the purple sails of Cleopatra's great galley and knew what it meant. With a few ships he followed her, abandoning the battle; within a few hours the fleet he had left behind had been destroyed or surrendered. A year later, defeated by Octavian's legions on land, Antony retreated to Egypt and tried to kill himself with his sword. Still alive, he was carried to Cleopatra and died in her arms. Soon after, Cleopatra, a prisoner of Octavian, also killed herself; it is said that she had an asp smuggled into her rooms, hidden in a basket of dates. Octavian received the title Augustus, the 'revered', and, though he never claimed the imperial title, became the first of the Roman emperors.

In a letter to his mother (September 1809), Lord Byron wrote, 'To-day I saw the remains of the town of Actium, near which Antony lost the world.'

The shocking news of Antony's defeat spread rapidly to every province of the Empire. And yet such a huge victory, changing history, can also be of relatively little importance to the people of a faraway city, an irony captured by Cavafy's 'In a Township of Asia Minor' (translated by Edmund Keeley and Philip Sherrard):

The news about the outcome of the sea-battle at Actium
was of course unexpected.
But there's no need to draft a new proclamation.
The name's the only thing that has to be changed.
There, in the concluding lines, instead of: 'Having freed the
    Romans
from Octavius, that disaster,
that parody of a Caesar,'
we'll substitute: 'Having freed the Romans
from Antony, that disaster [...]'
The whole text fits very nicely.

William Lithgow's book *The Total Discourse of the Rare Adventures
and Painefull Peregrinations of Long Nineteen Years Travayles
From Scotland to the most Kingdoms of Europe, Asia and Africa*
was published in 1632. The title admirably reflects its contents,
'painefull' being the right description of many of his adventures.
Little is known about Lithgow except that he was born in Lanark,
Scotland, in about 1585 and his father was a merchant. When very
young he became involved in a fight over a girl and had his ears cut
off – hence his nickname 'Lugless Willie'. It is not known how or
whether this affected him, but shortly afterwards he set out on a
series of journeys, mainly on foot, which carried him across much
of Europe and as far as Jerusalem.

John L. Tomkinson points out in his *Travellers' Greece: Memories
of an Enchanted Land* (2006) that Lithgow was an adventurer rather
than a scholar, but that in the early seventeenth century only an
adventurer could have survived in that anarchic and lawless region
of the Ottoman Empire and, 'as the first known traveller from
Britain to penetrate the interior of the country, he provides a very
valuable historical witness.'

Sailing south through the Ionian Islands, Lithgow wrote: 'I
embarked on a Greek *carmesalo* with a great number of passengers,

Greeks, Slavonians, Italians, Armenians and Jews, that were all mindful for Zante, and I also of the like intent; being in all forty-eight persons.' As strong winds swept the ship south along the coast of Kefalonia a sail was seen coming up behind them; a lookout from the masthead confirmed she was 'a Turkish galley of Bizerta, prosecuting a straight course to invade our barke; which sudden affrighted news overwhelmed us in despair.' In the panic that followed, the passengers urged the captain to surrender, most of them being confident of being ransomed by their friends. 'But I, the wandering pilgrim, pondering in my pensive breast my solitary estate, the distance of my country and my friends, could conceive no hope of deliverance. Upon the which troublesome and fearful appearance of slavery, I arose, and spoke to the Master.'

Lithgow reminded the captain that since he owned half the ship and most of the cargo, if he surrendered he would lose it all. His words inspired the captain to encourage the passengers and crew to fight. Soon:

> every man was busy in the work; some below in the gun-room, others cleansing the muskets, some preparing the powder and balls, some their swords and short weapons, some dressing the half-pikes, and other making fast the doors above, for the master resolved to make combat below, both to save us from small shot, and besides for boarding us on a sudden.

'After a long and doubtful fight, both with great and small shot (night parting us)', the battle was broken off and thanks to a violent storm they managed to beach their damaged and leaking ship in a bay in Kefalonia.

> In this fight there were of us killed three Italians, two Greeks, and two Jews, with eleven others deadly wounded, and I also hurt in the right arm with a small shot [...] Being all disembarked onshore, we gave thanks to the Lord for our unexpected safety, and buried the

dead Christians in a Greek churchyard, and the Jews were interred by the sea side [...] Leaving this weather-beaten *carmesalo* laid up, I hired two fishermen in a little boat, to carry me over to Zante, being twenty-five miles distant. Here a Greek surgeon undertook the curing of my arm.

William Lithgow was always complaining but had much to complain about in his 'rare adventures and painefull peregrinations', his experiences nevertheless a delight to the armchair traveller. Tomkinson remarks in his series *Grecian Journeys* (2008) that Lithgow 'displays all the narrow-minded bigotry we would expect from a Scottish Protestant of the period, disproving conclusively the thesis that travel broadens the mind' – amply demonstrated in the account of his visit to the southernmost of the Ionian Islands.

Cythera is an island of circuit three-score miles, having but one castle called Capsali, which is kept by a Venetian captain [...] At the time of my abode, at the village of Capsali (being a haven for small barkes, and situate below the castle) the captain of that same fortress killed a seminary priest, whom he had found with his whore in a brothel-house: for the which sacrilegious murder the governor of the isle deposed the captain and banished him, causing a boat to be prepared to send him to Crete.

Lithgow's Protestant sympathies were with the captain and he could not resist adding: 'Oh! If all the priests which do commit incest, adultery and fornication (yea, and worse, *il peccato carnale contra natura*) were thus handled and severely rewarded: what a sea of sodomitical irreligious blood would overflow the half of Europe, to stain the spotted colour of that Roman Beast.'

Lithgow was on the same boat as the condemned captain; pursued by three Turkish galleys and sailing across miles of 'dangerous and combustious seas', he was lucky to reach Crete.

In one of his dialogues, *Why Oracles Fail,* the Greek historian Plutarch, writing in the first century CE, repeats a story told by Epitherses, 'who lived in our town and was my teacher in grammar'. This gentleman was making a voyage to Italy and embarked on a ship carrying freight and many passengers:

> It was already evening when, near the Echinades islands, the wind dropped and the ship drifted near Paxi. Almost everybody was awake, and a good many had not finished their after-dinner wine. Suddenly from the island of Paxi was heard the voice of someone calling loudly, *Thamus!* so that all were amazed.
>
> Thamus was an Egyptian pilot, not known by name even to many on board. Twice he was called and made no reply, but the third time he answered; and the caller, raising his voice, said, 'When you come opposite to Palodes, announce that Great Pan is dead.' On hearing this, all, said Epitherses, were astounded and reasoned among themselves whether it were better to carry out the order or refuse to meddle and let the matter go. Under the circumstances Thamus made up his mind that if there should be a breeze he would sail past and keep quiet, but with no wind and a smooth sea about the place he would announce what he had heard. So, when he came opposite Palodes, and there was neither wind nor wave, Thamus from the stern, looking towards the land, said the words as he heard them: 'Great Pan is dead!' Even before he was finished there was a great cry of lamentation, not of one person but of many, mingled with exclamations of amazement. As many persons were on the vessel, the story was soon spread in Rome, and Thamus was sent for by Tiberius Caesar. Tiberius became so convinced of the truth of the story that he caused an enquiry and investigation to be made.

The story has always generated chatter among historians and mythologists, and not only because Tiberius showed so much interest. Aside from the unlikely suggestion that Plutarch simply made the story up, among the many theories on offer the most obvious is still the best. The death of Great Pan – Pan with his pipes, the goat-horned god of glade and pasture, leading the nymphs in dance – foretold the end of paganism and the coming of monotheism and Christianity, particularly since it was in the reign of Tiberius that Jesus lived and died.

It is not surprising that so much attention was given to Pan and the rumour of his death, for he was not a god to be taken lightly. Respected as the god of lust and nature uncontrolled, he made his rare appearances only in the heavy heat of a summer noon. Pan was feared for his terror-awakening shout, inspiring mindless panic that so easily infects crowds, and he was loved for his free spirit, poetry and dance and the seductive music of his pipes.

> What was he doing, the great god Pan,
> Down in the reeds by the river?
> Spreading ruin and scattering ban,
> Splashing and paddling with hoofs of a goat,
> And breaking the golden lilies afloat
>   With the dragon-fly on the river.

In Elizabeth Barratt Browning's 'A Musical Instrument' (1860) Pan 'tore out a reed [...] from the deep, cool bed of the river', fashioned the first pipe from it and, putting it to his mouth, made the first music:

> Blinding sweet, O great god Pan!
> The sun on the hill forgot to die.
> And the lilies revived, and the dragon-fly
> Came back to dream on the river.
>
> Yet half a beast is the great god Pan.
> To laugh as he sits by the river,
> Making a poet out of a man:

The true gods sigh for the cost and pain, –
For the reed which grows nevermore again
As a reed with the reeds in the river.

Edward Lear was 36 when he first stepped foot on Corfu, arriving from Italy in 1848. He wrote to his sister Ann, 'I wish I could give you an idea of the beauty of this island, it is really a paradise.'

Famous for his nonsense verse and limericks, Lear is less well known for his drawings and paintings. His watercolours are especially recognised today for their quality and skill. Much of his best work was done in Greece.

Lear was born in London of a middle-class family, the twentieth of 21 children. Emotionally abandoned by his mother, he was brought up mainly by an older sister. Unhappiness as a child was made more painful by epilepsy, which in those days was popularly considered to be possession by the devil (alternatively, brought on by masturbation). Desperate to conceal his illness, he learned to recognise the warning signs and did everything possible to be alone when the attacks came.

As a young man he had made his name as an illustrator of birds, but changed his profession to landscape painter. As he also suffered from asthma and bronchitis and easily became ill in the cold and damp of England, he spent as much time as he could in the warmer climate of the Mediterranean, travelling, sketching and painting. In a letter of 6 December 1857 to a friend in wintry England, Lear wrote, marvelling at the weather in Corfu: 'simply cloudless glory for 7 long days and nights. Anything like the splendor of olive-grove and orange-garden, the blue of sky & ivory of church and chapel, the violet of mountain rising from peacock-wing-hued sea, and tipped with lines of silver snow, can hardly be imagined. I wish to goodness grass-hoppers you were here.'

Over the following 16 years Lear travelled all over Greece, often alone, at a time when much of the northern part of the country, including what is now Albania, and also Crete, was still under Turkish rule, sketching, painting in watercolours and making notes. He returned to England to sell his work, raise money and plan further journeys. He was happy in Corfu and made the island his base, spending long hours tramping the olive-green hills with his sketchbook, preferring the company of 'trees, clouds & silence' to people.

Two of his best-known 'Views of the Ionian Islands' are of Corfu's dramatic north-west. In a letter dated Easter Sunday, 1862, Lear wrote: 'At this beautiful place there is just now perfect quiet, except only a dim hum of myriad ripples 500 feet below me, all round the great rocks that rise perpendicularly from the sea [...] On my left is the convent of Palaiokastritza, and happily as the monkery had functions at 2 a.m., they are all fast asleep now.' High above the 'many peacock-tailed bays here reflecting the vast red cliffs [...] the immense rock of St. Angelo rising into the air, on whose summit the old castle still is seen a ruin, just 1,400 feet above the water.' His solitude was soon to be broken: 'Accursed picnic parties with miserable scores of asses male and female are coming tomorrow, and peace flies – as I shall too.'

Though irritated by the 'drumbeating bothery frivolity of the town of Corfu', he got to know many of the officers and families of the garrison. In a letter to his friend Chichester Fortescue on 21 January 1862, he wrote how he was looking out of the window when the regiment marched by: 'I have a full palette & brushes in my hand: whereat Col. Bruce saw me & saluted – and not liking to make a formillier nod in presence of the hole harmy, I put up my hand to salute, – and thereby transferred all my colours into my hair & whiskers – which I must now wash in turpentine or shave off.'

Lear loved Corfu, but some of the houses or apartments that he rented were far from ideal for him to concentrate on his work. 'The constant walking and noise overhead prevents my application to any sort of work, and it is only from 6 to 8 in the morning that I can really attend to anything.' Lear considered installing a piano, but then remembered that 'Miss Henderson over my head has one, and plays jocular jigs continually. Then what the devil can I do? Buy a baboon and parrot and let them rush around the room?'

As John Freely, in *The Ionian Islands* (2008) suggests, 'it was probably in such a frustrated mood that Lear wrote one of his best known limericks.'

> There was an Old Man of Corfu
> Who never knew what he should do;
> So he rushed up and down,
> Till the sun made him brown,
> That bewildered Old Man of Corfu.

Only recently has Greece become a relatively easy place to move around; in the nineteenth century and well into the twentieth travelling by land or by sea was uncomfortable, difficult and often dangerous. Roads were bad and often impassable in winter, while the sea could be rough even in midsummer. Bandits threatened the roads, pirates the sea. The rich could secure a ship's cabin with some comforts attached, but no money could buy comfortable roadside inns that did not exist; and wherever one slept it was rare to spend a night without being steadily eaten alive by lice, bedbugs or fleas.

The problem called for imaginative solutions. Edward Lear described how, on arrival at a village and when a house had been chosen in which to stay the night, the servants unloaded the baggage from the mules and set up the beds, each one with 'a large muslin bag', attached to a wooden beam in the ceiling, 'into which I creep by a hole which is tied up directly I am in it, so that no creature gets in & one sleeps soundly in a room full of vermin. I thought I should have laughed all night long the first time I crept into this strange bag, but soon grew used to it.'

In *Travellers to an Antique Land* (1991) Robert Eisner notes that the 'great adventure writers, from Homer to the present, have known the romantic potential for a reader's imagination of a list, for it is like a plot distilled to only nouns, with the adjectives and verbs to be anticipated or filled in as the pages turn.'

Lear, who knew what he was talking about, advised the traveller to take with him plenty of cooking equipment, 'a light mattress, some sheets and blankets, and a good supply of capotes and plaids [...] some rice, curry powder and cayenne', while two sets of clothing were required, 'one for visiting consuls, pashas, and dignitaries, the other for rough everyday work'. Most important of all was 'some quinine made into pills'. Essentials were 'a Boyourldi, or general order of introduction to governors or pashas; and your Teskere, or provincial passport for yourself and guide'. The fewer luxuries the better, but Lear recommended 'a long strap with a pair of ordinary stirrups, to throw over the Turkish saddles [...] to save you the cramp caused by the awkward shovel stirrups of the country'. To avoid 'seceding bits of luggage escaping at unexpected intervals', he suggested that everything should be stowed in 'two Brobdignagian saddle-bags' to be hung on each side of the baggage horse. Recommendations for travelling equipment from other travellers and Murray's Guides include an umbrella (for protection mainly from the sun), an India rubber bath with bellows to inflate it, mathematical instruments, tinted spectacles and measuring tape.

Vivian Noakes, in *Edward Lear: The Life of a Wanderer* (2004), believed that Lear craved but never found the affection he lacked as a child. It is true that the intensity of his friendships with men was never returned to the same degree, while he hesitated to develop close relations with women for fear they would discover and be disgusted by his epilepsy. In 1862 he wrote, only half jokingly, 'I wish I was married to a clever good nice fat little Greek girl – and had 25 olive trees, some goats and a house. But the above girl, happily for herself, likes somebody else.'

Lear's nonsense songs and verse secured his place in the culture of English-speaking peoples; perhaps, if he had become the successful painter he so desperately wanted to be, he might never have written them. Yet he made many friends, most of whom were relatively rich and inevitably from the upper classes; they admired him for his painting and drawing skills, and loved him for his good nature and sense of humour. Lord Tennyson paid tribute to Lear in a poem especially dedicated to him. Like many an armchair traveller, he was able to enjoy Greece through Lear's eyes:

> With such a pencil, such a pen,
> You shadow forth to distant men,
> I read and felt that I was there.

Lear's favourite tipple was Marsala and water, and in his last years he drank too much of it. He had reason to be depressed as his sight was failing, his paintings were not selling, and he was increasingly lonely and affected by the 'morbids', as he called his moods of depression. It was in Cannes in 1867 that he met John Addington Symonds, and to entertain his daughter composed *The Owl and the Pussycat*.

In 1871 he moved to San Remo in northern Italy, where he built a house. Living alone at Villa Tennyson, named after the poet laureate's wife Emily, whom Lear had always admired, his health declined. His Greek servant Giorgio, who had been his companion for so many years of travel in Greece, and later in the Middle East and India, became ill and died from what today we would probably call dementia. Each year Lear still copied into the front of his diary, 'Always have 10 years work mapped out before you, if you want to be happy', but work was not going well, mainly because he was going blind.

Although friends wrote to him and he did receive a visit from the only woman he had ever thought seriously of marrying – but never could make up his mind to propose to her – his life became increasingly solitary. His beloved cat Foss, who appears in so many of his humorous drawings, died in September 1887. Four months later, attended only by his servant, Lear was dead.

On a little heap of barley
Died my aged uncle Arly,
    And they buried him one night:–
Close beside the leafy thicket;–
There, – his hat and Railway Ticket ;–
There, his ever faithful Cricket;–
    (But his shoes were far too tight).

My Dear Mother, – I have now been some time in Turkey: this place is on the coast, but I have traversed the interior of the province of Albania on a visit to the Pacha. I left Malta in the *Spider,* a brig of war, on the 21st of September, and arrived in eight days at Prevesa.

George Noel Gordon, Lord Byron, was 22 when he wrote this letter, dated 12 November 1809. He was taking the Grand Tour, with his friend from Cambridge University, John Cam Hobhouse. He was also trying to forget a failed love affair, and to escape his debts. Because most of mainland Europe was in the hands of Napoleon, Grand Tourists were restricted to countries of the Mediterranean: Portugal, Greece (part of the Ottoman Empire) and Turkey itself. This suited Byron, who had long been romantically attracted by the Islamic Levant. He began to write a long poem drawing on his travels, *Childe Harold's Pilgrimage*; the first part of the poem, published five years later, made him famous.

Ali Pasha, Byron noted, was 'one of the most powerful men in the Ottoman empire'. Nominally subject to the sultan, he was in fact virtually independent, ruling over most of north-western and central Greece. After crossing over the mountains from the coast, 'a country of the most picturesque beauty', Byron and Hobhouse were horrified as they entered Yanina (now Ioannina) to see hanging from a plane tree a man's torn side and arm. This was the remains of one of Ali Pasha's victims – criminal or enemy, much the same to him – who had endured one of the extreme tortures and agonising executions that Ali Pasha inflicted on his subjects and liked to watch himself.

Ali Pasha was away, but instructions had been left to look after the visitors and several days later they set off for Tepelni where the Pasha was with his army. After a nine-day journey 'much prolonged by torrents that had fallen from the mountains, intersecting the roads', Byron finally rode into Tepelni:

> I shall never forget the singular scene on entering Tepaleen at five in the afternoon, as the sun was going down [...] The Albanians, in their dresses, (the most magnificent in the world, consisting of a long *white kilt*, gold-worked cloak, crimson velvet gold-laced jacket and waistcoat, silver-mounted pistols and daggers,) the Tartars with their high caps, the Turks in their vast pelisses and turbans, the soldiers and black slaves with the horses [...] two hundred steeds ready caparisoned to move in a moment, couriers entering or passing out with the despatches, the kettle-drums beating, boys calling the hour from the minaret of the mosque.

The scene was translated to *Childe Harold* (II, 580):

> The wild Albanian kirtled to his knee,
> With shawl-girt head and ornamented gun.
> And gold-embroidered garments, fair to see;
> And crimson-scarfed men of Macedon
> The Delhi with his cap of terror on,
> And crooked glaive – the lively, supple Greek
> And swarthy Nubia's mutilated son;
> The bearded Turk that rarely deigns to speak,
> Master of all around, too potent to be meek

His account continued:

The next day I was introduced to Ali Pacha. I was dressed in a full suit of staff uniform, with a very magnificent sabre, etc. The vizier received me in a large room paved with marble; a fountain was playing in the centre; the apartment was surrounded by scarlet ottomans. He received me standing, a wonderful compliment from a Mussulman, and made me sit down on his right hand. I have a Greek interpreter for general use, but a physician of Ali's named Femlario, who understands Latin, acted for me on this occasion. His first question was, why, at so early an age, I left my country? – (the Turks have no idea of travelling for amusement). He then said, the English minister, Captain Leake, had told him I was of a great family, and desired his respects to my mother; which I now, in the name of Ali Pacha, present to you. He said he was certain I was a man of birth, because I had small ears, curling hair, and little white hands [...] He told me to consider him as a father whilst I was in Turkey, and said he looked on me as his son. Indeed, he treated me like a child, sending me almonds and sugared sherbet, fruit and sweetmeats, twenty times a day. He begged me to visit him often, and at night, when he was at leisure. I then, after coffee and pipes, retired for the first time. I saw him thrice afterwards [...] His highness is sixty years old, very fat, and not tall, but with a fine face, light blue eyes, and a white beard; his manner is very kind, and at the same time he possesses that dignity which I find universal amongst the Turks. He has the appearance of anything but his real character, for he is a remorseless tyrant, guilty of the most horrible cruelties, very brave, and so good a general that they call him the Mahometan Buonaparte. Napoleon has twice offered to make him King of Epirus, but he prefers the English interest, and abhors the French.

The Pasha showed Byron a snuff box that the French Emperor had sent him with Napoleon's picture on it

Byron had mixed feelings about Ali Pasha. He was delighted to be so well received by so important an international figure, but was aware of what a monster he could be and was shocked that he would watch with enjoyment his enemies being tortured to death. Byron was also wise not to accept the tyrant's invitation to visit him at 'night, when he was at leisure', as his sexual interests were known to be varied, and indeed bisexuality was commonplace in that part of the world. Elizabeth Longford writes in *Byron's Greece* (1975) that 'Byron was aware of Ali's erotic designs. A contemporary print shows the young Englishman sitting uneasily at the end of a cushioned divan, as far away as possible from his host and as close as possible to a group of voluptuous houris.'

While Byron was impressed by the wild beauty of the country and found the men handsome – 'all soldiers, and war and the chase their sole occupation' – he saw that the women were 'treated like slaves, *beaten*, and, in short, complete beasts of burden; they plough, dig, and sow. I found them carrying wood, and actually repairing the highways.' In Ali Pasha's reign women caught in adultery were sewn up in sacks and dropped into the deep waters of Lake Pamvotis, overlooked by the mountains on one side and the walls of the Pasha's palace on the other. Byron reflects his ambivalence towards the Pasha in *Childe Harold* (II, 62).

> In marbled-paved pavilion, where a spring
> Of living water from the centre rose,
> Whose bubbling did a genial freshness fling,
> And soft voluptuous couches breathed repose
> Ali reclined, a man of war and woes:
> Yet in his lineaments ye cannot trace,
> While Gentleness her milder radiance throws
> Along that aged venerable face,
> The deeds that lurk beneath, and stain him with disgrace.

Byron and Hobhouse felt obliged to travel with a guard of 50 Albanians, mainly from Souli (Suli), a savage region south of Ioannina which for years had refused to accept Ali Pasha's rule.

When in 1803, in a famous episode in Greek history, the Souliotes were eventually overcome by force of numbers, many of the women, rather than fall into the hands of their attackers, threw themselves, babies in their arms, over a cliff to instantaneous death. Travelling was dangerous and foreigners kidnapped by bandits risked being sold into slavery. The wild country through which Byron travelled is described by Elizabeth Longford:

> If a storm blows up in these passes, great swathes of slate-coloured cloud or transparent shreds of mist add beauty to the fantastic mountains. Or there may be a total black-out for the moment, with the sound of small bells close by but no sign of goats. Then comes a rent in the storm-cloud; a torrent far below appears as a pale streak of light; and on the turf by the roadside, goats and kids suddenly materialise in a vivid patchwork of brown, black, fawn, tawny and white.

Much has been written about Ali Pasha, and fictional characters based on him appear in novels such as *The Count of Monte Cristo* by Alexandre Dumas (the betrayal and slavery of the Pasha's wife and daughter) and in *The Ionian Mission* by Patrick O'Brian (the British Navy fighting the French over possession of Corfu).

François Pouqueville was France's representative at the court of Ali Pasha until the fall of Napoleon Bonaparte. Ali at one point considered an alliance with the French, until he was persuaded that friendship with the British was more in his interest. Consequently Pouqueville has not had a good press in English, especially from the likes of Byron and Hobhouse. His view of Tepelin, Ali Pasha's stronghold, in *Travels in Epirus, Albania, Macedonia, and Thessaly* (1820) was very different from Byron's, reflecting perhaps the very different treatment he received.

For my part I could see nothing but a gloomy valley, bounded by mountains naked and forbidding; the birth-place of storms and tempests, which rage with such fury that it has never been possible to raise a tree round the place. The palace has the repulsive air of a prison. When the day declines the gates are closed and barricaded: armed guards repair to their assigned posts; dogs of the famed Molossian breed, turned loose in the courts, make the air resound with their howlings. I was myself, in fact, mured in a chamber, without windows, with my servants; and an Albanian slept on the outside of the door to accompany any of us who desired to go out. In the abode of tyranny every thing is a cause of suspicion. Many times, during the long nights I passed in that place, did I hear the clanking of the chains of the miserable beings, groaning in the dungeons sunk, as well as the vaulted receptacles of Aly's treasures, in the solid rock, under the magnificently furnished apartments prepared for his accommodation.

Though disliked by some contemporary Englishmen, Pouqueville was a distinguished traveller and writer. Managing to survive the dangerous years of the French Revolution, he trained as a doctor and enlisted in Napoleon's vast enterprise to conquer Egypt and parts east. On his way back to France his ship was captured by pirates who sold him to the Ottomans. By 1801, when he returned to Paris after two and a half years' imprisonment in Constantinople, he had learned modern Greek and become an enthusiastic supporter of Greek independence. His books continued to further the cause.

A much later visitor to Greece, who wrote and sketched as he travelled, was Osbert Lancaster. Best known for his cartoons, mainly in the *Daily Express*, for which he provided more than 10,000 over a period of 40 years, he is also the author of *Classical Landscape with Figures* (1947), illustrated with his drawings. This is an account of his travels in Greece in 1945–6, just after the war, while press attaché to the British Embassy. Lancaster described the criteria and standards of judgement by which he worked as those of an 'Anglican graduate of Oxford with a taste for architecture, turned cartoonist, approaching middle age and living in Kensington'. This self-deprecation was taken at face value by the public for many years, and it is only recently that his qualities as a critic of art and architecture, and his skill as an artist have been recognised, together with his gentle sense of humour, which lightens up everything he drew or wrote.

Like Byron, Lancaster found Ioannina one of his favourite Greek towns and was fascinated by its colourful past when Ali Pasha ruled.

When Ali was at the height of his fame the Kastro, which today retains within its immense walls only two mosques, some ruinous Turkish baths and one wing of the palace [...] presented the most fantastic spectacle. In the principal courtyard, the great gates of which were generally ornamented with the crucified remains of at least one malefactor, a crowd of wasp-waisted and magnificently over-dressed Skipetars, the brave and ferocious Albanian tribesmen on whose loyal support the Pasha's power principally rested, mocked and badgered a throng of unfortunate petitioners desperately waving their various requests on the ends of long sticks in a jostling crowd by the entrance to the palace. Beyond this doorway, from which the eager supplicants were firmly held back by the sentries, lay an extraordinary world of kiosks and pavilions, painted saloons with plate-glass windows overlooking the mountains and lake, and women's apartments guarded by negro eunuchs with naked scimitars, filled with gold-embroidered divans and cages of nightingales provoked to unseasonable song by the green gauze with which they were enshrouded. Against this highly-coloured background moved a procession of inmates no less exotic: Ali's youthful personal attendants, bare-foot with their long golden hair flowing unrestrained to their waists, half-naked

dervishes [...] Greek advisors and Albanian mercenaries, Italian
doctors and French artillerymen, and, as often as not, an English
'milor' registering interest without approval.

Occasionally an extra stir and bustle in the ante-room
announced the arrival of some outstanding personage of the court:
Mukhtar, the Pasha's elder son, whose lust was so uncontrollable
that he frequently raped women in the public street in broad
daylight, or his younger son, the courteous and distinguished-
looking Veli, who possessed the largest library of pornography
in the whole of the Near East, or his favourite general, the
gigantic mulatto, Yusuf Arab, known, not without good reason,
as the Blood-drinker. But in the very heart of this gilded warren
– where the Pasha himself, reclining on a silk divan, puffed his
long pipe, dictated masterpieces of sycophantic insincerity to his
sovereign on the Bosphorus, counted up his hoarded millions or
simply meditated elaborate and enjoyable schemes of revenge for
injuries suffered forty years before – perfect peace and tranquility
habitually reigned.

That is, until fate caught up with him. By arranging to have one of
his political opponents murdered in Constantinople, Ali took a step
too far. The sultan used the opportunity to order Ali's deposition
and in 1822 sent an army to enforce the *firman*. Ten years earlier,
in the second canto of *Childe Harold*, Byron had foreseen his fate.

> Blood follows blood, and through their mortal span,
> In bloodier acts conclude those who with blood began.

Ali's followers rapidly deserted him and he withdrew to the
fortress of Ioannina. Here he was deceived as he had deceived so
many: promised that his life would be spared, he was allowed to
retire to the monastery of St Pantaleimon on the island in the lake.
When soldiers were sent with orders to behead him, Ali resisted
and it is said he was shot through the floor of a room where he

was defending himself. His head was sent to the sultan in Constantinople; he was 82. The island, scene of Ali's demise, parts of it unchanged since his time, is one of the many attractions of Ioannina today.

These weeks travelling with Hobhouse in the wild mountains of Epirus were decisive in forming Byron's attraction to this corner of the world and its peoples, the first steps on a road that came to journey's end 15 years later. In *Childe Harold* he told the story of his pilgrim's adventures; in letters to his mother he enjoyed recounting his own. Besides his armed Souliote escort he was always accompanied by his faithful servant Fletcher:

> Two days ago I was nearly lost in a Turkish ship of war, owing to the ignorance of the captain and crew, though the storm was not violent. Fletcher yelled after his wife, the Greeks called on all the saints, the Mussulmans on Alla; the captain burst into tears and ran below deck, telling us to call on God; the sails were split, the main-yard shivered, the wind blowing fresh, the night setting in, and all our chance was to make Corfu, which is in possession of the French, or (as Fletcher pathetically termed it) 'a watery grave.' I did what I could to console Fletcher, but finding him incorrigible, wrapped myself up in my Albanian capote (an immense cloak), and lay down on deck to wait the worst. I have learnt to philosophise in my travels; and if I had not, complaint was useless. Luckily the wind abated, and only drove us on the coast of Suli, on the main land, where we landed, and proceeded, by the help of the natives, to Prevesa again; but I shall not trust Turkish sailors in future, though the Pacha had ordered one of his own galliots to take me to Patras. I am therefore going as far as Missolonghi by land, and there have only to cross a small gulf to get to Patras.
>
> Fletcher's next epistle will be full of marvels. We were one night lost for nine hours in the mountains in a thunder-storm, and since

nearly wrecked. In both cases Fletcher was sorely bewildered, from apprehensions of famine and banditti in the first, and drowning in the second instance. His eyes were a little hurt by the lightning, or crying (I don't know which), but are now recovered.

He finished this letter to his mother with, 'When you write, address to me at Mr. Strané's, English consul, Patras, Morea.' Byron found living inexpensive in Greece compared with Malta and Spain, which was just as well as he was always short of money.

Yesterday, the 11th of November, I bathed in the sea; to-day is so hot that I am writing in a shady room of the English consul's, with three doors wide open, no fire, or even *fireplace*, in the house, except for culinary purposes [...] I am going to-morrow, with a guard of fifty men, to Patras in the Morea, and thence to Athens, where I shall winter.

2

NORTHERN GREECE

Was this the face that launch'd a thousand ships
And burnt the topless towers of Ilium?
(Christopher Marlowe, *Doctor Faustus*, 1604)

The *Iliad* and *Odyssey*, epics attributed to the blind poet Homer, are
thought to have first appeared in their present form about 700 BCE,
soon after the Greeks, adapting the alphabet of their Phoenician
neighbours, took to writing. An account of the dramatic events that
took place around 1200 BCE, the story was kept alive for some four
centuries by a tradition of oral poetry declaimed and sung by travelling bards to rapt audiences throughout the Greek-speaking world.

> Anger – sing goddess, the anger of Achilles son of Peleus, that
> accursed anger that brought the Greeks endless sufferings and
> sent the souls of many warriors to Hades, leaving their bodies as
> carrion for the dogs and a feast for the birds.

These are the opening lines of the *Iliad*, which tells of a few days
of passion, heroism, honour and revenge near the end of the ten-
year siege of Troy. In its frequent battle scenes it rivals even the
Old Testament in brutality and pitiless violence, and yet it is never
clear whether Homer intended to glorify war or emphasise its tragic
futility.

Peter Jones, writing in the introduction to E. V. Rieu's translation
which he also revised and updated (2003), calls the *Iliad* the first
work of Western literature, and also the world's first tragedy:

Two hundred years before the Greek tragic poets invented the medium for the stage Homer had grasped its essential nature in the figure of [...] Achilles – an initially wronged hero, of divine ancestry, who finds his world inexplicably turning to ashes as a result of the decisions he has freely, if intemperately, taken, whose greatness lies in his refusal to disclaim the responsibility for his actions, even though his own death will be the inevitable consequence.

But was any of this great story true? Most scholars and the general public had their doubts. The ruins of Troy – Ilium, as it was known to Homer – had never been convincingly identified, and the epic itself was so driven by the actions and rivalries of gods and goddesses that common sense would relegate it firmly to the category of myth.

One man, however, was convinced that Troy had existed and that Helen's abduction by Paris, the long siege, the 'wrath of Achilles', the words of Agamemnon, the death of Hector, the grief of his father Priam was all history rather than myth. That man was a wealthy German entrepreneur, Heinrich Schliemann.

Schliemann taught himself the rudiments of archaeology. His success as a businessman, he believed, came not from talent but from self-discipline and perseverance, qualities which he applied so effectively to uncovering the secrets of the past. And yet, as David Traill (*Schliemann of Troy, Treasure and Deceit*, 1995) tells us, no archaeologist has been more severely criticised.

He was accused by contemporary scholars of digging insensitively through important levels of history without properly recording finds on the way – though it must be said that such care and precision only became routine later. Much worse, he is accused of lying, fraud and deception, manipulating his finds to suit his instinct for self-promotion and his ambition for international recognition; he was also a cheat, concealing the most precious pieces from the Turkish and later Greek authorities. Was he little more than an unscrupulous treasure-hunter?

Schliemann was born in Neubukow, in northern Germany, in 1822. His father, a Lutheran minister, was accused of embezzlement and the family could not afford to send the young Heinrich to university. Instead he was apprenticed to a firm of grocers, went to sea, was shipwrecked, and at 22 joined a German import–export company in St Petersburg. Here he showed an extraordinary talent for languages – during his life he learned to write and speak a dozen, including ancient Greek. Another of his talents was for business. Following his brother to California at the time of the Gold Rush, he started a bank trading in gold dust; during the Crimean War he sold ammunition material to the Russians. By the age of 36 he was wealthy enough to retire and dedicate himself to a passion conceived earlier in his life: classical archaeology, and in particular the search for ancient Troy.

In 1867 Schliemann moved to Paris, and when his wife refused to join him, divorced her. Determined on his new career, he decided he needed a new wife, preferably one who was young, Greek and ready to share his interest in archaeology. If the internet had existed he would surely have used it: instead he advertised for a wife in an Athens newspaper. A friend, the archbishop of Athens, introduced him to a relative, Sophia Engastromenos; she was 17, 30 years Schliemann's junior. They married in 1869. Schliemann was ready to start his search for ancient Troy.

The site in general terms was not in dispute and was well known in ancient times. When Xerxes invaded Europe in 480 BCE he made a special detour to see it. According to Herodotus he climbed up to Priam's citadel and, 'when he had been told the full story of what had happened there, he sacrificed a thousand heifers to Athena of Ilium and the Magi poured out libations to the heroes.' Two hundred and thirty years later Alexander the Great, on his way east to conquer the Persian Empire, stopped over at Troy to sacrifice to the Homeric heroes whom he regarded as his ancestors.

Commanding the entrance to the Hellespont, as the Dardanelles used to be called, Troy was perfectly positioned to exploit the rich trade that flowed to and from the Black Sea. But the silting up of rivers over thousands of years had altered the coastline and made the landscape almost unrecognisable (as it had at Thermopylae). Tradition held that the great mound of Hissarlik covered the ruins of ancient Troy, and this is where Schliemann proceeded to dig, his workmen rapidly excavating a huge trench that passed though the layers of different cities that in the course of 3,000 years had flourished, fallen and been rebuilt on the same site.

When his workmen reached one of the settlement's lowest levels Schliemann was convinced he had reached Priam's city. In May 1873 he reported: 'In excavating this wall further and directly by the side of the palace of King Priam, I came upon a large copper article of the most remarkable form, which attracted my attention all the more as I thought I saw gold behind it.' He immediately called an early lunch break for his workmen. 'While the men were eating and resting, I cut out the Treasure with a large knife [...] It would, however, have been impossible for me to have removed the Treasure without the help of my dear wife, who stood by me ready to pack the things which I cut out in her shawl and to carry them away.' Although his wife's help in concealing and removing the treasure in her shawl was one of Schliemann's favourite stories, he was eventually obliged to admit he had made it up! Sophia was in Athens at the time, her father having just died.

Later, questions were asked as to the provenance of the various components of the treasure: were they really found together and at the same time? Schliemann had contracted with the Turkish authorities to hand over part of his archaeological finds. Instead, claiming that they would disappear in the corrupt hands of an Ottoman pasha, he smuggled them to Athens, where he famously photographed Sophia adorned with the fabulous diadem and dripping with ancient gold – jewellery, Schliemann suggested, that had probably last been worn by Helen of Troy herself.

Schliemann's discovery of the astounding collection of bronze, gold and silver objects – 'Priam's Treasure' he called it, and the name has stuck – electrified newspaper readers in Europe and America. In fact, the artefacts discovered by Schliemann are now thought to belong to a level of Troy at least a thousand years earlier than Priam's city.

The subsequent history of 'Priam's Treasure' is suitably dramatic. For a time it was displayed in London and from 1881 in museums in Berlin. During World War II the treasure was hidden in a bunker under the Berlin Zoo, but in 1945 when the Russians captured the city it disappeared, spirited away, it is said, by the Red Army. For years the Soviet government denied any knowledge of it, until in 1993 it showed up in the Pushkin Museum in Moscow. Russia is unwilling to return the treasure, claiming it as compensation for Nazi Germany's looting of Russian cities and museums. Ownership is of course also claimed by the Turkish government.

Cheat, liar, conman … were only some of the words used to describe Schliemann – and that was even before he became an archaeologist. Nevertheless his extraordinary success at Troy and later at Mycenae captivated the imagination of the public, suddenly bringing into focus Homer's *Iliad* and other great stories of far-off times that had previously been regarded as fiction. His finds also demonstrated that Greek civilisation was about 1,000 years earlier than anyone had imagined.

Schliemann's discoveries, however questionably obtained and presented, made him famous, earning him the admiration of men as different as Gladstone and Freud; his success also inspired a new generation of archaeologists and led to a whole series of excavations throughout the Middle East and elsewhere, initiating the popular interest in digging up the past which is still with us today.

The corridor of land along the north Aegean coast, from the Dardanelles to Thessaloniki (earlier called Thessalonica or Salonica, today often called Saloniki) has been a route into Europe from the east travelled not only by men with new ideas (like St Paul) but by invading armies. It was the route Xerxes, the king of Persia, took in 480 BCE when he invaded Greece, a first step in his ambition to add Europe to his empire.

Xerxes knew of the difficulties in moving large numbers of soldiers and ships over long distances, and the importance of planning ahead. A decade earlier a storm had wrecked his father's fleet as it tried to round the peninsula of Mount Athos. To avoid a similar catastrophe, for the King of Kings there was a simple answer. Where the peninsula joins the mainland there is an isthmus, mainly flat, about a mile and a half across. Xerxes gave the order: dig a canal. Herodotus tells us the work, carried out by countless slaves of different nations 'under the lash', took three years. Traces of the canal, which was broad enough to take two triremes rowing abreast, are still visible today.

To provide the army on its long march, depots were set up at strategic points on the land route from the Dardanelles and supplied by merchant ships and overland caravans with every kind of store for the men and animals of his huge army.

We know this, and of many other details of this massive invasion from the east, from the writings of one man, Herodotus. He was born at Halikarnassus (modern Bodrum, on the Aegean coast of Turkey) about 484 BCE and died in the Greek city of Thurii in southern Italy soon after 430 BCE. He wrote his history (*historia,* inquiries) he said, 'to keep alive the memory of men's achievements and to ensure that the great and famous actions of Greeks and barbarians will not be forgotten, and to explain why they fought each other'.

'There it is,' writes Justin Marozzi (*The Man Who Invented History: Travels with Herodotus,* 2008). 'The birth of history in one paragraph. With these few words, written in the fifth century BC, Herodotus first formulates humankind's burning interest in the past, an obsession that has remained with us ever since.'

Herodotus was known to the ancients as 'the father of history'. He was also a great traveller, and perhaps he should be awarded a second title, 'father of travel writing'. Indeed it sometimes seems that the story of the Persian invasion of Greece, which occupies only the last three of his nine books, is merely a convenient hook on which to hang his detailed and colourful descriptions of the peoples of his world that he had collected with such evident interest and enjoyment.

When the king of Persia went to war he was obliged to include contingents from every part of the empire, no doubt a sound policy. Herodotus enjoys telling us of the nations that took part in this expedition, marching westwards towards Therma (modern Thessaloniki) partly because he knew that for most Greeks their appearance would seem startling, to say the least:

> The Persians, who wore on their heads the soft hat called the tiara, and about their bodies, tunics with sleeves, of divers colours, having iron scales upon them like the scales of a fish [...] The Assyrians went to war with helmets upon their heads made of brass [...] They carried shields, lances, and daggers very like the Egyptians; but they had wooden clubs knotted with iron, and linen corselets [...] The Sacae, or Scyths, were clad in trousers, and had on their heads tall stiff caps rising to a point. They bore the bow of their country, and the dagger; besides which they carried the battle-axe or *sagaris* [...] The Indians wore cotton dresses, and carried bows of cane with iron at the point [...] The Caspians were clad in cloaks of skin, and carried the cane bow of their country, and the scimitar [...] The Sarangians had dyed garments that showed brightly, and buskins that reached the knee: they bore Median bows, and lances [...] The Arabians wore the zeira, or long cloak, fastened about them with a girdle; and carried at their right side long bows, which when unstrung, bent backwards.

Of particular fascination for Herodotus and his readers were the Ethiopians, who:

were clothed in the skin of leopards and lions, and had long bows made of the stem of the palm-leaf, not less than four cubits [about 1.8m] in length. On these they laid short arrows made of reed, and armed at the tip not with iron but with a piece of stone [probably agate], sharpened to a point, of the kind used in engraving seals. They carried likewise spears, the head of which was the sharpened horn of an antelope; and in addition they had knotted clubs. When they went into battle they painted their bodies half with chalk, and half with vermilion.

Ethiopians of the west

had straight hair, while they of Libya are more woolly-haired than any other people in the world [...] They wore upon their heads the scalps of horses, with the ears and mane attached; the ears were made to stand up straight, and the mane served as a crest. For shields this people made use of the skins of cranes.

Herodotus lists contingents of some 40 nations in Xerxes's army. Most wore very little body armour, in contrast to the Greeks opposing them. Perhaps it was felt that they made up for this by sheer numbers and by their strange and often terrifying appearance.

As the invading army marched west, the fleet following along the shore, it had to cross the Strymon. Here in the river's running water the magi, the Persian priests, cut the throats of nine white horses to propitiate the river god; then, crossing the bridges at Nine Ways, took nine local children and buried them alive. Human sacrifice was not part of Zoroastrianism; but when so much depends on the success of a great enterprise the king may have thought it wise to cover every angle.

> *And a vision appeared to Paul in the night; there stood a man from*
> *Macedonia, and prayed him, saying, Come over to Macedonia and*
> *help us.*

(Acts 16:9, King James Version)

It was 50 CE, Paul was in Troas just across the straits from Europe. And so, accompanied by his 'friend in faith' Silas, he crossed the Dardanelles; and after speaking in Philippi, where he was beaten up and imprisoned, he arrived in Thessalonica (Thessaloniki), where he stayed with a sympathiser by the name of Jason.

Whether or not one is a Christian it is hard not to find Saul of Tarsus, better known by his Roman name Paul, one of the most fascinating people of his time. He was the first great Christian theologian, and Christianity today is largely a result of his interpretation of the Gospels. A strict Jew and a Pharisee, he was full of contradictions. As a young man he was a passionate enemy of the new-fangled faith of a small but vocal minority of Jews who outrageously asserted that the recently crucified criminal, Jesus of Nazareth, was the son of god, that he was the Messiah, and that he had been resurrected from the dead. Paul was determined to stamp out this absurd and dangerous heresy, and when his friends and colleagues had the Jesus-preaching Stephen in their power, they stripped off their cloaks and gave them to Paul to keep while they stoned Stephen to death; and it was Paul who then went from house to house dragging out believers and throwing them into prison.

He was on his way to Damascus to continue the good work in that city when his famous vision of God triggered a dramatic reversal. From that moment, and for the rest of his life, which ended with execution and martyrdom in Rome, he dedicated his talents not to the suppression of Christ's teachings but to their proclamation, at first to his fellow Jews and then, with increasing impatience at their refusal to listen, to the gentiles – the rest of the world.

In 380 CE, by the Edict of Thessalonica, Christianity became the state religion of the Roman Empire. Christianity would never have achieved this extraordinary success, or gone on to become a worldwide religion without Paul's single-minded efforts: 'the good news' of the evangelists would have remained the property of a minor and obscure Judaic sect.

It was some 20 years after Jesus's crucifixion that Paul started his journeys. Despite repeated disappointment, he never abandoned hope that his fellow Jews would see the light and be persuaded of Jesus's divinity. Wherever he went – and in most major cities there was a flourishing Jewish community – his first destination was the synagogue, as it was when he came to Thessaloniki.

Chapter 17 of Acts of the Apostles tells us that:

Paul, as his manner was, went in unto them, and three sabbath days reasoned with them out of the scriptures [...] alleging, that Christ must needs have suffered, and risen again from the dead; and that this Jesus, whom I preach unto you, is Christ. And some of them believed, and consorted with Paul and Silas; and of the devout Greeks a great multitude, and of the chief women not a few.

But the Jews which believed not, moved with envy, took unto them certain lewd fellows of the baser sort, and gathered a company, and set all the city on an uproar, and assaulted the house of Jason, and sought to bring them out to the people. And when they found them not, they drew Jason and certain brethren unto the rulers of the city, crying, These that have turned the world upside down are come hither also ... and these all do contrary to the decrees of Cæsar, saying that there is another king, *one* Jesus.

And they troubled the people and the rulers of the city [...] And the brethren immediately sent away Paul and Silas by night unto Berea.

Verea, to give it its modern name, some 70 kilometres south-west of Thessaloniki, is usually visited by tourists on their way to Vergina to see the magnificent tombs of the ancient kings of Macedon –

more of which are being excavated with astonishing results today – in the plain below the city. Because of its position on the edge of the Mount Olympus range, with unlimited water from springs and streams, Verea has always been prosperous and important, and consequently the victim of conquest by Romans, Byzantines, Normans, Franks, Turks and Bulgars, being finally incorporated into the modern Greek state only in 1913.

William Leake (*Travels in Northern Greece*, 1835) remarked on its prosperity in the early 1800s, commenting on the number of its churches, many of which were concealed as barns, and the quantities of water available for the numerous *hammams* or public baths. Jute and flax were manufactured there, and it was the home of the famous macarana towels, four of which were needed for each bather, plus another two for his bed to rest on after the bath.

When Paul preached there 1,800 years earlier Verea had a flourishing Jewish community who listened to what he had to say with interest. But when the Jews of Thessaloniki heard that Paul was continuing to spread his blasphemies they followed him to Verea, 'and stirred up the people'. The Christian brethren saw that Paul was in serious danger; Silas and Timothy decided to stay but insisted that Paul should leave – he was hurried to the coast and put on a ship for Athens.

Thessaloniki was important in St Paul's time and is today the second city in Greece. Its turbulent past during the last 1,500 years has been much more dramatic than that of Athens, which after its days of classical glory gradually shrank into obscurity.

A little-known theatre of World War I was the hinterland of Thessaloniki, Macedonia, where French and British forces fought with Serbia against the Bulgarians. *The Times* of 16 December 2015 published a letter of a century earlier from an officer in an English regiment, part of the Balkan Expeditionary Force that landed at Thessaloniki in 1915.

On board ship in the Aegean, he wrote, he and his men were delighted by the warm weather at the end of November:

> when we were glad of every bit of shade on deck [...] On arriving in Salonika we found a difference in temperature, the nights being particularly cold. After two or three days' rain the place was a swamp, then snow and frost set in, so it looks more like a Polar expedition, and the men in their sheepskin coats add to the picture.
>
> It is extraordinary when you think that we are in a neutral country. In the town you see men of all nationalities – Greeks, Turks, Jews, Bulgars, French, and British – and all sorts and conditions of uniforms. It is a strange sight to see in the same street ancient carts drawn by a pair of buffaloes or yaks (great grey brutes) and numbers of the French and British motor lorries and dispatch riders, with boys selling an English newspaper called the *Balkan News*. It is quite nice to be near a town once more where one can get hot baths and shampoos and buy anything one may want, although naturally the shopkeepers' motto is to 'make hay while the sun shines'. It is no good trying to argue, it is take or leave it.
>
> There are a music hall and picture palaces, also cafes and hotels where you can get a good English dinner. The dining room of the hotel is full of people of all nations – Ambassadors with their wives and families, Turks and Germans in civilian clothes, but the majority officers of all ranks. With 10 or 12 degrees of frost and snow underfoot we want plenty of warm clothing, but personally I am well and fit, and much prefer it to being boxed up in Flanders. Of course, we do not know how long we shall be in camp, and we may spend Christmas in dugouts in the Serbian mountains.

Thirty years later, Osbert Lancaster arrived in Thessaloniki. It was early in 1945 and the city had been reduced to war-ruined poverty, the occupation ended but the civil war far from over. He found the city deeply depressing, its violent history further blackened by the horror and disaster suffered by the Jewish community. Of the 70,000 Jews in the city in 1941 only some 1,200 remained. In *Classical Landscape with Figures* he wrote, 'Of the rest a few had managed to escape abroad, others had been hidden by Greeks, but the vast majority had been carried away to Poland, where those who survived the foodless journey in cattle trucks perished in the labour camp and the gas chamber.'

Lancaster's gloomy view extended even to the White Tower, which he admitted was impressive but could not resist adding, 'even the most besotted antiquarian would be hard put to deny it bears a striking resemblance to a crenellated gasometer.'

In Thessaloniki he finally found relief in the old upper town under the great fortification walls, and above all in the ancient churches that had somehow survived. Many of these were built when the Byzantine Empire was in decline. 'No longer could the reduced Empire afford to decorate its shrines with gold and precious stones; fresco must do duty for mosaic, brick for marble.' Lancaster found one building quite without rival:

The Church of the Holy Apostles, standing in a little untouched square in the old quarter of the town, is an elaborated version of the cross-in-square dating from the early years of the fourteenth century [...] with no less than five domes rising on exceptionally tall drums [...] but it is to its texture and surface decoration that it owes its pre-eminence. Never, even among the chimney stacks of Elizabethan England, can the decorative possibilities of brick have been so lavishly exploited as they are here: eaves, window-surrounds, string courses all display a variety and ingenuity of treatment unparalleled elsewhere. But it is for the decoration of the apses that the bricklayers have reserved the ultimate flights of their skill and fancy; here the courses ripple and weave, twist and turn into every imaginable geometrical formation.

Lancaster admired many Greek churches but he was mainly interested in their architecture. He would have agreed that for a

Christian brought up as Roman Catholic or Protestant, the first experience of an Orthodox church and its rites of worship can be strange and even alarming. Yet one of the many pleasures of walking in the Greek countryside is to come across the unexpected chapel, its whitewashed walls and slate dome suddenly visible between the olive trees.

Some of these mini-churches are ancient, usually occupying a site that was holy long before Christianity and now dedicated to the saint considered the most suitable replacement for his or her pagan predecessor. Many are new, built as a thanksgiving by a pious family of the neighbourhood, maintained privately and visited only occasionally. They come to life once a year on the saint's day, when the dome will reverberate with the chanting of a priest and the enthusiastic responses of the congregation crowding in. The chapel can never hold so many and they will spill outside and sit with their families under the surrounding olive trees, sharing the food and wine they have brought, until night falls and even the priest tires, and someone brings out a bouzouki and the dancing begins ...

Patrick Leigh Fermor was one who delighted in these half-abandoned shrines, with their atmosphere of dereliction and dust, the frescoes fading on their walls. 'Above their regulation beards and their ineluctable attributes,' he wrote in *Mani* (1958):

> the saints gaze from the iconostasis and the walls of the narthex and katholikon with a strange, blank, wide-eyed fixity, and behind their hoary and venerable heads, the golden haloes succeed each other in vistas of gleaming horseshoes or, when a saintly host is assembled in close array, in a shining interlock of glory like the overlapping scales of a vast goldfish [...]
>
> Scenes of carnage often cover the walls of churches from vaulting to flagstone. Beheadings, flayings, burnings, roastings [...] redden the mural cartouches with blood and flame. But something serene and formal in the treatment of these orgies of martyrdom, a mild

and benevolent composure in the faces of both executioner and victim and even on the haloed faces of the decapitated martyrs, robs their impact of anguish and horror.

In *Sailing to Byzantium* (1969) Osbert Lancaster also writes of these countryside churches he has come upon, often on foot on his way to visit a classical site. They have given him great pleasure:

Always small and usually decayed, the wall-paintings green-veined with damp, the plaster dropping from the Pantokrator in the dome, the Holy Table bare save for a yellowing copy of last year's *Kathimerini* and a jam-jar half full of oil and dead flies, they are infinitely far removed from the pomp and glitter of S. Vitale [in Ravenna] or Haghia Sophia [Constantinople].

Or, he might have added, from many of the large churches built in Greece today.

Nevertheless at high noon, when the silence is broken only by the buzzing of the wild bees which have nested on top of the iconostasis, and the air is heavy with the smell of honey-wax candles and the wild thyme on the threshold, it is in such humble shrines as these that one may, perhaps, come closest to understanding the message of Orthodoxy.

There is a lament in the wind's talk [...] *Turn south, it says, astern* [...] *There, carried high on a bank of clouds, hovers a shape, a triangle in the sky. This is the Holy Mountain Athos, station of a faith where all the years have stopped.*

(Robert Byron, *The Station*, 1928)

So wrote the young Robert Byron, on a ship leaving Athos for the port of Kavalla. Robert (distantly related to Lord Byron) arrived for

his first short visit to the Holy Mountain in August 1926. He wrote
to his mother:

> At last, after a year's planning I am here, and the suitcase. It is
> too wonderful for words – this long narrow peninsula – a single
> wooded range of mountains stretching out into the sea – and
> ending in a terrific peak, six thousand feet high – with clouds
> wreathing around it – all around the fresh green of the gardens
> of the monasteries, the woods of planes and Spanish chestnut –
> and the sea an ethereal silvery blue, like the wing of a butterfly,
> always visible.
>
> We arrived at Daphni, the little port, at six this morning [...]
> Our breakfast consisted of liqueurs like fire, watermelon and
> tea [...] Then we got three mules, heaved the suitcases and the
> Gladstone bag – containing insect spray, 8 tins of sardines, 2 of
> tongue, 2 of pate de foie gras, marching chocolate, cooking stove
> etc. on to it – and getting on the others set off on a 3 hour ride to
> Caryes, the capital.

Mount Athos, part of Greece, but internationally recognised as a
self-governing theocracy, has been a centre of Christian Orthodox
worship for more than 1,000 years. An imperial edict of 1046 banned
the presence of women (and children) on the peninsula, a prohibition
applying to all female creatures. The first monastery, the Grand Lavra,
was built in 963, but monks are known to have sought the peace and
solitude of the remote peninsula hundreds of years earlier.

Robert Byron, who through his writing almost single-handedly
brought Byzantine art and history to the attention of the general
public, had on his first visit seen with his own eyes some of the
treasures of the monasteries. On his second expedition the
following year much of the weight carried by the mules was
photographic equipment, including films and plates, for he had been
commissioned to write a book about Mount Athos at the same time
as one on Byzantine art and architecture. His friend David Talbot

Rice, already an archaeologist, was to take the photographs. They were accompanied by Mark Ogilvie-Grant, their contemporary at Eton, and Gerald Reitlinger a friend from Oxford. Besides quantities of the insect spray Flit, the mules were also loaded with saddlebags and boxes bulging with delicacies to alleviate the harsh monastic diet – jars of chicken in aspic, a soda syphon – as well as each expedition member's personal effects.

Most of the 20 monasteries, founded in the early Middle Ages, followed a pattern, as Byron described:

> Within [...] fortified walls, sometimes rising hundreds of feet from precipitous spurs of rock, sometimes set amidst terraced gardens or on the sea shore, and entered by one gate which is locked every evening at sunset, stand the church, chapels, refectories, guest houses and numerous rows of balconied cells [...] At the back rises usually a square tower, with machicolated balconies, now used as a library.

For the next few weeks the party set about visiting the monasteries, travelling by foot or by mule on the rough forest paths, guests of the monks with whom they negotiated permission to photograph the ancient and often fading frescoes of church and refectory, the icons and mosaics and the illuminated manuscripts hidden in the libraries. Their work was complicated by the dating system followed by the monks, who still insist on keeping to the old Julian calendar, 13 days adrift from the Gregorian used in the rest of the world; the hours of the day are also different, as the monks live by Byzantine time, where each day begins at sunset rather than midnight. Byron and Talbot Rice were largely successful in seeing and recording what they wanted, but it was exhausting and uncomfortable work which eventually took its toll.

On 1 October 1927, he wrote to his mother:

> At last we are off that mountain. We all began to get so ill at Caryes – I had a frightful migraine and a sore throat that I felt

sure was the prelude to typhus, and David had dysentery and was
sick, that we suddenly resolved to leave no matter whither and rode
down *in the dark* with all the things to Daphni [...] the road being
absolutely precipitous, and mules quite unable to see – the baggage
mule fell into a gully – another ran off into the virgin forest –
David fell off and was sick on the way.

At Daphni there was no food at the inn until 'Mark pushed the
man out of the kitchen and scrambled 2 dozen eggs which he found
in a basket. Then we went to bed – at 10. At 11 I killed 46 large red
bed bugs squirting blood over sheets already covered with vomit
and by morning brought the score up to 95.' Robert Knox, in his
biography, *Robert Byron* (2003), adds that eventually Robert and
Mark threw their mattresses out of the window. Mark's, which was
stuffed with hay, was eaten by a donkey.

Robert Byron's visits to Mount Athos were as nothing to the
great journeys he undertook in the following years, to Persia and
Afghanistan, India, Tibet and China. Among his many publications
the most outstanding is *The Road to Oxiana* (1937), judged one of
the best travel books ever written and deeply admired by writers
such as Patrick Leigh Fermor and Eric Newby, Bruce Chatwin and
William Dalrymple. Travel, and his passionate interest in humanism
and civilisation, helped him to outgrow the petty snobberies of
his contemporaries at Eton and Oxford, and unlike many of the
'Brideshead' set he was quick to see through Stalinism and was from
the first an outspoken enemy of both Mussolini and Hitler.

In October 1940 when Italy attacked Greece, he spoke to the
Greek people on the BBC. Apologising for his poor Greek, he
recalled his journeys in the Pindus mountains, at that moment
theatre of a savage war in which Greek forces were throwing back
the Italian invaders. The following year, from a military base in
Scotland, he was posted to Egypt. On 24 February, two days before
his thirty-sixth birthday, the ship he was on was torpedoed by a
U-boat off the Scottish coast. His body was never found.

More recently there has been a revival of interest in Mount Athos and monasticism in general. The number of novitiates enrolling in the 20 monasteries has grown and, since the opening up of Eastern Europe and Russia, funds have flooded in to repair and maintain the old foundations cut off for so long by the 1917 Revolution and the Iron Curtain. Today there are about 2,000 monks in the monasteries or living as hermits alone in caves or in small groups on the mountain's steep slopes.

Friends who have visited Athos in recent years report the existence of roads, wheeled traffic, even a bus and taxis, mobile phones … It was very different when I was there, fresh out of Cambridge, in September 1956, travelling, in the direction of India, with a good friend from university, David Gaunt. In our hands, of course, was a copy of Robert Byron's *The Station*.

Like every arrival on the Holy Mountain we reported first to the administrative offices at Karyes to receive our papers. We then decided to separate, each taking a different route round the peninsula. Surely, alone, without the distractions of each other's company, we would more easily absorb the spirituality radiating from this ancient centre of religious faith and learning.

A long day's walk and one mistaken direction along the paths that wound through the forest high above the sea took me to the walls of Iviron. Too late: the great gate was shut, and no amount of thumping on it drew any response. I could hear muffled chanting and guessed that the monks were in chapel where, I knew, they spent much of every night. Hungry but otherwise not too concerned, I set off downhill in the twilight towards the sea and was happy to scoop a bed out of pebbles still hot from the sun; only to wake a few hours later, surprised at how quickly they had lost their warmth and were now as cold as the stars wheeling slowly overhead.

Some days later David and I met up by chance in the courtyard of the Grand Lavra. We were delighted to see each other. Deciding that travelling alone was not as illuminating as expected, we continued our tour of the monasteries together, marvelling at these dramatic structures perched on the top of cliffs or clinging to their sides hundreds of feet above the sea. We were grateful for the hospitality of the monks and the simple food and wine generously offered, taken often in silence sitting at long refectory tables while a monk stood at a lectern reading aloud. At night, after keeping the monks company for part of the night's service, we slept in the moonlight on courtyard walls and benches – indeed anywhere outside, to avoid the fleas and bedbugs which were otherwise impossible to escape.

The plague of bedbugs was a hazard in the past shared by every pilgrim to the Holy Mountain, as were the toilet arrangements. Mark Ogilvie-Grant, travelling with Robert Byron, wrote home that 'sometimes they are triangles in the floor hanging over precipices so that the wind blows the paper up and it eddies round the room.' Thirty years later in the monasteries of Dionysiou and Simonopetra nothing had changed.

But pilgrims to the Holy Mountain are rightly expected to be above such mundane irritations, their minds raised to the consideration of higher things, whether their aim is to become closer to God through prayer and separation from the world, or through the appreciation of great art, or by creating it. One of the latter, who came to Athos to draw and paint in 1856, was Edward Lear.

Lear arrived by walking across the isthmus where Xerxes had built his canal. Lear was not feeling his best, having fallen down some stairs in Athens and hurt his back, while his servant Giorgio had become ill with a fever which he passed on to his master. Yet Lear, ever the dedicated professional, refused to let up – he had work to do and a living to make. 'I persisted & persisted': he walked at least eight hours a day and visited most of the main monasteries. In a letter to his friend Chichester Fortescue he mixed the admiration he felt for the stupendous scenery with outrage that men could perversely shut themselves away from life, banning the presence of women and anything female:

I never saw any more striking scenes than those forest screens and
terrible crags, all lonely, lonely, lonely: paths leading to hermitages
where these dead men abide, – or to the immense monasteries
where many hundred of these living corpses chant prayers nightly
and daily: the blue seas dash against the hard iron rocks below –
and the oak fringed or chestnut covered height above, with always
the great peak of Athos towering over all things, and beyond all
the island-edged horizon of wide ocean.

While he admitted that some of the monks were kind to him,
his general opinion of them was low, happily referring to them as
'muttering, miserable, mutton-hating, man-avoiding, misogynic,
morose and merriment-marring [...] mournful, minced-fish and
marmalade masticating Monx'. Nevertheless the drawings and
sketches he made of the Holy Mountain and its monasteries are
among the most beautiful he ever did.

The complete absence of women from the whole of the Athos
peninsula was a dramatic fact that struck many visitors. One of
the many who came in the nineteenth century, hoping also to buy
valuable manuscripts (at a low price) from the monks, was Robert
Curzon. He recounted his journey in *Visits to Monasteries in the
Levant* (1849) and never forgot his conversation with 'a magnificent-
looking man of thirty or thirty-five years of age, with large eyes and
long black hair and beard' who, like many of the monks, had spent
almost all his life on Athos. 'He did not remember his mother, and
did not seem quite sure that he ever had one; he had never seen a
woman, nor had he any idea what sort of things women were, or
what they looked like. He asked me if they resembled the pictures of
the *Panagia*, the Holy Virgin which hang in every church.' Anyone,
Curzon went on:

conversant with the peculiar conventional representations of the
Blessed Virgin in the Greek church, which are all exactly alike,
stiff, hard and dry, without any appearance of life or motion, will

agree with me that they do not afford a very favourable idea of the grace and beauty of the fair sex; and that there was a difference of appearance between black women, Circassians, and those of other nations, which was, however, difficult to describe to one who had never seen a lady of any race.

He listened with great interest while I told him that all women were not exactly like the pictures he had seen [...] but I did not think it charitable to carry on the conversation farther, although the poor monk seemed to have a strong inclination to know more of that interesting race of beings from whose society he had been so entirely debarred. I often thought afterwards of the singular lot of this manly and noble-looking monk; whether he is still a recluse, either in the monastery or in his mountain farm, with its little moss-grown chapel as ancient as the days of Constantine; or whether he has gone out into the world and mingled with its pleasures and its cares.

I suppose that motor vehicles and mobile phones are not necessarily barriers to godliness, but nor is there convincing evidence that better communications between earthly beings result in closer contact with God. But despite the arrival of modern times, some things on the Holy Mountain have not changed: women are still forbidden on the peninsula, though the embargo which extended to female animals such as hens and cats has been relaxed.

Only a few women are known to have successfully evaded the keen eyes of the monks. A couple of Victorian women managed to land on the peninsula, one being Lady Stratford de Redcliffe in 1852. The 1930s were enlivened by the first Greek to win the Miss Europe title, who shocked the world when she smuggled herself into Athos dressed as a man. In 1953 an American Fulbright Program teacher from Athens, Ohio, landed briefly, along with two other women, greatly upsetting the monks.

Perhaps the most bizarre female visitor was the prolific French writer Maryse Choisy, born in 1903, a follower of psychoanalysis and for a period a patient of Sigmund Freud. As far as possible she based her novels on firsthand experience, for example writing *Un mois chez les filles* (*A Month with the Girls*) only after spending time in a Marseilles brothel. In the 1920s she balanced this with *Un mois chez les hommes* (*A Month with the Men*), an account of her entry into Mount Athos disguised as a sailor, for which, with her boyfriend's agreement, she undertook what she called the 'Amazonian' surgical procedure. Despite this she still had to ward off advances from one of the monks, though she does not specify whether she was pursued as a boy or as a girl. It might have been coincidence, but after her experiences on the Holy Mountain she underwent a religious conversion, withdrew her books from publication and bought up any copies in circulation. She continued to write, however, with considerable success, dying in 1979.

The *avaton*, the exclusion of women from Athos, is increasingly questioned and in 2003 the European Parliament demanded the ban on women be lifted, since it violated 'the universally recognised principle of gender equality'. But the last words of Robert Byron's book – 'Athos, station of a faith where all the years have stopped' – still ring true, and it is unlikely that such a request will be granted any time soon.

When our world was young it was known that Giants existed, and according to the Greeks it was in the mountains of Pelion, Ossa and Olympus that they lived. It is said that the Giants resented the growing dominance of the new gods that had recently come down from the north. Hating the order that these arrogant foreign deities sought to impose upon their own agreeable anarchy, they attacked them with massive clubs and spears, hurling rocks and burning oak trees. The gods retreated to the heights of Mount Olympus. To get at their cowardly opponents, the Giants lifted up Mount Pelion, piled it on top of Ossa, and attacked again. In the long and terrible battle that followed, the Giants were picked off, one by one, by arrows shot by Apollo and Heracles, by the red-hot iron rods forged and flung by Hephaestus and by the death-dealing thunderbolts of Zeus.

The battle of the Giants with the Olympian gods is one of the most ancient of all myths, and writers who described the conflict, each offering his own interpretation of its significance, include Homer, Hesiod, Euripides, Sophocles, Pindar and Ovid, to mention only a few, while the details of individual combat in that epic war were sculpted on the friezes of temples throughout the Greek world. Defeated, the Giants' huge-boned bodies – beautiful, once, but now torn and disfigured – were buried deep under the mountains to ensure that even their spirits could not escape. Today, when the earth shakes and cities tremble, seismologists rush to measure, record and chart the grind and clash of tectonic plates, but we who understand the ancient myths know that it is the giants, bitter and angry, gathering their strength to rise up and challenge the gods again.

Anyone who has been to Volos, the seaport sheltering under the shoulder of Mount Pelion, will know that from this shore was launched perhaps the most famous ship of all time, *Argo*, which carried Jason and his heroic crew on a spectacular journey of adventure in quest of the Golden Fleece.

Today there are few secrets of geography left. Outer space has become our ultimate unknown, the theme of science fiction and the destination of our most perilous and costly expeditions. For the Greeks of ancient times little was known beyond the boundaries of the Mediterranean. Rumours reaching them of unscalable mountain ranges, burning deserts and vast oceans guarded by monsters not only aroused fantastical speculation but also inspired voyages of discovery as dangerous and dramatic to them as today's rocket-propelled missions to Mars. Of these the voyage of *Argo* was the first.

The story is an old one, known to Homer and Hesiod, told and retold by poets of the past, and as with all such legends few agree on the details. The only full account that has come down to us is by Apollonius of Rhodes, who lived and wrote mainly in Alexandria at the beginning of the third century BCE, perhaps nine centuries after the heroes set out.

There are always compelling reasons for the launching of such dangerous undertakings and in this case it was fear of a prophecy coming true. King Pelias, guilty of usurping the kingdom of Iolkos, as Volos was known in those times, had been warned that he was in mortal danger from a man arriving at his palace *with one foot bare.* As it happened, the young Jason (whose father, incidentally, should have been on the throne) had accepted the royal invitation to a banquet. On the way Jason, crossing a river, lost a sandal in the mud and reached the palace wearing only one. Noticing this horrific fact, the King's first instinct was to have Jason killed, but because the young man was so well known, he decided on a longer-term but equally effective solution. He would give Jason an impossible task – to bring him the Golden Fleece, the treasured possession of the king of Colchis. To the Greeks of that time, Colchis, on the eastern shore of the Black Sea, was on the very edge of the world; to reach this remote kingdom involved a sea journey into the unknown, beset by insuperable obstacles and fearful and unpredictable dangers. No man making the attempt could hope to return alive.

Jason accepted the challenge, as King Pelias expected he would, and set about his preparations. His first requirement was a suitable vessel, and in this he was helped by the goddess Athena, who put its design and construction in the willing hands of the famous craftsman Argus (who gave the ship its name).

Diodorus Siculus, writing in the first century BCE, explains that *Argo* was no ordinary ship, being 'much larger in every respect than was usual in those times, for then they used to sail only in boats and little skiffs'. *Argo*, built of wood from the great forests of Mount Pelion, was probably the first penteconter, a 50-oared galley (25 oars on each side), a class of warship not superseded in size and speed until the launching of the earliest trireme (170-oared) in about 550 BCE.

Diodorus tells us that as the news spread around Greece of the building and purpose of such an amazing ship, the bravest and most active young noblemen dropped everything and set off for Volos to enrol among the Argonauts and 'partake of the honour in this expedition'.

Jason's first choice of companion was Orpheus, who could 'with the music of his voice enchant stubborn mountain rocks and rushing streams [...] Testifying to the magic of his song,' Apollonius says, 'there are wild oaks growing on the coast of Thrace which he lured down from Pieria with his lyre, rank on rank, like soldiers on the march.'

Another to join early was Tiphys, 'an expert mariner, who could sense the coming of a swell across the open sea and learn from sun and stars when storms were brewing or a ship might sail.' The challenge proved irresistible to the great Heracles (Hercules). At the time he had just caught and was carrying on his broad shoulders, roped up and alive, the Erymanthine boar, but as soon as he heard of the expedition, 'he dropped the boar at the entrance to the market of Mycenae and promptly set out,' accompanied by the young Hylas 'to carry his arrows and serve as keeper of the bow'. Ancaeus, with his two older brothers from Tegea, 'came clad in a bearskin brandishing a huge two-edged axe in his right hand' because his grandfather, reluctant to see him go, had hidden his armour and weapons. Iphiclus came, 'a good fighter both with the javelin and hand-to-hand', and Euphemus, the son of Poseidon and Europa, the fastest runner in the world, who 'could run across the rolling waters of the grey sea without wetting his swift feet – his toes alone sank in as he sped along his watery path'. Against King Pelias's orders even Argus came, wearing the skin of a huge black-haired bull, followed by 'the mighty Polydeuces (also known as Pollux), the patron of boxing, and his twin brother Castor, 'that famous master of the racing horse', and Augeias, lord of the Eleans, said to be the richest man in Greece, 'who wished for nothing better than to see the land of Colchis', keen no doubt to compare its king's legendary wealth with his own. These and many others skilled in seamanship and war arrived to join Jason in his epic quest.

Most visitors to Volos today are either about to head up into the cooler air of Mount Pelion to escape the summer heat among the villages clinging to its slopes or about to take ferryboat or hydrofoil to the islands of the Sporades – Skiathos, Skopelos and Alonnisos. A bronze sculpture of *Argo* decorates the quay and if you sit at one of the many cafés along the splendid *paralia* (harbour front), a coffee or better still an ouzo in front of you, you can look past the yachts, beyond and across the water to the headland of ancient Pagasae. If in your mind's eye you scroll back a few thousand years, you will see the Argonauts, thronged by an excited crowd of eager townsfolk and weeping women, as they make their way 'through the city to the ship where it lay on the shore called Magnesian Pagasae'. The address has hardly changed in those millennia: as any map will tell you Volos is still to be found in the province of Magnesia, at the head of the Gulf of Pagasae.

Apollonius describes how the crew sat on the folded sails and the mast as it lay beside the ship high on the beach, and waited for Jason to address them. *Argo*, Jason said, was ready and fully equipped for the long voyage. But there was one thing still to be done – to choose a leader, an important decision, he emphasised, considering the dangers ahead and that they all wished to return safely.

> As he finished speaking the young men's eyes sought out the dauntless Heracles where he sat in the centre, and with one voice they called on him to take command. But he, without moving from his seat, raised his right hand and said: 'You must not offer me this honour. I will not accept it for myself, nor will I let another man stand up. The one who assembled this force must be its leader too.' The crew applauded his magnanimity and accepted the decision.

'Warlike Jason' was delighted, and following his instructions the crew prepared for *Argo*'s launch. 'At a word from Argus, they strengthened the ship by girding her with stout rope, which they drew taut on either side, so that her planks should not spring from their bolts but stand any pounding that the seas might give.' Next they dug a trench in front of the ship, a wide runway down to the sea, lined it with rollers of greased logs, and took their places alongside the ship. 'And now Tiphys leapt on board to tell the young men when to push. He gave the order with a mighty shout [...] At the first heave they shifted her [...] and then strained forward [...] to keep her on the move. And move she did. Between the two files of hustling, shouting men, Pelian *Argo* ran swiftly down.'

With the logs on which she rolled smoking from friction, the ship made a great splash on entering the sea and the crew had to keep hold of the ropes to haul her back to the beach. They shipped the oars, put all the stores on board, stepped the mast and drew lots for their places on the benches, which held two oarsmen each. 'But the midships seat they gave to Heracles, selecting as his mate Ancaeus [...] leaving this bench for their sole use [...] and they all agreed that Tiphys should be the helmsman of their gallant ship.'

'Next, piling up shingle on the beach, they made a seaside altar for Apollo as god of shores and embarkation,' spreading dry olive wood on top. Two oxen from Jason's herd had been brought for sacrifice. As Jason sprinkled barleycorn he prayed to Apollo for:

fair weather and a gentle breeze to carry us across the sea; Heracles stepped forward killing an ox with a single blow of his club, while Ancaeus decapitated the other with one stroke of his bronze axe. The oxen were promptly skinned and cut up for roasting on the fire – with careful attention to the sacred pieces from the thighs, and Jason poured libations of unmixed wine [...]

When radiant Dawn with her bright eyes beheld the towering crags of Pelion, and the headlands washed by wind-driven seas stood sharp and clear, Tiphys awoke and quickly roused his comrades to embark and fix the oars.

Even *Argo* cried out, the voice coming out of a magic beam made from an oak at Dodona that Athena had made sure was carpentered into the ship's stem.

So they followed one another to the rowing benches and, taking their allotted places, sat down in proper order with their weapons by them. Ancaeus sat amidships beside the mighty bulk of Heracles, who laid his club near by and made the ship's keel underfoot sink deep into the water. And now the hawsers were hauled in and they poured libations to the sea.

The poet Pindar, writing a couple of centuries before Apollonius, records (translated by Peter Levi) Jason's prayer as *Argo* is launched:

> The captain on the stern
> held in his hand
> a cup of gold,
> called on the Father of the sons of heaven:
> Zeus, his spear the lightning flash,
> on the swift rush of waves and on the winds,
> the nights, and the sea's roads,
> serene days and beloved homecoming;
> assenting thunder answered out of clouds
> and tearing through them flashed the bright lightning.
> And the heroes breathed courage again.

'Jason wept', Apollonius tells us,

> as he turned his eyes away from the land of his birth. But the rest struck the rough sea with their oars in time with Orpheus's lyre [...] Their blades were swallowed by the waves, and on either

side the dark salt water broke into foam, seething angrily in answer to the strong men's strokes. The armour on the moving ship glittered in the sunshine like fire; and all the time she was followed by a long white wake which stood out like a path across a green plain [...]

All the gods looked down from heaven that day [...] and from the mountain heights the nymphs of Pelion admired Athene's work and the gallant Argonauts themselves, tugging at the oars.

Typhis is at the helm, his hand on the 'polished steering-oar', when now:

they stepped the tall mast in its box and fixed it with forestays drawn taut on either bow; then hauled the sail up to the masthead and unfurled it. The shrill wind filled it out; and after making the halyards fast on deck, each round its wooden pin, they sailed on at their ease past the long Tisaean headland, while Orpheus played his lyre and sang a sweet song of highborn Artemis, Saver of Ships [...] Fish large and small came darting out over the salt sea depths and gambolled in their watery wake [...] and the wind, freshening as the day wore on, carried *Argo* on her way.

Modern travellers on hydrofoil, ferryboat or yacht, bound for the islands of the Sporades, traverse the same waters as *Argo*, with the capes and headlands on either side hardly changed by the passing millennia. With the summer *meltemi* blowing fresh behind them, the vessel's white wake streaming astern, the launch of *Argo* could all have happened yesterday, or even today.

On board ship leaving the Gulf of Volos, if heading for the islands, you must turn left, as *Argo* did, passing close by the small harbour of Trikeri. With his usual care and attention to detail, William Leake describes in *Travels in Northern Greece* the village on its hilltop, safe from surprise attack from pirates, and the way Aegean shipping was financed in the early nineteenth century:

> Trikeri, called Bulbulje by the Turks, contains three or four hundred houses, constructed in the same manner as those of the district of Volo [*sic*], and situated on the summit of a high hill at the eastern entrance of the gulf. The people live entirely by the sea; some of the poorer classes [...] cut sponges and catch starfish. The others are sailors, ship or boat builders, and traders. The highest rank are ship-owners, or captains of ships. The richest lend money at a high interest upon maritime traffic, or make advances upon bills, drawn upon Constantinople, where the cargoes which are chiefly of corn are generally sold. The Trikeriotes usually fit out their ventures in the same manner as the people of Ydhra, Spetzia, Poro and many other maritime towns; that is to say, the owner, captain, and sailors, all have shares in the ship and cargo, the sailors generally sharing a half among them, which is in lieu of all other demands. During the scarcity of corn in France at the beginning of the Revolution a sailor's share for the voyage amounted sometime to three purses, which at that time was equivalent to 150*l.* sterling.

Apollonius went on to chronicle *Argo*'s legendary voyage, how the beautiful witch-princess Medea, daughter of the king of Colchis, falls passionately in love with Jason, how he finally acquires the Golden Fleece, the quarrels and betrayals among his crew, how *Argo* escapes being crushed between the Cyanean rocks and traverses the rivers of Europe before finally returning, in reasonable shape but minus several of her original crew, to Pagasae. The Greeks believed that in honour of Jason's achievement the gods carried the *Argo*, 'finest of all ships that ever braved the sea with oars', up into the sky, placing it beside Sirius as a constellation where, on a clear Aegean night, it is still visible with the naked eye.

When Apollonius first wrote his *Argonautica* it was badly received in Alexandria, where the writers and critics whom he most

admired derided his efforts. Particularly harsh was Callimachus of
Cyrene, the poet, critic and scholar who worked with Apollonius
at the great Library of Alexandria. Callimachus favoured short,
compact writing; one of his epigrams, as valid then as it is today,
was: 'Big book, big evil.' He was against long Homeric epics – such
as the *Argonautica* – and made his feelings to the young man clear,
starting a feud between the two that lasted the rest of their lives.
Apollonius felt so humiliated that he left Alexandria for Rhodes
and rewrote the entire book. The second attempt is the one we can
read today and its success – still in print after 2,300 years – must
be an encouragement to rejected writers everywhere. When the
new version was published in Alexandria, all was forgiven (except
by Callimachus) and Apollonius returned to work at the Library.
It was now the turn of Callimachus to be humiliated: Ptolemy
II appointed Apollonius chief librarian, over the head of his
older colleague.

Argo ended her seagoing days pulled up on shore at the isthmus
of Corinth. In *The Golden Fleece* (1944), Robert Graves's account of
the great voyage, this is how Jason died:

> Jason was overcome with grief at the death of his four children [...]
> and that he was now undisputed king of the double kingdom of
> Corinth gave him no comfort. He went down one early morning
> to the shrine of Poseidon on the isthmus, and there lay brooding
> under the prow of the *Argo*, wrapped in his figured cloak, and
> without either sacrificing to Poseidon or speaking a civil word to
> any of the priests who came out to greet him.

The Chief Priest tried to talk to him. 'Jason turned his head, but
still would not answer. There was a dazed look in his eyes and his
mouth stood open, like a child who is about to cry, but no cry came.'
Dismissing the others, the priest 'sat watching from the temple
steps, warned by his own heart that some strange event was about to
take place that he could neither hasten not hinder'.

Jason's head sank lower. He fell asleep. And presently the Chief Priest saw from the corner of his eye what he could not have seen directly – the pale forms of a man and a hound coming at a shambling run along the road from Megara [...]

The hound made straight for Jason and stood over him, baring its fangs in a snarl, the fur at its neck rising; but the shepherd clambered up into the bows of the *Argo*, as a lizard runs up a wall.

Then, as the Chief Priest watched, holding his breath, the shepherd shoved hard with his shoulder at the curved prow; and as he strained, his foot braced against a stanchion, the eight winds ceased their sport and all rushed with a roaring noise along the gunwale on both sides of the ship.

There was a tearing sound, and a loud crash. Down fell the tall prow, and the muzzle of the Ram figure-head struck Jason upon the skull and crushed it miserably to a pulp. Yet the prudent Chief Priest did not move from his seat until both shepherd and dog had satiated themselves with the blood and brains of their enemy; for had he baulked these phantoms of their vengeance they would have haunted the enclosure insufferably. Now, however they trotted away in perfect contentment.

Robert Graves wrote the ending to *The Golden Fleece* when he had just received the news that his eldest son David, fighting in Burma, was reported missing, presumed dead. In the last paragraph of his book Graves tells also of the violent death of Jason's companion Orpheus: 'The Ciconian women one night tore him to pieces during their autumnal orgies in honour of the Triple Goddess. Nor is this to be wondered at: the Goddess has always rewarded with dismemberment those who love her best, scattering their bloody pieces over the earth to fructify it, but gently taking their astonished souls into her own keeping.'

The King with half the East at heel is marched from lands of morning;
Their fighters drink the rivers up, their shafts benight the air.
And he that stands will die for nought, and home there's no returning.
The Spartans on the sea-wet rock sat down and combed their hair.

(A. E. Housman, 'The Oracles', 1922)

The need to speed along the national road which links northern and southern Greece means that certain places of historical significance are easily passed unnoticed. Thermopylae, the 'Hot Gates' as it was called because of its thermal springs, is one. The sea, which once lapped the edge of the ancient road, has receded across what is now flat agricultural land to the distant horizon. Yet it was here, in 480 BCE, defending the narrow stretch of road between the sea and the cliffs of Kallidromos, that a king of Sparta, Leonidas, and his Three Hundred came, leading some 7,000 allied troops, to defend the pass against an immense Persian army. What happened in the next few days, told by Herodotus and other Greek and Roman writers, has caught the imagination of every generation since.

When Xerxes sent out cavalry to spy out the enemy position, they could see little because the Greeks were camped on the other side of an old wall that stretched across the pass from the cliff-face to the edge of the sea. One of the horsemen rode as close as he dared and saw in front of the wall men, naked, engaged in gymnastic exercises, washing, and caring for their long hair; their weapons were piled beside bright crimson cloaks. Mystified, and also surprised that they paid him no attention whatsoever, he reported back to the King. Xerxes asked for an explanation from Demaratus, the exiled king of Sparta who by accompanying Xerxes hoped to regain power when the Persians triumphed. Demaratus may have smiled to himself when he heard the description – by their red cloaks he knew who they were. They were Spartans, he said to the King, and they always paid great attention to their appearance before battle.

When Xerxes asked why there were so few of them at Thermopylae he was told that the rest were attending an important religious festival, and that most other Greeks were celebrating the sacred Games at Olympia. The King was not impressed. Herodotus tells us that the Persian nobles joked that the prize for winning at the Games must be valuable indeed, to keep men from defending their homes; on the contrary, Demaratus answered, the prize was a wreath of olives. This reply further annoyed the company present and the Spartan felt it wise to retire.

Earlier in the campaign when Xerxes had asked Demaratus about the resistance his invading army could expect, Demaratus had told him that the Greeks who would never give in to him were the Spartans; they were free men and would never be slaves, and as soldiers, when fighting together, they were the best and bravest in the world. But though they valued their freedom, they were not completely free: 'their freedom is governed by law, which they fear even more than your subjects fear you, O King. And their law commands that in battle they never surrender, however many are against them; they must stand firm, and conquer or die.'

Demaratus knew what he was talking about. The only professional soldiers in the Greek world, the Spartans were brought up from boyhood to eat, fight and sleep with the same friends in the same military group, developing not only first-rate discipline and fighting skills but also an unbreakable bond between themselves. He guessed that Leonidas had been ordered to hold the pass, if need be to the death.

And so it proved. Several days of continuous assault on the Greeks, who fought in relays in front of the wall, made no impression, thanks to Spartan discipline and the Greeks' superior armour. The Spartans faced a multitude of archers but they had their large round shields to give some shelter. When they were warned of the avalanche of arrows that would soon fall upon them, one of them replied, 'So much the better, we shall fight in the shade.'

The traitor Ephialtes, who told the Persians of the path through the mountains, broke the deadlock. It was dusk, Herodotus tells us, 'at about the time the lamps were lit', that Hydarnes and his 10,000 'Immortals' set off, guided by Ephialtes, on their night march to cut off the Greeks.

When a scout brought Leonidas the news that the Persians had broken past the Phocians guarding the mountain path, he asked Megistias the famous seer for his opinion. Megistias examined the entrails of a sacrificed goat and pronounced that death would come in the evening. Leonidas dismissed his allies, who were glad to escape southwards while the road was still open. As Demaratus had known they would, Leonidas and his Spartans stayed.

Herodotus writes that when Leonidas learned that the Persians had reached the coast, and the trap was closed, he abandoned the wall and brought his men out to fight in front of it; and when he was killed how the survivors retreated to the mound where, with weapons broken, they fought on with hands and teeth to the end.

The battle was a bitter defeat for the Greeks, but as an enduring symbol of courage in the face of overwhelming strength it has few equals. William Golding, author of *Lord of the Flies* and Nobel Prize-winner, visited Thermopylae in the early 1960s. In *The Hot Gates*, a collection of essays published in 1965, he writes of his experience as he walked over the scene of the ancient battle.

I came to myself in a great stillness, to find that I was standing by the little mound. This is the mound of Leonidas, with its dust and rank grass, its flowers and lizards, its stones, scruffy laurels and hot gusts of wind. I knew now that something real happened here. It is not just that the human spirit reacts directly and beyond all argument to a story of sacrifice and courage, as a wine glass must vibrate to the sound of a violin. It is also because, way back and at the hundredth remove, that company stood right in the line of history. A little of Leonidas lies in the fact that I can go where I like and write what I like. He contributed to set us free.

The famous epigram for the Spartan dead was written by the poet Simonides of Ceos, a rival of Pindar, who was alive at the time. His words are inscribed under the colossal bronze statue of Leonidas who today stands tall, shield in hand, spear raised, beside the old road.

> Go tell the Spartans, stranger passing by,
> That here, obedient to their laws, we lie.

 3

ATHENS

*One clear image will stand in my mind forever: the Parthenon, stark,
stripped, economical, violent, a clamorous outcry against a landscape of
grace and terror.*

(Le Corbusier, *Towards an Architecture*, 1923)

*Here sky is everywhere, on all sides the sun's ray,
And something all around like the honey of Hymettus;
The lilies emerge unwithering from the marble;
Divine Penteli flashes, begetter of an Olympus.*

*The excavating axe stumbles on beauty;
In her entrails Cybele hold gods instead of mortals,
Athens gushes violet blood
Each time the shafts of twilight strike her.*

(Kostis Palamas, 'Songs of My Fatherland', 1886)

If every famous city has its symbol – New York the Statue of
Liberty, Paris the Eiffel Tower – then Athens has the magnificently
columned Parthenon crowning the Acropolis. Cyriac of Ancona,
papal diplomat and traveller, was delighted by his visit to Athens
in 1436, but what pleased him most (quoted by Mary Beard in
The Parthenon, 2002) was 'the great and marvelous temple of
Pallas Athene on the topmost citadel of the city, a divine work
by Phidias, which has 58 towering columns, each seven feet in
diameter, and is splendidly adorned with the noblest images on
all sides'.

When the Englishman George Wheler and his friend Jacob Spon were in Athens in 1676, Greece had been a province of the Ottoman Empire for 200 years; they had difficulty in getting permission from the governor to visit the Acropolis and only succeeded with a present of 'three *Oka's* of *Coffee*' (about 4 kilos). And yet the beauty of the Parthenon had not diminished. Wheler wrote in his *A Journey into Greece* (1682) that the temple of Minerva, as the Parthenon was then known, 'is not only the chief ornament of the citadel; but absolutely, both for matter and art, the most beautiful piece of antiquity remaining in the world. I wish I could communicate the pleasure I had in viewing it.' The friends' next objective was the Erechtheion, but 'we could not have permission to go into the temple, to see it, because the Turk that lives in it, hath made it his seraglio for his women; and was then abroad.'

Visitors today who marvel at the bare beauty of the buildings rising from the bedrock of its summit may be surprised to know that the Parthenon was a temple to the goddess Athena for only eight of its 24 centuries of existence. For the next 1,000 years it was a Christian church, and then for 400 a Turkish mosque.

The Parthenon had been protected as a place of worship under Christianity and Islam, but in 1687 when the Venetians were besieging the Acropolis a shell hit the Turkish stock of gunpowder stored inside. The explosion killed 300, blew the roof off and hurled down many of the ancient columns. The half-ruined building, still with its minaret, continued to stand, together with a massive tower erected earlier by the Florentines, surrounded by the packed houses of a Turkish village.

After Greek independence in 1821 it was decided by the newly installed Bavarian monarchy that the fledgling nation should best represent itself by its classical past, and that everything in between – Byzantine and especially Turkish – should as far as possible be forgotten or set aside. As Michael Llewellyn Smith put it in *Athens: A Cultural and Literal History* (2004): 'The priority for nineteenth century Greece was to assert Greek identity as a member of the

European family with roots firmly planted in ancient classical soil.' Consequently, from the 1830s, the Acropolis was subjected to a dramatic facelift that painstakingly erased, cut and smoothed away every trace of building later than the fifth century BCE. Today the buildings towering above you are the basic constructions of Periclean Athens. Except that Pericles, if he were alive today, would notice that a lot was missing.

Lord Byron was in Athens while many of the Parthenon's best bits were torn down, carted to Piraeus and shipped to England. At the time he was on friendly terms with Lord Elgin's agent Lusieri who coordinated the work, as well as with Lusieri's rival the Frenchman Fauvel (who would have done exactly the same, except that the destination of the looted – or saved? – sculptures would have been Paris rather than London). While the sculptures were collected – many of them hacked and sawn off the great marble slabs of the building's upper levels, Lord Elgin remained most of the time at his ambassadorial post in Constantinople, plying Lusieri with instructions and sending money to sweeten the Turkish authorities and pay the workmen.

> Cold is the heart, fair Greece! that looks on thee
> Nor feels as lovers o'er the dust they loved;
> Dull is the eye that will not weep to see
> Thy walls defaced, thy mouldering shrines removed
> By British hands.

Byron, who had begun to write *Childe Harold's Pilgrimage,* had been mulling over the rights and wrongs of what he had witnessed in Athens, and came down fiercely against Elgin. By the time he returned to England in 1811, ironically travelling the first part of the journey on a ship carrying some of Elgin's marbles, he had made up his mind. In March *Childe Harold* was published in London to unexpected acclaim ('I woke up one morning and found myself famous'). Byron's newly acquired celebrity ensured that his vicious attack on the Scottish Lord Elgin, in the second canto of the poem was widely read; it set the tone for the controversy over the theft – or rescue? – of the marbles, a subject with cultural and political implications that have inspired passionate debate ever since.

Byron's friend Hobhouse found an inscription carved by a wit on a wall of the Erechtheion which read: QUOD NON FECERUNT GOTI HOC FECERUNT SCOTI – 'What the Goths did not do has been done by the Scots'. It was Hobhouse who noted with uncommon prescience the 'singular speech of a Learned Greek of Iannina, who said to me, "You English are carrying off the works of *the Greeks*, our forefathers – preserve them well – as we Greeks will come and re-demand them!"'

But William Turner, assigned to the British Embassy at Constantinople and in Athens during 1812–14, had a different view of Lord Elgin's activities (*Journal of a Tour in the Levant*, 1820). Considering the damage already done to the sculptures on the Acropolis, he felt that Elgin should have carried off more: 'At all events, I think that Athens and England are both under infinite obligations to him for what he has saved. The very metal found inside the columns, for which the seller can procure thirty piastres, is a strong temptation to the barbarians, under whose custody the splendid ruins of Greece are unfortunately placed.'

Greece was first looted of its statues and sculptures on a grand scale by the Romans. The second major assault came in the eighteenth century, before the start of any serious interest in archaeology, and before even the word was invented, when Greece was one of the poorest regions of the Ottoman Empire and so under-populated, according to Thomas Peachem in *The Compleat Gentleman* (1634) that in parts 'there were more Statues than men living'. In any case there was every justification for taking them away, 'for by reason of the barbarous religion of the Turks, which alloweth not the likeness or representation of any living thing, they have been for the most part buried in ruins or broken to pieces'.

Terence Spencer notes in *Fair Greece Sad Relic* (1954) that:

Elizabethan visitors were not above bringing a keepsake home. Indeed Thomas Dallam, the organ-builder who in 1599 was sent to Constantinople with one of his instruments as a present from Queen Elizabeth to the Sultan, provides us with the first recorded example of the British souvenir-hunter in Greek lands; on the way to Constantinople he and some of the merchants went ashore at 'Cape Janissary' to make a tour of the ancient sites. 'We saw more at large the ruins of the walls and houses in Troy, and from thence I brought a piece of white marble pillar, the which I broke with my own hands, having a good hammer, which my mate Harvie did carry ashore for the same purpose; and I brought this piece of marble to London.'

Dallam's diary, first published by the Hakluyt Society, can now be enjoyed in modern English thanks to John Mole (*The Sultan's Organ*, 2012), who describes the instrument Dallam took to Constantinople as a 'chiming clock with jewel encrusted moving figures combined with an automatic organ, which could play tunes on its own for six hours'. Dallam went on to build less exotic instruments, including the organ in the Chapel of King's College, Cambridge, though only a fraction of the original now remains.

Dallam's minor pilfering was nothing to the wholesale looting and destruction of ancient sites that took place in the eighteenth century, as can be guessed from the *Gentleman's Magazine* of November 1793, which advised the traveller, 'if he meet with any statues or Colossus too great to be carried away whole, he must employ men to saw it asunder with iron saws and sharp sand.'

As foreseen by many, the sculptures not carried off by Elgin and which remained on the Parthenon did suffer further damage, most of it caused by a more modern enemy, pollution. With the knowledge we have of those times and circumstances, Byron's attack on Lord Elgin seems unfair, and yet if Byron were alive today he would surely support Greece's claim to have the marbles returned, especially now that they would be safe, and perfectly presented, in the modern museum newly built just below the Acropolis.

The arrival of the marbles in England and their public exhibition revolutionised European taste in classical sculpture, which until then had preferred the polished and idealised copies made by the Romans. William St Clair, in *Lord Elgin and the Marbles* (1967), reflected: 'These large mutilated marbles with the intimate knowledge of anatomy that they revealed [...] set an entirely new standard in the appreciation of ancient art.'

Sue Brown, biographer of the painter Joseph Severn, who nursed John Keats on his death bed in Rome, tells us how the young poet went to see the Elgin Marbles several times in 1817 'and would sit for an hour or more at a time beside them rapt in reverie'. It is easy to believe that some of the images in his 'Ode on a Grecian Urn' were inspired by the sculptures:

> Who are these coming to the sacrifice?
> To what green altar, O mysterious priest
> Leadest thou that heifer lowing to the skies [...]?

Mary Beard in *The Parthenon* asks the key question governing the controversy: to whom does the Parthenon belong?

> Does it count as the possession of all those who would love to see themselves as the inheritors of the values of fifth-century Athens? Or those whose capital city it dominates? Can a single monument act as a symbol both of nationhood and of world culture? [...] Paradoxically its status as international icon can hardly be disentangled from its diaspora that so many of us lament. Not just from London to Athens, but from Uppsala to Rome, Nashville to Paris, the Parthenon is literally a wonder of the world.

Suddenly, at a turn of the road between the low green hills, I saw standing huge before me a great flat rock, like a platform raised by Titans to assail the gods from. Upon its top, glowing bright in the westering sunlight, stood

a royal palace, the columns russet red, the pink-washed walls picked out
with white and blue squares. So high it stood against the sky, the guards
on the ramparts looked as small as goldsmith's work, and their spears as
fine as wire. I caught my breath. I had guessed at nothing like this.

(Mary Renault, *The King Must Die*, 1958)

This is how Theseus, in Mary Renault's *The King Must Die*, first saw the Acropolis as he came from Eleusis to claim his heritage from the father he had never met, Aegius, king of Athens.

Renault's novels opened up ancient Greece to a new and wider reading public, but she had been writing long before the publication of the first of her historical novels, *The Last of the Wine*, in 1956. Born Eileen Mary Challans in 1905, she adopted her pen-name (which she pronounced 'ren-olt') soon after leaving Oxford University. To earn a living and gain experience of life she trained as a nurse at Oxford's Radcliffe Infirmary, working with survivors of Dunkirk and later with patients suffering brain damage. Here she met the 22-year-old Julie Mullard who was to be her companion for the rest of her life. Despite the long hospital working hours, Renault managed to write in her free time, publishing five novels, before winning a major MGM cash prize for *Return to Night* in 1946.

The prize changed her life. With Julie Mullard she began to travel in Africa and Europe. Of all places visited she found Greece 'incomparably the most moving and memorable'; she found it 'a man's country', however, not ideal for unmarried women, especially if they were foreign. Instead, she and Julie made their home in South Africa, first in Durban and then in Cape Town, where they could live together without shocking the neighbours.

During her lifetime Mary Renault became, unwillingly, something of an icon to gays of both sexes, though neither she nor Julie Mullard ever referred to themselves as lesbians. Many years later she told the late David Sweetman, her biographer: 'I think a lot of people are intermediately sexed. It's like something shading from white to black with a lot of grey in the middle.'

She had already written of homosexual relations in *The Charioteer* (1953), a brave story of two young servicemen finding their identity in wartime England, drawing for their ideas on Plato's Dialogues; the novel was positively received but shocked many: it had to wait six years before publication in America, and only after the success of *The Last of the Wine*, claimed to be the best novel ever written about ancient Greece.

The historical novelist Sarah Dunant (author of *Blood and Beauty*) wrote in the introduction to the reissuing by Virago of some of Renault's early novels: 'From the opening sentence of *The Last of the Wine*, ancient Greece and the male voices through which she enters it burn off the page with an immediacy and power that will characterize all her historical fiction. Homosexual love, sacrifice, companionship and heroism abound in a culture which accepts, encourages and celebrates sexual diversity.'

Renault had found the perfect stage on which to launch her favourite heroic actors of myth and history, recreating a world that she brought passionately to life by her talent for storytelling and the care she took in researching historical detail. She had also found a time and a place where emotions were not governed or distinguished by gender, and where homosexual love was often a simple and natural extension of personal relations.

The Last of the Wine was followed by the two novels about the hero Theseus (*The King Must Die* and *The Bull from the Sea*, 1962). *The Mask of Apollo* was published in 1966. Her last novels were the celebrated trilogy on the life of Alexander the Great: *Fire from Heaven* and *The Persian Boy*, completed by *Funeral Games*, two years before her death.

Mary Renault visited Greece only twice, in 1954 and 1962, returning always to Cape Town and her house overlooking the ocean where she lived with Julie Mullard, her dogs and an expanding library of books on Greece and ancient history. It was there that in 1983 she died of lung cancer; she was 78. Her books have never stopped selling and recently there has been renewed acclaim for her work from critics, fellow novelists and historians. No writer has been so effective in bringing alive to so many people Greece of the distant past.

Athens in its long life has seen more than its share of dramatic events. One that I keep returning to in my mind occurred in those fateful few days in the late summer of 480 BCE when Xerxes, King of Kings, determined to destroy Athens, was approaching from the north with a vast army and fleet, carrying all before him. As news of the Persians' rapid progress filtered south, it must have been obvious to all that the little world of Greece, with its city-states, gods and traditions, was about to be extinguished forever.

The Athenians knew they were marked down by the Great King for destruction. Ten years before, at Marathon, the army sent against the Athenians by Xerxes's father Darius had been heavily defeated. Now, the son was coming to take his revenge. Torn by anxiety about what action to take in face of the disaster about to overwhelm them, the Athenians had sent a delegation to Delphi to ask the oracle's advice. Herodotus says:

> As soon as the customary rites were performed, and they had entered the shrine and taken their seats, the Priestess Aristonice uttered the following prophecy:
>
>> Why sit you, doomed ones! Fly to the world's end [...]
>> All is ruined, for fire and the headlong God of War
>> Speeding in a Syrian chariot shall bring you low.
>> Many a tower shall he destroy, not yours alone,
>> And give to pitiless fire many shrines of gods,
>> Which even now stand sweating, quivering with fear,
>> While over the rooftops black blood runs streaming
>> In prophecy of woe than needs must come.

Appalled by the god's words the Athenian envoys were about to abandon themselves to grief, when they were advised to approach the oracle once more, 'with branches of olive in their hands, in the guise of suppliants'.

'Lord Apollo,' they said, 'in consideration of these olive boughs we have brought you, can you not give us some better prophecy about our country? Otherwise we will never leave this holy place and will stay here till we die.' Reluctantly the oracle returned a second response, slightly less unfavourable: there was to be no escape from destruction, but the Athenians were advised that their 'wooden wall' would not fail them:

> But wait not the host of horse and foot coming from Asia,
> Nor be still, but turn your back and withdraw from the foe.
> Truly a day will come when you will meet him face to face.

And then came the two critical lines:

> Divine Salamis, you will bring death to women's sons
> When the corn is scattered, or the harvest gathered in.

On their return to Athens the envoys made public the oracle's answer. Herodotus tells us of the intense and anxious debate that followed: what did the god mean? The older men thought that the Acropolis would escape destruction 'on the grounds that it was fenced in the old days with a thorn hedge, and that this was *the wooden wall* of the oracle'. Others thought the wooden wall meant the Athenian fleet, but there was a serious problem here, as 'death to women's sons' must surely mean they would be defeated in a sea battle at Salamis.

Not for the first or last time Themistocles, elected archon, came to the rescue of his city. He pointed out that if the god meant that the Athenians would be defeated he would have said something like 'hateful' Salamis, not 'divine'; the slaughter foreseen, therefore, referred not to the Athenians but to the Persians. Themistocles' interpretation carried the day, and it was agreed that the entire population of Athens must now be immediately evacuated to friendly cities in the Peloponnese and also to Salamis. Now the city was empty, except for a few priests of the temple of Athena, the poor who could not afford to leave the city and those who believed they would be saved by the 'wooden wall', the barricade surrounding the Acropolis which they had hastily reinforced with doors and planks.

Hardly had the last stragglers, their possessions bundled onto mules and donkeys, left the city, when the first messengers reached Athens with the dreadful news: Leonidas was dead with all his Spartans – the Persians had broken through at Thermopylae. For those on the Acropolis it was now a matter of waiting to see the first dust cloud thrown up by the hooves of the Persian cavalry galloping through the gap between Parnes and Pendeli ... Who, peering northward over the thorn barriers of the Acropolis, would not have felt his stomach tighten with fear?

'The Persians', says Herodotus, 'occupied the hill which the Athenians call the Aeropagus [Areopagus], opposite the Acropolis, and began the siege, wrapping their arrows with tow, setting them alight and shooting them into the barricade.' Even with their wooden wall in flames the defenders refused all offers of surrender and by rolling rocks down upon their attackers prevented them from approaching the gates. But the Persians found the solution.

There was a place 'in front of the Acropolis, behind the way up to the gates, where the ascent is so steep that no guard was set, because it was not thought that any man would be able to climb it.' But Xerxes, whose army included soldiers from every part of the empire, sent his crack mountain troops to scale the cliff. They reached the top and ran to open the gates. Some of the defenders now threw themselves down from the walls, the others fled for sanctuary to the inner chamber of the temple. But there was to be no escape. The Persians broke into the temple and killed everyone inside. 'The barbarians then plundered the shrine of all its treasures and set fire to the Acropolis.' Herodotus adds: 'Now absolute master of Athens, Xerxes sent a messenger to Susa with the news of his success.'

The smoke from the burning Acropolis was visible to the Athenians who had abandoned their city and taken refuge on the island of Salamis; it was also seen by the rowers of the Greek fleet now assembling in the straits – an ominous reminder of the oracle's direst prophecy.

Looking south from the Acropolis you will see to the right of Piraeus the grey-blue hump of the island of Salamis. Here in the straits between the island and the mainland took place one of the most significant sea battles of the Western world. Today the enclosed waters are scattered with oil tankers and cargo ships peacefully at anchor; in 480 BCE those same waters were churned by thousands of oars rowed in anger, as two great fleets of triremes clashed together. And on a hilltop on the mainland, by the present Perama shipyards, Xerxes, king of Persia, King of Kings, heard the roar of battle and watched in horror as his magnificent fleet was destroyed, and his dream of conquering Greece and Europe died before his eyes. Byron imagined the scene in 'The Isles of Greece', his poem within a poem in *Don Juan:*

> A king sate on the rocky brow
> Which looks o'er sea-born Salamis
> And ships, by thousands, lay below,
> And men in nations; – all were his!
> He counted them at break of day –
> And when the sun set where were they?

Aeschylus in his play *The Persians,* which was performed in Athens only a few years after the battle, has a messenger recount the catastrophic disaster to Xerxes's mother, Queen Atossa, who is waiting for news in faraway Susa. The messenger tells how, as the

Persian fleet entered the bay of Salamis, they expected the Greek ships trapped there to surrender – instead the Greeks attacked:

> with a united sweep and rush of oars
> on order they struck the deep water of the sea [...]
> At once ship against ship its bronze ram
> struck. A ship of the Hellenes began
> the attack and broke off completely the beak
> of a Phoenician ship: ship rushed against ship.
> At first at this point the mass of the Persian force
> resisted but the bulk of the fleet in a narrow strait
> was confined and ship could not help ship
> but they with their bronze-mouthed rammings
> struck each other and broke the banks of oars [...]
> [...] and the sea could not be seen
> but was full of shipwrecks and the death of men.
> The beaches and rocks were full of corpses.
> Each ship in disorder rushed for flight [...]
> Like mackerel or a catch of fish,
> with scraps of oars and fragments of wreckage
> they struck, hacked them while moaning
> and mourning filled all the waters of the sea
> until the black eye of night removed them.

As the Queen and the court listened appalled at his account, the messenger concluded:

> The total of evils, not even if for ten days
> I enumerated them, could I tell you in full.
> For know this well: never in a single day
> did so great a number of men die.

Most of the dead were Persians; unlike the Greeks, they could not swim.

🔳

The plays of Aeschylus and the other great dramatists of the fifth century BCE were first performed in Athens in the theatre of Dionysus. From the south-eastern ramparts of the Acropolis the theatre, shaped like a seashell, lies directly below you.

Dionysus, the patron god of tragedy, is the foreign deity that came from the east, his followers dancing beside him, bringing the grape and joy, riot and ecstasy to the Homeric world of reason, order, honour and pride. Dionysus was also the god of trees and fruit, and generation – represented by the phallus, by bulls and goats, satyrs and *sileni*. Legend links him with birth and violent death, and rebirth. One of the secrets of Greek influence through the centuries was its ability to embrace Apollo's moderate and reasoned 'nothing too much' and 'know yourself' on the one hand, and the unreason, emotion and passionate frenzy of Dionysus on the other. The Greeks understood that the human character and condition, for good or ill, is composed of these two opposing elements always struggling for balance and always in conflict, a conflict rarely absent from the great plays of ancient Athens.

> Tiers of wooden benches; a round dancing floor some sixty feet across, backed by a wooden stage-building – that was all. Yet above towered the walls of the immemorial Acropolis, over which, in place of the older temple of Athena burnt by the Persians, from 447 BCE there began to climb, white against the blue Mediterranean sky, the columns of the Parthenon.

This was the view, as F. L. Lucas describes it in *Greek Drama for Everyman* (1954), of the audience, often several thousand at a time, who watched the spring drama festival of the Great Dionysia, the simple stage lit not by torches but by the rays of the early morning sun. It was not until about 330 BCE that wooden seating was replaced with stone.

'The audience', writes Lucas,

was vast (say fourteen thousand); it seems to have been lively, noisy, emotional and demonstrative. They ate, they applauded, they hissed, they kicked their wooden seats in disgust. It appears that women were admitted to tragedy, and probably also to comedy. From the later fifth century the poor had their admission paid for by the state. Therefore the Attic dramatists, like the Elizabethans, had a public of all classes, not of one; intelligent but not composed of 'intellectuals'; democratic, not precious. One can understand that it should have been impressed and awed by Aeschylus; amused (rather too easily) by Aristophanes; suspicious of Euripides. That it should have made a favourite of Sophocles remains remarkable. Yet one great excellence of the Greek mind was its power to combine simplicity and subtlety; just as the lines of Greek temples are made to look perfectly straight by being, in reality, delicately curved.

Aeschylus, known as the 'father of tragedy', is the earliest dramatist whose work has come down to us – though only seven plays have survived out of the ninety he wrote. When he first began writing, Greek theatre had just begun to evolve. He added a second actor, allowing for greater dramatic variety, while the chorus played a less important role. He is also said to have made the costumes more elaborate and dramatic, and to have had his actors wear platform boots to make them more visible to the audience. According to a later account, as they walked on stage in the first performance of the *Eumenides*, the chorus of Furies were so frightening in appearance that young children fainted, old men became incontinent, and pregnant women went into labour.

Aeschylus eventually moved to Sicily, where he died at the age of 70; he was given a magnificent burial in the public tombs of Gela. His epitaph makes no mention of his fame as a playwright but that – to him something much more important – he had fought at the Battle of Marathon.

As a poet his voice has been heard in very different ages and in countries far from Greece. In 1968 Robert F. Kennedy was campaigning for the US Democratic Party's presidential nomination when he learned that Martin Luther King had been assassinated in Memphis, Tennessee. Despite fears of riots and concerns for his safety, Kennedy insisted on attending a rally in Indianapolis in the heart of the city's African-American quarter. Many in the crowd had not heard about King's assassination and instead of the rousing campaign speech they expected, they heard a speech that is one of the most memorable in American history.

Acknowledging the audience's emotions, Kennedy referred to his own grief at the murder of his brother five years before, and quoting a passage from Edith Hamilton's translation of the play *Agamemnon*, said: 'My favorite poet was Aeschylus. And he once wrote: *Even in our sleep, pain which cannot forget falls drop by drop upon the heart, until in our own despair, against our will, comes wisdom through the awful grace of God.*'

Making an impassioned and eloquent plea for peace, love and unity among all Americans, white and black, Kennedy continued, 'Let us dedicate ourselves to what the Greeks wrote so many years ago: to tame the savageness of man and make gentle the life of this world.'

That night furious riots erupted in more than 100 major cities across the United States. Some 70,000 army and National Guard troops were called out to restore order, 35 people were killed and more that 2,500 injured. By contrast, in Indianapolis, after Kennedy's speech, the crowd dispersed quietly.

Two months later Robert Kennedy was himself assassinated. The quotation from Aeschylus is inscribed on the memorial at his grave in Arlington National Cemetery.

In his *Agamemnon*, the first part of the *Oresteia*, first performed in Athens in the theatre of Dionysus under the Acropolis in 458 BCE,

Aeschylus has the herald from the Greek army, finally victorious after ten years besieging Troy, report to the court of Clytemnestra at Mycenae. The herald is describing conditions in the field, perhaps based on the experience of the Athenians' recent siege of Thasos. Anyone who has been a soldier will recognise that not much has changed. In Philip Vellacott's translation:

To think what we went through! If I described it all,
The holes we camped in, dirt and weariness and sweat;
Or out at sea, with storms all night, trying to sleep
On a narrow board, with half a blanket; and all day,
Miserable and sick, we suffered and put up with it.
Then, when we landed, things were worse. We had to camp
Close by the enemy's wall, in the wet river-meadows,
Soaked from the dew and mist, ill from damp clothes, our hair
Matted like savages'. If I described the winter, when
In cruel snow winds from Ida birds froze on the trees;
Or if I told of the fierce heat, when Ocean dropped
Waveless and windless to his noon-day bed, and slept […]

Well, it's no time for moaning; that's all over now.
And those who died out there – it's over for them too;
No need to jump to orders; they can take their rest.

Hundreds of tragedies, comedies and satires were written and performed in Athens, and later throughout the Greek world, yet only a few have come down to us. Shreds of ancient papyrus still come to light with fragments of lost dramas but we only know for sure the texts of a few of the plays of Aeschylus (6), Sophocles (7) and Euripides (17), their survival depending as much on chance as on the public tastes of later antiquity.

Peter Levi in *A History of Greek Literature* (1985) tells us how tragedy was shaped by the social and political changes that utterly transformed the city and society of Athens in the course of the fifth century BCE. It flourished in the confident youth of the Athenian democracy, though by the Persian wars in 490 BCE Aeschylus was already producing plays, and theatrical festivals were already an institution. Throughout the century, democracy extended and state-regulated patronage increased. The rich were selected to compete for honour in mounting the tragedies just as they were directed to build and equip ships. The last great tragic poets died about the time of the fall of Athens at the close of the century.

Levi adds in *The Hill of Kronos*: 'The truth probably is that the deaths of Sophocles and Euripides in 406 not only marked the end of an age in Athenian theatre but made that end inevitable. Euripides and Sophocles were the greatest poets alive and they were very old men.'

A fragment from *Electra*, a play by Euripides, by a strange chance may have saved Athens from total ruin. In 404 BCE the city fell to the Spartan league; but, says the story, as its leaders debated whether to raze Athens from the earth and enslave her people, as she had enslaved others, they were touched to sudden pity by the voice of a man of Phocis casually chanting a choral passage from *Electra*, about the heroine's 'desolate home'. As F. L. Lucas notes in *Greek Drama for Everyman* (1954), much of the effect may have lain in the music which was specially composed for his words by Euripides, and is lost to us now.

The defeat of the Persian fleet at Salamis in 480 BCE, followed by the destruction of the Persian army at Plataea the following year, made Athens suddenly the dominant power in the Aegean. In a surge of self-confidence from its astounding victory, and rich from the tributes it was collecting from the city-states of Greece, Athens embarked on a dramatic and unprecedented construction programme to beautify the city and especially the Acropolis.

Plutarch, a Greek from Chaeronea, a city not far north of Athens, was deeply impressed by the result, and he knew Athens well, having studied mathematics and philosophy there in 66–67 CE. His *Lives of the Noble Greeks and Romans* made him known throughout the ancient world and is still read today; one of the great men he wrote about was the Athenian statesman Pericles.

Writing five centuries after the Parthenon was built, he explains how at the inspiration of Pericles, the city's elected leader, and under the direction of his sculptor and architect friend Phidias, the massive works went ahead. No expense was spared on the quality and variety of materials brought in to build and adorn the temples, including 'stone, bronze, ivory, gold, ebony and cypress wood'. Skilled craftsmen were needed to work these materials, and many others were involved, 'such as merchants, sailors, and pilots for the sea-borne traffic, and wagon-makers, trainers of draught animals, and drivers for everything that came by land. There were also rope-makers, weavers, leatherworkers, road builders and miners.' The hard labour would have been done by slaves, as it always had been – too obvious to be worth mentioning.

And all of it happened, Plutarch adds (in Michael Llewellyn Smith's translation):

> in the high summer of one man's administration [...] It is this, above all, which makes Pericles' works a wonder to us – the fact that they were created in so short a span, and yet for all time. Each one possessed a beauty which seemed venerable the moment it was born, and at the same time a youthful vigour which makes them appear to this day as if they were newly built.

It was in about 460 BCE that Phidias finished his colossal statue of the goddess Athena. Her core was wood, her flesh ivory and the rest of her gold – 1,100 kilos of it. Cicero says that she stood 11 metres tall. The point of her spear, caught by the sun, could be seen by ships far out to sea.

🔲

Looking down from the walls of the Acropolis, beyond the now-landscaped agora and the temple of Hephaestus is the area known in ancient times as the Kerameikos. The part of it just beyond the boundaries of the classical city was where the Athenians buried their dead.

Pericles was still the city's leader 20 years after the building of the Parthenon, but despite his political skills and experience he allowed Athens to be drawn into the long and devastating war with its old rival Sparta. It was here in the Kerameikos that he gave his famous oration to the Athenians mourning their dead after the first year of the war. We know this, and what Pericles said, thanks to Thucydides, who wrote the history of the conflict between Athens and Sparta known as the Peloponnesian War.

Born about 460 BCE, Thucydides was from a wealthy family with land in Attica and also in northern Greece. He commanded an Athenian squadron of triremes at Thasos in 424 but, having failed to save Amphipolis, was exiled. Although he eventually returned to Athens, he used his time in exile to interview participants and collect material for his account of the conflict.

Describing the funerals of those Athenians who had died in the first year of the war, Thucydides tells us that 'the bones are laid in the public burial place, which is in the most beautiful quarter outside the city walls. Here the Athenians always bury those who have fallen in war. The only exception is those who died at Marathon, who, because their achievement was considered absolutely outstanding, were buried on the battlefield itself.'

The Athenians were the first to honour the Unknown Soldier: 'Then there is a funeral procession in which coffins of cypress wood are carried on wagons [...] One empty bier is decorated and carried in the procession: this is for the missing, whose bodies could not be recovered.' It was not until 1916 that the concept was revived – by an army chaplain on the Western Front in World War I,

David Railton, who officiated at the burials of hundreds of British soldiers and was decorated for his bravery in comforting the dying under fire. After the war his proposal was enthusiastically endorsed by both the military and politicians, and in 1920 the body of an unidentified soldier was brought back from Flanders and buried with ceremony in Westminster Abbey.

The next year the Americans did the same, followed by the French and Italians, and over the years by many nations. The Greeks have their own monument to the Unknown Soldier in Constitution Square in Athens at the parliament building, guarded day and night by *evzones* (the Presidential Guard) in full dress. Engraved on the stone are quotations from Pericles's oration: 'For famous men have the whole earth their memorial' and 'Happiness depends on being free, and freedom depends on being courageous' – words that can be found on war memorials all over the world, translated into as many languages; perhaps its most recent appearance is on the memorial for Royal Air Force Bomber Command, in London's Green Park, unveiled in 2012.

Thucydides was a historian who took care to base his story on facts and evidence. In those days news of events, and political debates, were made known by word of mouth, and what was said and how it was said were important records of history. He makes it clear that the speeches he records are not quoted word for word, but are nevertheless accurate in their meaning and sense.

When Pericles began his oration he spoke first, with pride, of the qualities and achievements of his city. While to our eyes Athens of the fifth century BCE was far from perfect – the existence of slavery, for example, the low position of women in society – many of our values and ideals were set out by the Athenians 2,500 years ago. Listen to what Pericles has to say: 'Our constitution is called a democracy because power is in the hands not of a minority but of the whole people.' 'When it is a question of settling private disputes, everyone is equal before the law.' 'We are free and tolerant in our private lives; but in public affairs we keep to the law; this is because it commands our deep respect.' 'Our love of what is beautiful does not lead to extravagance; our love of the things of the mind does not make us soft.' 'We regard wealth as something to be properly used, rather than as something to boast about. As for poverty, no-one need be ashamed to admit it: the real shame is not to take practical measures to escape from it.'

'I declare', said Pericles, 'that our city is an education to Greece.' He could not have foreseen that Athens would also be an education to the world. Yet we know only too well that the ideals and values signalled by the Greeks were just that – ideals. They were hard to live up to then and have proved equally elusive since; and always will be, 'as long as human nature stays the same'. The war between Athens and Sparta ended, 25 years after Pericles' death, in the total defeat and humiliation of Athens and, for a time at least, in the extinction of democracy.

As in every war there was courage and heroism, but also brutality, cruelty and betrayal. W. H. Auden in his poem 'September 1st, 1939' wrote:

> Exiled Thucydides knew
> All that a speech could say
> About Democracy,
> And what dictators do.

And yet, in those faraway days a flame was lit, and though often in the centuries since it has flickered only dimly, it has never been extinguished.

The Kerameikos burial ground, where Pericles and other distinguished citizens were invited to give funeral orations, was to be the scene of unprecedented activity early on in the war between Athens and Sparta:

The plague originated, so they say, in Ethiopia and upper Egypt, and spread from there to Egypt itself and Libya, and much of the territory of the King of Persia. In the city of Athens it appeared suddenly, and the first cases were among the population of Piraeus, so that it was supposed by them that the Peloponnesians had poisoned the reservoirs. Later, however, it appeared in the upper city, and by this time the deaths were greatly increasing in number.

This is how Thucydides begins his account of the plague that ravaged Athens in 430 BCE. He was not a doctor and would leave the medical aspects to others. What he could do, however, was describe the symptoms 'so that they might be recognized should it ever break out again'. He knew what he was talking about: 'I had the disease myself, and saw others suffering from it.'

The first signs, he tells us, were headache, inflamed eyes, bleeding from throat and tongue, foul breath. Next came stomach ache, vomiting, followed by spasms of ineffectual retching. 'Externally the body was not very hot to the touch,' he recalls, 'yet the skin was reddish and livid, breaking out into small pustules and ulcers. But inside there was a feeling of burning, so that people could not bear the touch of even the lightest linen clothing, but wanted to be absolutely naked and most of all would have liked to plunge into cold water.' Many of the sick did exactly that, jumping in the water tanks.

If by the seventh or eighth day those affected were still alive,

the disease then descended to the bowels, producing violent ulceration and uncontrollable diarrhoea, and most of them died later of the weakness caused by this [...] Even when people escaped its worst effects, it still left its traces on them by fastening on the extremities of the body. It affected the genitals, the fingers, and the toes, and any of those who recovered lost the use of these members. Some, too, went blind.

Alarmingly, the attacks appeared to be random: those in good health struck down as quickly as the sick and the frail. 'The most terrible thing of all was the despair into which people fell when they realized they had caught the plague [...] Terrible, too, was the sight of people dying through having caught the disease as a result of nursing others.'

What made the situation worse was the influx of people from the countryside. To escape the Spartan army that had invaded Attica, the Athenians were crowded into the city and the narrow space between the Long Walls and the port of Piraeus. 'There were no houses for them, and, living as they did in the hot season in badly ventilated huts, they died like flies. The bodies of the dying were heaped one on top of the other, and half-dead creatures could be seen staggering about in the streets or flocking about the fountains in their desire for water. The temples in which they took up their quarters were full of the bodies of those who had died there:

> All the funeral ceremonies which used to be observed were now disorganized, and they buried the dead as best they could. Many people [...] adopted the most shameless methods. They would arrive first at a funeral pyre that had been made by others, put their own dead upon it and set it alight; or, finding another pyre burning, they would throw the corpse they were carrying on top of the other one and go away.

A consequence of the plague was 'a state of unprecedented law-lessness'. Seeing that the plague struck rich and poor equally, and that some people became suddenly wealthy through inheriting from a dead relative,

> they resolved to spend their money quickly and to spend it on pleasure, since money and life alike seemed equally ephemeral [...] No fear of god or law of man had a restraining influence. As for the gods, it seemed to be the same thing whether one worshipped them or not, when one saw the good and the bad dying indiscriminately.

As for offences against human law, no-one expected to live long enough to be brought to trial and punished.

Two sons of Pericles died of the disease in 429 BCE; Thucydides tells us that at their funeral their father was for the first time seen in tears. Pericles himself succumbed to the plague later the same year.

Modern excavations of the area have already revealed one mass grave, containing 250 bodies of men, women and children, dated from the early years of the Peloponnesian War. Despite our knowledge of the symptoms, so carefully described by Thucydides, modern experts are still divided as to what the disease actually was. There is a strong case for it being an epidemic of typhus fever; it is also possible that it was an outbreak of haemorrhagic viral fever, reaching Piraeus through trade with the upper Nile and Africa. There are many types of HVF, of varying deadliness, Ebola being just one.

Another war, another invasion: the streets of Athens were not to be the scene of such concentrated suffering for 2,400 years, though this time death came not from plague but from starvation and malnutrition. During the Nazi occupation, from October 1941 to October a year later as many 40,000 lost their lives, that first winter at a rate of 300 a day. Edmund Keeley, in *Inventing Paradise* (2002), describes the scene:

> Those who died at home might be buried in unmarked shallow graves or dumped in cemeteries by their weakened relatives and their ration cards used to help the living, but those who collapsed in the streets lay for hours where they fell, their emaciated bodies eventually hauled away by municipal carts barely able to cope with the weight of their anonymous cargo.

It is not known for sure how or when Thucydides died; some say that he came to a violent end, perhaps murdered, soon after 400 BCE. He died before he could finish the last book of his history; it is said that his daughter completed it and took care of his writings after his death.

Thucydides warns his readers in advance that there is little of the romantic in his history. He had written it for those 'who want to understand clearly the events which happened in the past and which, human nature being what it is, will, at some time or other and in much the same ways, be repeated in the future'. His book, he hoped, would therefore be 'a possession for all time'.

Recognised as the founder of modern history, he was the first historian to ascribe events to human psychology and individual choice, rather than to ancestral curse, dreams, omens or intervention of the gods – in contrast to Herodotus (about 30 years older than him and whom he had probably met in Athens). Robin Lane Fox in *The Classical World* (2005) describes Thucydides as a hard and penetrating realist, exposing 'through speech and action, the amoral reality of inter-state politics, the verbal distortions of diplomatic speakers and factional leaders, and the terrifying violence which political revolution unleashes *as long as human nature stays the same* [...] His diagnosis is still only too recognizable.' Which is why *The Peloponnesian War* was so admired in ancient times, still fascinates and entertains, and remains recommended reading for the US and British military and for politicians today.

In recent years the Kerameikos has been rescued from modern construction and is a pleasant area to walk among the tombs and grave *stelae* commemorating the dead of those distant centuries. Michael Llewellyn Smith, in *Athens*, quotes the poet Odysseus Elytis reflecting on these mysterious headstones, often a single name carved in simple capitals.

> It is never night or morning, since time no longer has any meaning. But it is always the home, the family, the loved ones, the thread we held onto that keeps unwinding directly from our

heart. That girl who looks out with resignation; and the other one opening the jewel box; and the one who prepares to offer the mirror but hesitates, as if she sensed the uselessness of it [...] the little boy is there and looks about to fall asleep ... and the dog that smells the edge of the cloth [...] How puzzling! These capital letters in stone, nothing else mentioned, no further comment; these trace us back and locate us. They create the calm of a shadow within the blinding light of death [...] A kore, so young, so beautiful – it's not possible – surely she's still somewhere combing away at her hair.

Elytis died in 1996. He was the second Greek to have received the Nobel Prize for Literature, which he was awarded in 1979 (the first was Seferis, in 1963).

There is a statue of Plato in front of the Academy building in Akhadimias Street, close to the groves of olive and plane trees – long ago covered by the bricks and cement of the city – where the philosopher and poet founded his Academy in 385 BCE. Now the word for institutions of education the world over, 'academy' of course also gives us 'academics', those admired and respected collectors and dispensers of knowledge. One of Plato's pupils was Aristotle, who went on to tutor Alexander the Great and also to found his own school 50 years later – the Lyceum, a common word now for schools of every kind.

Next to Plato's statue is one of Socrates. The two will always be linked since we know about Socrates (who wrote nothing himself) only from the work of Plato, and to a lesser extent from Xenophon, both many years younger than Socrates and both his pupils.

Socrates was born in Athens in 470 BCE; his father was a stonemason, his mother a midwife. He fought for Athens as a hoplite (heavy-armed infantryman) and was known for his bravery and endurance in battle. From sculptures of his face, and descriptions in Plato's *Symposium*, we know that Socrates was broad-faced, blunt-nosed, bald and ugly; he usually went barefoot, walking with a strange strutting movement, and liked to stand in a trance of concentration for hours at a time. His appearance and mannerisms made him an easy object of satire by contemporary writers, most famously Aristophanes in *The Clouds.*

Socrates was often to be found in the Agora, where he walked and talked, usually the centre of a group of mostly young men, many of them from aristocratic families. Conversation – question and answer, dialogue or dialectic – was the way Socrates taught, teasing out the true meaning of ethical and moral values such as goodness, virtue and justice, at the same time providing the basis for today's scientific methods of inquiry. His original and exceptional mind and his contribution to Western philosophy will never be forgotten.

When a pupil of his asked at Delphi: who is the wisest of men? The oracle replied: Socrates, because he knows how little he knows.

In 399 BCE, at a time when Athens, defeated by Sparta, was in political turmoil, Socrates was charged with impiety and the corruption of Athenian youth. He was condemned to death. The condemned were allowed to propose an alternative sentence, and often the jury agreed a compromise – a heavy fine, imprisonment, or exile. Socrates suggested that because he had always helped the youth of Athens to seek the truth in all things he should be rewarded – with free meals for life, at state expense.

It is not difficult to see what a stubborn and irritating person he could be; the court was duly irritated and confirmed the death penalty. His many friends wished him to escape, and he was given every opportunity to do so; he refused – he was 70 years old, he said, was never going to stop teaching and in any case as a citizen of Athens it was his duty to respect its laws.

In his *Phaedo,* translated by Hugh Tredennick, Plato describes the last moments of Socrates, when the cup of hemlock had been put in his hands:

Up till this time most of us had been fairly successful in keeping back our tears; but when we saw that he had actually drunk it, we could do so no longer; in spite of myself the tears kept pouring out, so that I covered my face and wept broken-heartedly – not for him but for my own calamity in losing such a friend. Crito had given up even before me, and had gone out when he could not restrain his tears. But Apollodurus, who had never stopped crying even before, now broke out into such a storm of passionate weeping that he made everyone in the room break down, except Socrates himself, who said:

'Really, my friends, what a way to behave! Why, that was my main reason for sending away the women, to prevent this sort of disturbance; because I am told that one should make one's end in a tranquil frame of mind. Calm yourselves and try to be brave.'

This made his friends feel ashamed and they did their best to compose themselves. The man who had given Socrates the poison had advised him to walk about and that when he felt his legs were heavy to lie down on his back. The hemlock would slowly numb him from the feet up, and when it reached his heart he would be gone.

The coldness was spreading about as far as his waist when Socrates uncovered his face – for he had covered it up – and said (they were his last words): 'Crito, we ought to offer a cock to Asclepius. See to it and don't forget.'

'No, it shall be done,' said Crito. 'Are you sure there is nothing else?'

Socrates made no reply to this question, but after a little while he stirred; and when the man uncovered him, his eyes were fixed. When Crito saw this, he closed the mouth and eyes.

Of all those whom we knew in our time, he was the bravest and also the wisest and most upright man.

No one has been able to explain the last words of Socrates. Why offer a cock to Asclepius, the god of healing? Perhaps it was his last joke.

Another dramatic view from the great balcony that is the Acropolis is down on to the Areopagus, the rock site of the ancient criminal court of Athens and once the seat of the city's governing body. If you had done so in around 51 CE, not many years after Plutarch had been a student in Athens, you might have seen a crowd gathering around a speaker who was beginning to attract attention. Just arrived by ship from Macedonia, Paul had already argued with his fellow Jews in the synagogue and preached in the Agora to anyone who would listen to him; what he said made people curious. The Acts of the Apostles recounts:

> Then certain philosophers of the Epicureans, and of the Stoicks, encountered him. And some said, What will this babbler say? other some, He seemeth to be a setter forth of strange gods: because he preached unto them Jesus, and the resurrection.
>
> And they took him, and brought him unto Areopagus, saying, May we know what this new doctrine, whereof thou speakest, is? For thou bringest certain strange things to our ears: we would know therefore what these things mean. (For all the Athenians and strangers which were there spent their time in nothing else, but either to tell, or to hear some new thing.)

Paul knew that Athens was the cultural centre of the Roman Empire and wanted his visit there to make an impression. Yet he must have been taken aback at the multitude of statues of gods and goddesses decorating every part of Athens, a 'city wholly given to idolatry', especially shocking to a Jew. In any case he seized on this as his theme in addressing a highly sceptical audience:

Ye men of Athens, I perceive that in all things ye are too superstitious. For as I passed by, and beheld your devotions, I found an altar with this inscription, *To The Unknown God*. Whom therefore ye ignorantly worship, him declare I unto you. God that made the world and all things therein, seeing that he is Lord of heaven and earth, dwelleth not in temples made with hands [...] as though he needed any thing, seeing he giveth to all life, and breath, and all things; And hath made of one blood all nations of men for to dwell on all the face of the earth.

Here, in these words to the 'men of Athens', were heard for the first time the fundamental beliefs of Christianity. 'And when they heard of the resurrection of the dead, some mocked: and others said, We will hear thee again on this matter. So Paul departed from among them. Howbeit certain men clave unto him, and believed: among the which was Dionysius the Areopagite, and a woman named Damaris, and others with them.'

Paul did not stay long in Athens and set off by road to Corinth, where there was a thriving Jewish community and where he hoped to find an audience more amenable to the concept of monotheism and the startling new faith that was now his life's work to make known to the world.

Little is recorded of Athens in the Dark Ages under Byzantine rule. *Pope Joan,* however, a novel by Emmanuel Royidis (or Rhoides) written in the eighteenth century, and adapted by Lawrence Durrell in 1948, provides a convincing picture of Athens in the ninth century:

Deprived of its idols and altars Athens resembled nothing so much as a blind Polyphemus. In every niche where once a statue had stood they found a cross; instead of temples they now found small ugly domed churches resembling stone periwigs. These had been built by the Athenian Eudocia, who, wishing to honour every saint with a private residence, had been compelled to undertake this horde of chapels, giving more honour, it would seem, to the industry of the beaver than to the 'Unknown God'. At the porches of these chapels were seated the monks and anchorites of the town, scratching at old parchments or at ulcers and weaving rush baskets as they breakfasted on onions. Only the classic beauty of the Athenian girls was left for the two strangers to admire. In that age, of course, Athens was the harem of the Byzantine emperors. They gathered the loveliest girls from the town as later the Sultans did from Circassia.

Athens had long been a focus for the imagination of English writers. John Milton was one of the first to emphasise the cultural importance of Greece, acknowledging that 'whatever literary advance' he had made was due to his 'intimacy' with the literature of ancient Athens. In the fourth book of *Paradise Regained* (1671) he points to:

Where on the Aegean shore a City stands [...]
Athens, the eye of Greece, Mother of Arts, And Eloquence.

As a young man on his cultural Grand Tour, Milton had planned to visit Greece. By December 1638 he had reached Naples, but there the 'sad news' reached him of the outbreak of the Civil War in England (*tristis ex Anglia belli civilis*) and he immediately left for home.

In 1774 the London Society of Dilettanti, to which we owe many of the rare descriptions of Greece at that time, sent Richard Chandler, a distinguished antiquarian, with an architect and a painter, to explore the antiquities of Ionia and Greece. In Athens in 1775, they bought two fragments of the Parthenon frieze which they had found 'inserted into the doorways of the town' and were presented with 'a beautiful trunk which had fallen from the metopes, and lay neglected in the garden of a Turk'.

A favourite landmark of old Athens is the Tower of the Winds in the Roman Agora, perhaps the first clock tower ever built, though of course the time it told was calculated by water and the sun. Chandler, who wrote of his journey in *Travels in Greece* (1766), was one of the first travellers in the east to record the spectacle of the 'whirling dervishes'. 'The Tower of the Winds is now a *teckeh*,' he wrote:

> or place of worship belonging to a college of dervishes. The chief dervish, a comely man, with a grey beard and of a fine presence, began the prayers, in which the rest bore part, all prostrating themselves, as usual, and several times touching the ground with their foreheads. On a sudden, they leapt up, threw off their outer garments, and, joining hands move round slowly to music, shouting Allah, the name of God. The instruments sounding quicker, they kept time, calling out *Allah Al illa Al Allah*. God. There is no other God but God. Other sentences were added to these as their motion increased; and the chief dervish, bursting from the ring into the middle, as if in a fit of enthusiasm, and letting down his hair behind, began turning about, his body poised on one of his great toes as on a pivot, without changing place. He was followed by another, who spun a different way, and then by more, four or five in number. The rapidity, with which they whisked around, was gradually augmented, and became amazing; their long hair not touching their shoulders but flying off; and the circle still surrounding them, shouting and throwing their heads backwards and forwards; the dome re-echoing the wild and loud music; and the noise as it were of frantic Bacchanals. At length, some quitting the ring and fainting, at which time it is believed they are favoured with ecstatic visions, the spectacle ended. We were soon after introduced into a room furnished with skins for sofas, and entertained with pipes and coffee by the chief dervish, whom we found, with several of his performers, as cool and placid, as if he had been only a looker-on.

The Napoleonic Wars closed off much of the continent to travellers and culture tourists, broadening the range of their destinations to Greece, Constantinople and the Levant. Scholars, soldiers and artists began to visit Greece in increasing numbers despite the difficulties of moving around this mountainous country which lacked inns and other amenities, and whose poor roads were beset by bandits – the *klephts* who played such a large part in the war of independence that was soon to break out. The foreigners came from every country in Europe, most from the British Isles, diligently exploring ancient ruins and writing up their observations. They admired the stupendous scenery and with Greek texts in hand imagined themselves in classical times, and were disappointed. For this they blamed the Greeks, making no allowance for a population impoverished by more than a millennium of foreign domination, the last few centuries under Turkish rule.

C. M. Woodhouse, in *The Philhellenes* (1971), wrote of these tourists:

> They loved the Greece of their dreams: the land, the language, the antiquities, but not the people. If only, they thought, the people could be more like British scholars and gentlemen; or failing that, as too much to be hoped, if only they were more like their own ancestors; or better still, if only they were not there at all. Some treated them as if they were not there, but it was not easy to ignore them. Only when Byron arrived in 1809 did the idea first dawn, and then only slowly, that the Greeks too were people.

François-René de Chateaubriand, the French writer and politician (*Travels in Greece ...*, 1811), approached Athens from the direction of Eleusis in 1806.

> The first thing that struck my eyes was the citadel lit by the rising sun: it was right in front of me, on the other side of the plain, and

seemed to be propped up on Mount Hymettus, which formed the background. It exhibited, in a confused mixture, the capitals of the Propylaea, the columns of the Parthenon and of the Erectheum, the embrasures of a wall loaded with canons, the gothic debris of the Christians, and the hovels of the Muslims [...]

At the foot of the Acropolis, Athens was revealed: its flat roofs, intermixed with minarets, cypress trees, ruins, isolated columns: the domes of its mosques, crowned with big storks' nests, made an agreeable effect in the sun's rays. But, if one could recognize Athens in its ruins, one could see also, that the town of Minerva was no longer inhabited by its own people.

We were walking towards this little town of which the population was not even equal to that of a Paris faubourg, but whose renown equals that of the Roman empire.

Patrick Anderson writes in *Dolphin Days* (1963) that when Chateaubriand and Byron visited Athens it was 'quite a small town of ten thousand inhabitants; Hobhouse could walk round it in forty-seven minutes. A tall Florentine watchtower dominated the Acropolis hill; there was a small mosque inside the Parthenon and a Turkish barracks outside.'

Byron and Hobhouse arrived in December 1809. They stayed at the house of the British vice-consul, a Greek called Makris, whose daughter was immortalised in Byron's poem:

> Maid of Athens, ere we part,
> Give, Oh give me back my heart!

After a voyage with Hobhouse to Constantinople, on the way swimming the Hellespont in memory of Leander, Byron returned to Athens the following year, this time staying at the Capuchin monastery, built round the ancient monument to Lysicrates at the base of the Acropolis. He wrote to his friend Francis Hodgson, no doubt with the intention of making him envious: 'I am living in the

Capuchin Convent, Hymettus before me, the Acropolis behind, the temple of Jove to my right, the Stadium in front, the town to the left, eh, Sir, there's a situation, there's your picturesque! nothing like that in Lunnun, no not even the Mansion House. And I feed on Woodcock & red mullet every day.'

Here Byron spent an enjoyable year with the young male students – 'nothing but riot from Noon till night', as he told Hobhouse, who had returned to England. He worked on his poetry, rode and swam every day, studied demotic Greek and mixed with the growing number of foreigners passing through.

Many of the foreigners visiting Greece at that time despised not only the Greeks but the everyday language they spoke. Byron was one of the first to learn and appreciate Romaic, as the spoken language was then called. Among the Greek poets he translated was the revolutionary writer Rigas Feraios, who had been executed by the Turks in 1798. Feraios had penned a Greek version of the French revolutionary anthem the *Marseillaise*, which may have inspired Byron's 'Sons of the Greeks, arise'.

'At daybreak on the 12th of September we weighed anchor. The wind was fair, the day delightful, and by twelve o'clock we were at the entrance of the Piraeus.' So wrote Charles Meryon in his diary, later published as *Travels of Lady Hester Stanhope, by her Physician* (1849).

> The fame of Lord Byron's exploit in swimming across the Hellespont, from Sestos to Abydos, in imitation of Leander, had already reached us, and, just as we were passing the mole-head, we saw a man jump from it into the sea, whom Lord Sligo recognized to be Lord Byron himself, and, hailing him, bade him hasten to dress and to come and join us.

Lord Sligo borrowed one of Byron's horses and rode with him into Athens, while Lady Hester Stanhope's party waited on the shore. Meryon recorded: 'The country immediately adjoining the port seemed bare and without verdure. Some remains of the quays, which once bordered the Piraeus, lay scattered at the water's edge, and a few ill-constructed boats, made fast by rush hawsers, showed how low the navy of Athens had declined.'

When they finally set off for Athens, the scenery improved,

> but while musing on the goodly prospect around me, on temples and demigods, on the Parthenon and Socrates [...] my reflections were interrupted by the loud smack of a whip, applied by Aly the Tartar to the back of a poor Greek, accompanied by a louder oath, which at once dissipated my vision and brought me back to the reality of things around me.

John Galt, a Scottish writer and a friend of Byron, was in Piraeus at about the same time. In *Voyages and Travels* (1813) he noted that two ships were at anchor in the harbour:

> One of them was destined to receive the spoils of the Parthenon; and the other had lately arrived with a cargo of human beings from the coast of Africa. The Athenians were always great slavemongers; and, at present, there are between two and three hundred in the city: they are chiefly females, servants of the Turks, who have the reputation of being indulgent and kind-hearted masters. About a week ago, a black girl brought a duck to our convent for sale, and the friar asked her how she came to be made a slave. She gave a shrill ludicrous laugh, and said she was taken by the catchers when she was at the well for water. She was born in Egypt, and caught in the neighbourhood of Alexandria.

The only other trade at Piraeus, Galt added, 'besides the little that is done in the human commodity', was in the export of olive oil.

In 1830 the French writer and politician Alfonse de Lamartine, whom we shall hear more of later, visited Athens on his way east but was not impressed by the Parthenon. He wrote in his *Voyage en Orient* (1839), 'As a monument it lacks life [...] beautiful it undoubtedly is, but of a cold and deadly beauty which only an artist can divest of its pall and free from dust [...] For me, I admire it, and depart without the least desire to see it more.'

Robert Eisner, in *Travellers to an Antique Land* (1991), noted that 'most of the finest travel writers on Greece, especially in the twentieth century, have been only amateurs of the classics.' They were therefore not spoiled 'by the burdens of academic professionalism' or weighed down by the challenge to write better than their classical predecessors. William Makepeace Thackeray, who wrote up his visit to Greece in *From Cornhill to Cairo* (1846), was undoubtedly burdened by the classics he had been taught at school and which he had learned to hate and associated with his unhappy childhood: born in India, he had been sent to school in England at the age of four.

> If papa and mamma (honour be to them!) had not followed the faith of their fathers, and thought proper to send their only beloved son [...] into ten years' banishment of infernal misery, tyranny, annoyance [...] if, I say, my dear parents instead of giving me the inestimable benefit of ten years' classical education, had kept me at home with my thirteen dear sisters, it is probable that I should like this country of Attica, in sight of the blue shores of which the present pathetic letter is written; but I was made so miserable in youth by a classical education that all connected with it is disagreeable in my eyes; and I have the same recollection of Greek in my youth that I have of castor oil.

Unlike Thackeray, Edward Lear was not burdened by the classics. His first sight of the Acropolis was in 1848 when he was a guest of Sir Stratford Canning, who was on his way out to Constantinople as British ambassador to Turkey. In a letter to his sister Ann, Lear wrote how:

> the manner that huge mass of rock [...] stands above the modern town with its glittering white marble ruins against the deep blue sky is quite beyond my expectations [...] I wish you could see the temple of the Parthenon, or the Acropolis by sunset – I really never saw anything so wonderful. Most of the columns being rusty with age the whole mass becomes like gold & ivory – & the polished white marble pavement is literally blue from the reflection of the sky. You walk about in a wilderness of broken columns – friezes, etc., etc. Owls, the bird of Minerva, are extremely common, & come & sit very near me when I draw [...]
>
> All the little comforts of dear old Italy – ice, fruits etc, are quite unknown [...] The Areopagus is now only inhabited by sheep and goats.

In an oil painting he completed a few years later, Lear captured 'the immense sweep of plain with exquisitely formed mountains down to the sea'. Today that 'immense sweep' is now almost entirely covered by the modern city, a transformation made in little more than 100 years.

In 1867 Samuel Langhorne Clemens (pen-name Mark Twain) sailed from New York on the *Quaker City* on a voyage to the Mediterranean and the Holy Land. Mark Twain was 32 at the time; his job as a Mississippi riverboat pilot had been interrupted by the American Civil War and he had taken up journalism, with some success. He was determined to be a writer, and like many before and since, he hoped to make a book out of his travels. That book, *The Innocents Abroad*, was published in 1869 and was Mark Twain's first 'bestseller'. The famous Tom Sawyer and Huckleberry Finn novels followed. William Faulkner called Twain 'the father of American literature'. In *The Innocents Abroad* Twain recorded:

> We arrived, and entered the ancient harbour of the Piraeus at last. We dropped anchor within half a mile of the village. Away off, across the undulating Plain of Attica, could be seen a little square-topped hill with a something on it, which our glasses soon discovered to be the ruined edifices of the citadel of the Athenians, and most prominent among them loomed the venerable Parthenon. So exquisitely clear and pure is this wonderful atmosphere that every column of the noble structure was discernible through the telescope, and even the smaller ruins about it assumed some semblance of shape. This at a distance of five or six miles.

The high hopes of the passengers of visiting the Acropolis were dashed when they were informed by the port authorities that the ship was in strict quarantine, and no one was allowed ashore. Deeply disappointed, Mark Twain and three friends made enquiries as to the penalties of breaking the quarantine laws in Greece, and though being told they risked several months' imprisonment, decided to take a chance. At 11 p.m., with clouds masking the moon, they were put ashore in a small rowing boat. Skirting the village of Piraeus, they headed across country, dogs barking at their heels, and reached the Acropolis about two hours later without having been stopped. With 'the prodigious walls of the citadel towering above our heads [...] we passed at once through a great arched passage like a railway tunnel, and went straight to the gate that leads to the ancient temples. It was locked!'

They contemplated breaking in. 'Xerxes took that mighty citadel four hundred and eighty years before Christ [...] and if we four Americans had remained unmolested five minutes longer we would have taken it too.' But force was unnecessary, for when 'the garrison' of four Greeks appeared, 'bribery and corruption' won the day and they were let in to wander freely among the ruins.

Here and there, in lavish profusion, were gleaming white statues of men and women, propped against blocks of marble, some of them armless, some without legs, others headless – but all looking mournful in the moonlight, and startlingly human! They rose up and confronted the midnight intruder on every side – they stared at him from unlooked-for nooks and recesses; they peered at him over fragmentary heaps far down the desolate corridors; they barred his way in the midst of the broad forum, and solemnly pointed with handless arms the way from the sacred fane; and through the roofless temple the moon looked down, and banded the floor and darkened the scattered fragments and broken statues with the slanting shadows of the columns.

From the battlemented edge of the Acropolis they looked down on Athens lit by the full moon:

every house, every window, every clinging vine, every projection was as distinct and sharply marked as if the time were noonday; and yet there was no glare, no glitter, nothing harsh or repulsive – the noiseless city was flooded with the mellowest light that ever streamed from the moon, and seemed like some living creature wrapped in peaceful slumber [...] Overhead the stately columns, majestic still in their ruin – underfoot the dreaming city – in the distance the silver sea – not on the broad earth is there another picture half so beautiful!

Twain and his companions had to leave in a hurry if they were to get back to their ship undetected before dawn. Helping themselves to grapes from vineyards on the way, they were stopped and accosted by armed and outraged farmers. Mark Twain hid his grapes by the roadside, feeling that 'it was not right to steal grapes. And all the more so when the owner was around.'

'When far on our road, we had a parting view of the Parthenon, with the moonlight streaming through its open colonnades and touching its capitals with silver. As it looked then, solemn, grand, and beautiful it will always remain in our memories.' They managed to evade police and customs officials and finally got back on board their ship, exhausted after having walked, stumbled and scrambled some 13 miles during the night. Next morning they learned that two other passengers, who had gone ashore and simply hired a carriage, 'went and came safely, and never walked a step'.

Samuel Barrows was one of those who accompanied the archaeologist Wilhelm Dörpfeld, who as a young man had worked with Schliemann on his excavations of Troy in 1893. While in Athens Barrows saw in a corner of the theatre of Herodes Atticus under the Acropolis an enormous earthenware jar. He wrote in *The Isles and Shrines of Greece* (1898):

> One day, as Professor Dörpfeld was concluding his lecture to a group of archaeologists in the ruins of the old theatre, they were suddenly startled by seeing a head thrust out of the jar which lay on its side. Then shoulders, body and legs slowly emerged. Inquiry showed that a half-witted man, driven about by the persecutions of a rabble of boys, had taken refuge in the old wine jar and lived there most of the time for two weeks. A kind woman had brought him food and covered the mouth of the jar with a curtain. The poor wretch sadly lacked the wisdom of Diogenes and was more in need of merciful than of honest men.

Barrows stayed in Athens long enough to note that it was mainly goats that supplied the citizens with milk:

> One of the commonest sights in Athens is that of six or eight sober-looking goats marching through the streets, driven by a goatherd, who carries the milk measure in his hand. He has a regular route morning and afternoon. When he comes to the house of

a customer, he milks one of the goats, receives the milk into his measure, and pours it into the servant's pitcher.

Barrows was happy to recognise the advantages of supplying milk this way – the customer always got his milk fresh, and 'with a roof of cream on it'. Also, 'the milkman is not obliged to carry cans. Each goat transports her own supply.'

One morning, from his house in Athens, Barrows had just observed the arrival of the goats, who were lining up against the garden wall opposite, when:

> a man came out on the lower roof of the house behind it and shot himself. The fact that he held a prominent position in a bank, and was the victim of this sudden impulse in a moment of depression, did not serve to delay his funeral. The stigma attached to suicide cannot be removed. In fact, in the longer catechism of the Greco-Russian Church suicide is said to be 'the most criminal of all murders. For if it be contrary to kill another man like unto ourselves, much more is it contrary to nature to kill our own selves.' The funeral of a suicide is always held as soon as possible. In this case the man was buried without a priest at four o'clock the same afternoon, and of course in unconsecrated ground. Two of my friends had left that morning on an excursion for Marathon. They started after breakfast, and got back to a seven o'clock dinner. When they left, this man was living, when they came back, he had been buried three hours.

One of the most beautiful of all burial places must surely be the First Cemetery in Athens, near the Panathenaic Stadium, opened in 1837. Cremation until very recently was forbidden by the Orthodox Church and is still rarely practised. Burial space is therefore in short supply and normally bodies are dug up after three to five years (thanks to the climate they are by this time reduced to skull and bones, which can be fitted easily into a handy wooden box, for storage in a chapel or ossuary).

Patrick Leigh Fermor, writing in *Mani* at a time when most Greeks died in their own homes, reminds us that:

> the physical fact of death has no palliations or disguises. The sealed coffin of western Europe and the cosmetics and mummifications of North America are undreamed of. Every Greek child has heard again and again the agony of the death rattle and seen the shrunken gray chaps, the fallen jaw and closed eyelids of their elders. The coffin is left open until the last minute and lowered into the grave when everyone has kissed the dead cheeks goodbye.

Hence the valued existence of the First Cemetery, where the rich and famous have found places where they can lie undisturbed.

Walking the paths of this peaceful Mediterranean garden, between some of the best and often most moving of neo-classical sculpture – statues, tombstones and mausoleums – visitors can find themselves spellbound by the sunlit white marble and the dark green of pine and cypress set against blue sky, conscious that here inscribed in stone on these graves of prominent and influential Greeks and foreigners, politicians and poets, artists and generals, is also written a history of modern Greece. In Cavafy's poem 'Voices' (1904):

> Ideal and dearly beloved voices
> Of those who are dead
> Or of those who are lost to us like the dead.
>
> Sometimes they speak to us in our dreams;
> Sometimes in thought the mind hears them.
>
> And for a moment with their echo
> Other echoes return from the first poetry of our lives –
> Like music that extinguishes the far-off night.

Perhaps the most conspicuous tomb in the cemetery is that of Heinrich Schliemann, whose discoveries at Troy (see Chapter 2) and at Mycenae (Chapter 5) astonished the world and gave such impetus to modern archaeology.

Robert Byron came to Greece in love with Byzantine architecture and with a jaundiced view of the classical achievement, blaming the dreary prints and drawings of the Parthenon, common to every school in England – 'a row of grooved cinnamon ninepins against a sky the colour of a butcher's apron' – for being responsible for the 'loathing with which the very thought of a Greek ruin fills the mind of an educated person'.

His first ascent of the Acropolis, described in *Europe in the Looking Glass* (1926), changed his mind. 'Strewn in all directions lay blocks of white marble gleaming in the brilliant sunshine, their broken sides displaying the oldest, and at the same time the most modern architectural conventions, varied with now and then a fragmentary bas-relief, the hindquarters of a horse, a human arm, or draped hip.'

Determined to 'pit his pen against the lens of the Victorian photographer', he wrote:

The pillars of the Parthenon are Doric, plain, massive and fluted from top to bottom. They are composed of separate blocks of marble, three and a half feet deep and five in diameter, which, at the time of construction, were forcibly ground to fit one another, only the topmost having previously been fluted. Then, when a succession of blocks had become a pillar, the whole fluting was carried out by hand. The marble is still as smooth as vellum, its surface hard as basalt, its edges sharp as steel. And for all the chips and flakes and holes, there is a certain quality about this handwork, which by handwork can always be distinguished, be it on metal, wood or stone – a textural quality that renders every imperfection not only superfluous but invisible. Picture these pillars, then, with their surface of vellum and their colour of sun-kissed satin, rising massive and radiant from the marble plinth of the whole building, against the brazen turquoise of the sky behind. At their feet the grey slabs of rock and the wreck of the innumerable statues and monuments with which the whole acropolis was once adorned; behind, the tall spike of Lycabettus rising from the white blocks of the town beneath its veil of dust; in front, the chimneys and promontory of Piraeus; finally the sea and the islands.

World War II, the Italian and then the much harsher German occupation, followed by the years when Greeks fought, killed and tormented each other, affected the country's poets; in their work the shadows of death and devastation of that terrible decade were inevitably reflected.

Besides the older poets such as Palamas, Seferis and Elytis, there were younger men coming into their maturity during these bitter years. Nikos Gatsos was one whose long poem *Amorgos* (translated by Edmund Keeley and Philip Sherrard) was written during the horrors of the winter famine of 1941–2:

> In the griever's courtyard no sun rises
> Only worms appear to mock the stars
> Only horses sprout upon the ant-hills
> And bats eat birds and piss out sperm.
>
> In the griever's courtyard night never sets
> Only the foliage vomits forth a river of tears
> When the devil passes by to mount the dogs
> And the crows swim in a well of blood.
>
> In the griever's courtyard the eye has gone dry
> The brain has frozen and the heart turned to stone.

The brutality and melancholy of these lines contrast with a glimmer of hope:

> For years and years, O my tormented heart, have I struggled with
>   ink and hammer,
> With gold and fire, to fashion an embroidery for you,
> The hyacinth of an orange tree,
> A flowering quince tree to comfort you –
> I who once touched you with the eyes of the Pleiades.

Yiannis Ritsos was another, more prolific, poet who survived the war years. His 'Women' (translated by Edmund Keeley) describes:

> Women are very distant. Their sheets smell of 'good night.'
> They set the bread down on the table so that we don't feel they're
>   absent.
> Then we recognize it is our fault. We get up out of our chair and
>   say:
> 'You worked awfully hard today,' or 'Forget it. I'll light the lamp.'
>
> When we strike the match she turns and slowly moves off
> with inexplicable concentration toward the kitchen. Her back
> is a bitterly sad hill loaded with many dead –
> the family's dead, her dead, your own death.
>
> You hear her footsteps creak on the old floorboards,
> hear the dishes cry in the rack, and then you hear
> the train that's taking the soldiers to the front.

Greeks have always turned to their poets in times of despair or crisis: in the war of independence from the Turks, in World War II under Nazi occupation, in the civil war which followed and under the military dictatorship of the Colonels. In *City and Loneliness* (translated by Alex Moskios), Kostis Palamas wrote:

This year's harsh winter brought me to my knees,
For it found me without youth and caught me without fire,
And time and time again as I walked the snowy streets,
I felt I would fall and die.

But yesterday I was encouraged by the laugh of March,
And I went to find again the roads to the ancient sites,
The first fragrance of a distant rose in my path
Brought tears to my eyes.

In February 1943, in occupied Greece, Palamas, the country's best-loved poet and author of the Olympic Hymn which is sung at every Olympic Games, died aged 84. His funeral became the occasion for a public release of national feeling as the crowds filled the paths of the First Cemetery and gathered round the grave. Angelos Sikelianos, who now inherited the dead poet's mantle of national poet, put his hand on the coffin and recited a poem which he had written the night before in memory of Palamas. Katsimbalis threw a handful of earth into the grave and then began to sing out in his booming voice the verses written by the nineteenth-century poet Dionysios Solomos, an invocation of freedom that had become the national anthem of Greece and which was banned by the German authorities on pain of death. At first Katsimbalis sang alone, then the crowd joined in, hesitantly, then in full voice. Michael Llewellyn Smith wrote in *Athens*, 'The funeral enabled the mourners to express in public what could not be expressed at other times. Ioanna Tattoos, Seferis's sister, ended her diary entry for the day of the funeral, "We are free."'

Palamas himself had written in the preface to his *The Twelve Words of the Gypsy* (1907, translated by T. P. Stephanides and G. C. Katsimbalis): 'it cannot be that I am the poet of myself alone; I am the poet of my age and of my race; and what I hold within me cannot be divided from the world without.'

Another dramatic funeral was that of George Seferis in 1971. Seferis had, like Sikelianos, condemned the Colonels' regime. It too was recorded by Michael Llewellyn Smith in *Athens*:

The service took place in the crowded Church of the Transfiguration on the edge of the Plaka [...] As the body in the hearse made the long, slow journey ... to the cemetery, the crowds spilled out and stopped the traffic. As with Palamas, music took over. In snatches, spontaneously, and then together, the crowd, mainly young people, sang the well-known Theodorakis setting of *Epiphaneia*. It is a very personal love poem, which on this occasion expressed the nostalgia for freedom that the poet represented for the crowd.

To me a poem by Bernard Spencer, 'A Spring Wind', though written in 1959, brings today's Athens to life, more than any other. Bernard Spencer is a much-neglected poet who died, aged 53, in 1963. A friend of Lawrence Durrell and one of the group of writers in Cairo during World War II, Spencer worked for the British Council in Thessaloniki and in Athens.

Spring shakes the windows, doors whang to,
The sky moves half in dark and half
Shining like knives: upon this table Elytis' poems lie,
Uttering the tangle of sea, the 'breathing caves'
And the fling of Aegean waves.

I am caught here in this scattering, vagrant season
Where telephones ring;
And all Greece goes through me
As the wind goes searching through the city streets.
Greece, I have so much loved you
Out of all reason;
That this unquiet time

Its budding and its pride
The news and the nostalgia of Spring
Swing towards you their tide:

Towards the windmills on the islands;
Alefkandra loved by winds,
Luminous with foam and morning, Athens
Her blinded marble heads,
Her pepper trees, the bare heels of her girls,
Old songs that bubble up from where thought starts,
Greek music treading like the beat of hearts;
Haunted Seferis, smiling, playing with beads.

Greek music, 'treading like the beat of hearts', has always been closely linked to Greek literature, in a way unknown in any other Western culture. All of the best-known Greek writers – Solomos, Cavafy, Palamas, Elytis, Sikelianos, Ritsos, Gatsos, Kazantzakis – all have had their work, mainly poetry but often opera and film, set to music by Greek composers, with many of their songs becoming greatly loved not only in Greece but also abroad.

The composers best known internationally are Manos Hatzidakis (1925–94) and Mikis Theodorakis (also born in 1925). Both joined the left-wing resistance against the Germans during the war, where they met and became friends. Hatzidakis wrote the music for the 1960 film *Never on Sunday* starring Melina Mercouri; her singing of 'Ena, kai dio, kai tria, kai tessera paidia' made her, the song and the film famous. Four years later a novel by Nikos Kazantzakis, *Alexis Zorbas*, became a film directed by Michael Cacoyannis with music by Theodorakis. *Zorba the Greek* and *Never on Sunday,* delighted audiences all over the world and suddenly drew their attention to this little country in southern Europe with its brave and animated people and renowned past, surrounded by spectacular mountains, islands and clear seas.

4

CENTRAL GREECE

Edward Lear was the perfect traveller, patient and good-natured, quick to forget discomfort in the pleasure of novel surroundings. After hours of walking and riding in the mountains, soaked by icy rain, he might allow himself a moment's complaint at the difficulty of changing his clothes in a crowded wayside khan or rest-house, but, he wrote in a letter, 'this done, a good dinner of rice, pilaf, and kebabs, with coffee and a cigar are beyond description refreshing; and the wayfarer soon forgets the inconveniences of travel while recording with pen or pencil its excitements and interests.'

Vivian Noakes in *Edward Lear: The Life of a Wanderer* quotes Charles Church, a companion on an early Greek journey, who noted how, even exhausted and in extreme heat, Lear 'was at work all the time, from 3 o'clock in the morning, only resting during the midheat […] intent upon his work, with infinite patience and unflagging good humour.' It was on this journey that they passed through Lamia, at that time a town on the frontier with Turkey. 'The strangest feature of the place is the *immense* number of storks it contains,' Lear wrote. 'Every house has one or more, some 8 or 10 nests, & the minarets – (now only in ruins) & other ruined houses are all alive with them. The clatter they make with their bills is most curious, & makes you fancy all the town are playing at backgammon.' Lamia had only been part of the Greek state for 16 years. Storks seem to have been well liked by the Turks, and perhaps for this reason, storks – and minarets – are rarely seen in Greek towns today.

These rocks rise tormented
Like the Byzantine soul to the sky.
Wounded obelisks, beasts of a granite
Nightmare, towering cubes and tablets
Fit for the Ten Commandments to be carved upon,
They move disdainful away
From the ashen pestilent plain.
Monasteries cling to their slopes
Deserted in a world that has forgotten
How to pray.

C. A. Trypanis in his poem 'Meteora' (in his collection *The Pompeian Dog*, 1964) wonders, like many of us who have contemplated these remote and beautiful 'fortresses of the soul', at the thoughts of those monks engaged:

In the sad fight of man to trample
His flesh – the look
In the upturned eyes of the ascetic
And saints on their pale, fading frescoes.

[…] And did they escape?
Did they not carry up the frowning face of the stone
The blind precipice, their last enemy,
The human blood? Or, lashed
By solitude, the winds and prayer
Did the storm of the flesh die down,
And the soul when called, move untroubled
From the fringe of the sky where it had nestled
Into the luminous blue?

But far below the villages of Thessaly
Bathed in the fever of the plain,
Cling to the earth, watching in awe the huge
Hewn steps that lead from their fields to the sky.

In the 1830s Robert Curzon, who spent years of travel in search of antique manuscripts (see also Chapter 2), describes in his *Visits to the Monasteries of the Levant* a frustrating experience at the monastery of St Barlaam at Meteora. Out of an ancient chest the old librarian had dug out for him a number of eleventh- and twelfth-century manuscripts, on vellum, of the Gospels. Particularly exciting was 'a large quarto, and one of the most beautiful manuscripts of its kind I have met with anywhere [...] as richly ornamented as a Romish missal [...] in excellent preservation, except for one miniature at the beginning, which had been smeared over by the wet finger of some ancient sloven.' Another volume of the Gospels which he greatly admired was smaller, 'in a very small, clear hand, bound in a kind of silver filigree'.

To Curzon's delight the *agoumenos* (abbot) agreed to sell both books to him, and several pieces of gold were handed over. Unfortunately for Curzon, a fierce quarrel then broke out between the abbot, the librarian and the monks as to how this unexpected windfall was to be distributed. Deadlock! With great reluctance the abbot handed back the gold and Curzon, deeply disappointed, returned the books, which he had already counted on being the chief ornaments of his library in England:

> My bag was brought forward, and when the books were extracted from it, I sat down on a stone in the courtyard, and for the last time turned over the gilded leaves and admired the ancient and splendid illuminations of the larger manuscript, the monks standing around me as I looked at the blue cypress trees, and green and gold peacocks, and intricate arabesques, so characteristic of the times of Byzantine art [...] It was a superb old book. I laid it down upon the stone beside me and placed the little volume with its curious silver binding on the top of it, and it was with a sigh that I left them there with the sun shining on the curious silver ornaments.

Nearly 20 years after his first Greek book, Osbert Lancaster was in Greece again, this time to write about Byzantine art and architecture, published in 1969 as *Sailing to Byzantium*. Visiting the celebrated monasteries of Meteora, he found them much more accessible than in Curzon's day. They could now be reached by road; and much else had changed.

He found little of architectural distinction at the Meteoron or St Barlaam's and thought they were best viewed from below:

> S. Stephanos is even less interesting and has the disadvantage of being a nunnery. Greek nuns are almost invariably bossy and frequently off their heads; these, who are no exception, have long since abandoned contemplation for the promotion of sales of the hideous local embroidery. All three churches can boast, and do, the possession of carved, wooden iconostases of a fiendish ingenuity better employed in the decoration of cuckoo clocks.

In *Roumeli* (1966), Patrick Leigh Fermor recalls peering up at the monasteries, perched on their pinnacles of rock, from a Bren gun carrier as the British army retreated southwards in the spring of 1941, 'and thinking, inspite of the plunging Stukas overhead, how remote and detached they looked, and how immune'. He had made a memorable visit to Meteora in 1935, staying at St Barlaam's, where he made friends with the abbot Christopher and the monk Bessarion (and their cat Makry) and attended one of the monastery's nightlong services:

> The hair of both monks, usually twisted into buns and tucked under their headgear, now tumbled in long twists half way down their backs. From below, the candle-light threw peculiar shadows on the waxen features of Bessarion and sharply defined the deep eyesockets, the fiercely bridged nose and quizzically wrinkled brow of Father Christopher, when, censer in hand, a magnificent colossus in splendid and threadbare vestments, he emerged from the altar. His deep voice groaned responses to the higher pitch of Bessarion. At a pause in the liturgy [...] Makry the tom cat stalked slowly into

the church and up to the rood-screen; the light from the central arch cast his elongated shadow portentously across the flagstones. Nimbly he leapt on the high, mother-of-pearl-inlaid octagonal table supporting the lectern and, curling his tail neatly round his haunches, sat gazing at the page. Without a break in the chanting, Bessarion pushed the raised paw away from the margin and gently stroked the tortoiseshell head as he sang; and slowly the long liturgy unfolded.

On his way back into the main church, Leigh Fermor caught a glimpse of Bessarion:

kindling a fire of thorns in the sooty depths of the kitchen. A blaze lit up the lenses of his spectacles and the minute bronze saucepans for Turkish coffee with which he was busy. Beyond, over the outer door to the narthex, the souls of the dead were being weighed in great painted scales. On one side, the righteous were conducted to paradise by angels. They floated heavenwards on rafts of cloud, and the interlock of their haloes receded like the scales of a goldfish. But on the other side, black-winged fiends were leading the dead away haltered and handcuffed, and hurling them into a terrible flaming gyre. This conflagration, peopled with prelates and emperors, swirled them into the shark-toothed mouth of a gigantic, glassy-eyed and swine-snouted monster. Giant dolphins and herrings and carp, each one with human limbs sticking out of its mouth, furrowed a stormy sea in the background [...]

Something pressed my shoulder. Looking round, I saw the great horny hand of the abbot resting there and, above and beyond it, his eyebrows raised high. 'There you are,' he observed severely, 'Hell' (he pointed at each in turn) 'and Heaven'. His index finger was aimed at the airborne swarm. 'Let's hope *that's* where you go.' As he turned towards the stairs, I thought I could divine the ghost of a wink. 'Up we go,' the abbot continued, 'Bessarion's ready with the coffee.' We halted half-way up the stairs. In my preoccupation with the frescoes I had forgotten to look down into the gulf. The lower world was hidden beneath a snowy mass of cloud that rose in a solid waste to the edge of the parapet. Only the monasteries rose like outposts in a Polar wilderness, as if one could cross the half mile to the Transfiguration on snow-shoes. The bridge, the tiles and the rotunda of St Barbara were just visible. The rest was snowed under. St Stephen and Holy Trinity rode high on the pale billows, and a bell sounded over the intervening distance like the signal of an ice-bound ship in distress.

Leaving Meteora a few days later, Leigh Fermor noted how few of the twenty-six foundations now remained, and reflected on the crumbled 'shells of the extinct monasteries':

Poised on their pinnacles, they are no longer accessible. No steps ascend and no monks are left to cast their nets into the surrounding gulf. They disintegrate in mid-air, empty stone caskets of rotting timber and slowly falling frescoes that only spiders and owls and kestrels inhabit or the occasional family of eagles. How distinct the rocks of the Meteora appear from all that surrounds them! They have a different birth, and bear an alien, planetary aspect, like a volley of thunderbolts embedded in the steep-sides hollow [...] As the shades of evening assembled, the monasteries began to float [...] Their massive supporting pillars became irrelevant appendages: wavering tendrils that tapered and dwindled and vanished in the dusk until the clusters of domes and cypresses and towers, like little celestial cities, seemed only to be held aloft in the void by the whirring and multiple wings of a company of seraphim.

Pouqueville on his expeditions into Thessaly paints a somewhat idealistic picture of the countryside in the first years of the nineteenth century. He clearly enjoyed his work, collecting social and geographical data in those happy days when he had the freedom to travel where he wished, before Ali Pasha switched sides from the French to the British. In *Travels in Epirus, Albania, Macedonia and Thessaly* (1820), he wrote:

> Each season brings round its labours, and each change of labour produced a change of enjoyment. In the time of seed-sowing, mounted on their antique carts they repair to the prepared field. The spring is introduced by festivals and *panegyres* or fairs, which attract for business or for pleasure the inhabitants of the surrounding villages. The heats of summer pass away under the cool shade of their hills and woods. The vintage, the cotton-harvest, are seasons of joy and expectation. The winter, in such a climate, invites the Thessalian to the chace. Thus passes round the year for the Thessalian husbandman; and the general regularity of the climate highly favours the unfolding of the faculties of both body and mind, among a race of men who want only a proper system of government to be happy.

Cape Sounion (also known as Cape Colonna or Sunium) remains one of the great dramatic sites of Greece. The drama, of course, is in its position. Surmounted by the ruins of the ancient temple dedicated to Poseidon, god of the sea, the high rocky cape points like an outstretched arm into the Aegean to the first islands of the Cyclades – Kea, Kythnos and Seriphos, with the promise of those sister islands with their magic names – Syros, Paros, Milos, Naxos, Mykonos and Santorini – trailing beyond the blue horizon.

The marble columns of the temple, scoured gleaming white by wind and sun, are visible for miles out to sea, a famous landmark for sailors who for 2,500 years have rowed and sailed round the cape.

Lord Byron was fascinated and deeply affected by Sounion, its beauty and savage history perfectly matching his romantic requirements. 'In all Attica,' he writes in a note to *Childe Harold*, 'if we except Athens itself and Marathon, there is no scene more interesting than Cape Colonna.' The hero of his later poem *Don Juan* exclaims:

> Place me on Sunium's marbled steep,
> Where nothing save the waves and I
> May hear our mutual murmurs sweep.

And later Juan recalls with pleasure,

> 'Twas oft my luck to dine,
> The grass my table-cloth, in open air,
> On Sunium.

Byron rounded the cape once by sea and made two visits by land. On the second occasion, he writes in a note to *Childe Harold*:

> we had a narrow escape from a party of Maniotes, concealed in the caverns underneath. We were told afterwards by one of their prisoners subsequently ransomed, that they were deterred from attacking us by the appearance of my two Albanians: conjecturing, very sagaciously, but falsely, that we had a complete guard of these Arnauts at hand, they remained stationary, and thus saved our party, which was too small to have opposed any effectual resistance.

Edward Dodwell, Irish painter and writer, travelled in Greece in the early years of the nineteenth century and recorded his journey in *Tour Through Greece* (1819). He remarks that the headland used to be called 'Xylophagos, devourer of wood, from the number of ships which are lost upon its rocks.' He and his party camped there for four days, in a cave under the cliffs:

> The promontory of Sunium is exposed more than any other ... to the violence of the winds. It is assailed by every rude gust which blows from the north, south and west [...] During our stay, scarcely

a moment intervened without a violent gale; and it is almost as ill-famed for shipwrecks as the Malean promontory nor is it less dreaded by the mariner.

Here Dodwell was comparing Sounion to Cape Matapan on the southern extremity of the Peloponnese.

Standing on Sounion's 'marbled steep' on a windless day of summer it is hard to imagine the fury of winter storms and the scenes of terror, destruction and death that have unfolded at one's feet. A special characteristic of high winds in the Aegean is the short, violent, battering seas that they create. Even in summer the *meltemi*, the ancient Etesian wind, while mercifully cooling the cities, can whip up waves of such violence that in World War II destroyers were discouraged from taking to sea, and today when it blows hard ferryboats are prohibited from leaving port.

Of the thousands of ships destroyed on the rocks of Cape Sounion, one of the best recorded is that of *Britannia*, a trading vessel on her way from Alexandria to Venice in October 1761. A member of the crew, a midshipman, was a young Scotsman, William Falconer. From a poor family in Edinburgh, he had become a seaman early in life, and also a poet. In *The Shipwreck* (1762) he describes the terrible storm that drove the ship towards the cape:

> But now Athenian mountains they descry,
> And o'er the surge Colonna frowns on high,
> Where marble columns, long by time defaced,
> Moss-covered, on the lofty cape are placed [...]
> The circling beach in murderous form appears,
> Decisive goal of all their hopes and fears:
> The seamen now in wild amazement see
> The scene of ruin rise beneath their lee.

Wind and surging sea hurled *Britannia* broadside at the cliffs, smashing her hull repeatedly on the rocks. Desperate sailors not already swept overboard climbed the rigging, vainly hoping to escape.

> The ship hangs hovering on the verge of death,
> Hell yawns, rocks rise, and breakers roar beneath! [...]
> Uplifted on the surge, to heaven she flies [...]
> As o'er the surge the stooping main-mast hung,
> Still on the rigging thirty seamen clung;
> Some, struggling, on a broken crag were cast,
> And there by oozy tangles grappled fast,
> Awhile they bore th'o'erwhelming billows' rage,
> Unequal combat with their fate to wage;
> Till all benumb'd and feeble they forgo
> Their slippery hold, and sink to shades below.
> Some, from the main-yard-arm impetuous thrown
> On marble ridges, die without a groan.

Falconer was one of only three survivors. Incredibly, he had just recently survived a shipwreck – in the English Channel. In February 1760 Falconer had been a midshipman on board the warship *Ramillies*. A navigation error drove the ship onto the rocks. The captain ordered the masts to be cut away, and dropped his anchors; but the storm raged with such fury that the cables parted and the ship was driven among the breakers and dashed to pieces. Out of 734 men, only Falconer and 25 others saved themselves by jumping from the stern to the rocks.

Falconer dedicated *The Shipwreck* to the Duke of York, and thanks to his patronage obtained the post of purser on a royal warship. The poem became popular and went through a number of editions; Byron knew it well and particularly wanted to see the site of the disaster. The poem was also used as a technical primer for sailing, as it contained clear and detailed descriptions of navigation, sails and rigging. Patrick O'Brian almost certainly read *The Shipwreck*, and other of Falconer's nautical works, including his *Universal Marine Dictionary* (1780); a character in O'Brian's well-known Aubrey–Maturin series is a poet who draws on Falconer's verse.

Falconer continued his career on the high seas and to write; his *Marine Dictionary* was much in demand. Having survived two shipwrecks he had surely suffered more than his fair share of nautical disasters. But ten years later he embarked as purser on an East Indiaman, the *Aurora;* the ship put in to Cape Town on her way east, left the port in December 1769 – and was never seen again. According to East India Company records:

> on the 19th of November, 1773, a Black was examined before the East India Directors, who affirmed, 'that he was one of five persons who had been saved from the wreck of the *Aurora*; that the said frigate had been cast away on a reef of rocks off Mocoa; and that he was two years upon an island after he had escaped; and was at length miraculously preserved by a country ship happening to touch at that island.'

Falconer was not one of those five; his luck had run out.

Errors in navigation were the cause of two of Falconer's shipwrecks and accounted for many of the huge number of vessels and sailors lost at sea every year in the eighteenth century. With trade and empire growing together, and increasing numbers of British ships on the high seas, it is not surprising that so much painstaking effort was given by the Royal Navy to mapping the world's oceans, including the Aegean, resulting in the detailed charts that are still used and respected today.

In September of 490 BCE the first recorded battle between East and West made its indelible mark on history. And for good reason, since all the essential ingredients were present: despotic East, all-powerful and with overwhelming numbers, attacks brave free citizens of small Western democratic state – and is soundly defeated. Perhaps the most famous battle in European history, it had no need of emphasis from Lord Byron. However his special touch in 'The Isles of Greece'

influenced Western public opinion just as the Greeks began their fight to free themselves from the Ottoman Empire.

> The mountains look on Marathon –
> And Marathon looks on the sea;
> And musing there an hour alone,
> I dream'd that Greece might still be free;
> For standing on the Persians' grave
> I could not deem myself a slave.

According to Herodotus, when the Persians disembarked their army including cavalry in the bay of Marathon, the Athenians, mustering every fighting man, marched north to confront them. A wait of several days followed, the Greeks blocking the road to Athens. Herodotus tells us that before the battle, the runner Pheidippides was despatched to Sparta, a distance of 225 kilometres (140 miles), in a desperate call for help. On the way he was accosted by the goat-footed Pan, who asked why the Athenians did not worship him. When Pheidippides promised, breathlessly, that this error would be immediately corrected, the god seemed satisfied: during the battle he appeared on the side of the Greeks, instilling his own special frenzy of fear, *panic,* among the enemy. After the Persian defeat a shrine was duly dedicated to him on the Acropolis.

As it happened, the Spartans were celebrating an important religious festival, but as soon as it was concluded an army set out and by forced marches reached Marathon the day after the battle. Like the Athenians, they had not seen Persian soldiers before. Ever professional, the Spartans inspected the weapons of the defeated, briefly congratulated the Athenians and marched home.

Later historians, probably starting with Plutarch, confused the magnificent run of Pheidippides to Sparta with another story, that of the runner who carried the message of victory from the battlefield of Marathon to Athens, with the vital information that the defeated Persian army had embarked on their ships and were heading south to attack the city. Blurting out the news, he dropped dead. The Athenians at Marathon, exhausted after hours of vicious fighting, marched home at the double, arriving just as the Persian fleet put in to the bay of Phaleron, a few miles from Athens. Discouraged by the arrival of the Athenian hoplites, the Persian fleet turned away and rowed back to Asia.

The distance run by this second messenger was about 42 kilometres (25 miles). For the first of the revived Olympic Games, held in Athens in 1896, a race was included to be run from Marathon to Athens. Appropriately, this first of the modern marathons was won by a Greek, Spiridon Louis. Another Greek came third, but was disqualified because he had taken a horse and carriage part of the way.

Runners like Pheidippides were vital to the smooth administration of the far-flung corners of the ancient world. And not just in Greece: Herodotus said of the Persian couriers, 'Neither snow nor rain nor heat nor gloom of night stays these couriers from the swift completion of their appointed rounds.' Harry Mount, in *Harry Mount's Odyssey* (2015), adds: 'The line is inscribed in enormous letters on the huge classical post-office on Eighth Avenue in Manhattan.'

> *I am the eye with which the Universe*
> *Beholds itself and knows itself divine;*
> *All harmony of instrument or verse,*
> *All prophecy, all medicine is mine,*
> *All light of art or nature*
> (Percy Bysshe Shelley, 'Hymn of Apollo', 1824)

For Shelley, Delphi belongs to Apollo, the sun god.

In his *Records of Shelley, Byron and the Author* (1858), Edward Trelawny recounts a conversation he had with Byron about travelling in the area of Delphi. Byron had been with his great friend John Cam Hobhouse:

Hobhouse and I wrangled every day [...] he had a greed for legendary lore, topography, inscriptions [...] He would potter with map and compass at the foot of Pindos, Parnes, and Parnassus, to ascertain the site of some ancient temple or city. I rode my mule up them. They haunted my dreams from boyhood; the pines, eagles, vultures, and owls were descended from those that Themistocles and Alexander had seen, and were not degenerated like the humans; the rocks and torrents were the same. John Cam's dogged perseverance in pursuit of his hobby is to be envied. I have no hobby and no perseverance. I gazed at the stars and ruminated. I took no notes, asked no questions.

Trelawny said, 'Your memory did more than his notes. You wrote *Childe Harold*; what did his notes produce?'

Osbert Lancaster was not as diligent an explorer as John Cam, but he was impressed by Delphi, recounting in *Classical Landscape with Figures*:

It is not difficult to understand how the ancients came to consider Delphi the very centre of the earth, for even if they had not Zeus's pair of eagles to guide them (that still wheel and circle endlessly above the cliffs), the whole conformation of these mountains gives to the landscape a magnificently ultimate look as of a point to which all the routes of the world must ultimately converge.

He was struck by the international character of the shrine, dominated by the great temple of Apollo, 'above the portal of which was carved the useful but discouraging injunction, *Know thyself* [...] To the oracle all the various cities and states looked for guidance in war, in foreign policy and in colonial expansion, and at the conclusion of any enterprise they were accustomed to express their gratitude and score off their rivals by the erection in the sacred precincts of monuments of competitive magnificence.'

Nowadays it is best to see Delphi, as every site in ancient Greece, in the early morning before the coaches from Athens unload their thousands.

'Delphi in the days of its greatness was something much more than a glorified Lourdes with a first-rate fortune-teller thrown in,' Lancaster writes. Visitors included 'merchants, artists and architects on the look-out for contracts, diplomats and international financiers making contact with their opposite numbers from the other end of the Mediterranean, philosophers in search of pupils and pupils in search of philosophers, and a large smart element who were accustomed to visit Delphi regularly during the season.' In addition there were the athletes come for the Pythian Games and, accompanying the genuine pilgrims, a 'vast crowd of religious touts who derived a profitable living from the interpretation of the frequently cabbalistic pronouncements of the oracle for the benefit of the less sophisticated consultants.'

> Standing on the terrace of the small inn in the village [this was in 1946] and looking out over the valley the impression of being at the very centre of things, both in place and time, remains curiously overpowering. Down below the vast unbroken sea of olives [...] stretches all the way to the real sea that appears strangely solid and metallic by contrast [...] Beyond, the barren and lofty mountains of Aetolia [...] stretch away down the Gulf to the little walled port of Navpaktos, whence the Turkish fleet sailed out to its doom at Lepanto. The skyline to the south is broken by the jagged peaks of the Peloponnese, among which Hercules hunted and destroyed the Erymanthine boar, and the mountains to the east are an outcrop of Helicon, sacred to the muses ... and the slopes on which one is suspended are those of Parnassus itself.

George Seferis visited the site some 20 years after Lancaster and in a 1961 article (later translated by C. Capri-Karka in *The Charioteer*, 1993–4), he wrote:

As one comes from Athens to Delphi, after Thebes and Livadia, where the road meets the road to Daulis, there is the crossroads of Megas, the 'bandit-killer' as he was called in the popular novels of the last century. In the years of Pythia, this crossroad was called 'split road.' It was a very significant crossroads for the emotional complexes of people in those days; and, in other ways, for us too. There begins the story of Oedipus, the ultimate suppliant. Pythia in her oracle had given her answer to his father: 'Laius, you ask me for a son; I will give him to you; but it is your fate that from his hands you will lose the light of day.'

The oracle at Delphi delivered its often cryptic replies to questions of state asked by kings and rulers from across the Mediterranean and beyond. Pythia, the priestess, intoxicated with fumes of laurel, overcome by the presence of the god, muttered, intoned or frenziedly screamed her responses, her words carefully recrafted by the attendant priests and proclaimed in measured hexameters or laconic prose to the awestruck suppliant.

To the many personal questions asked of the oracle, few answers could have had more dramatic consequence than the Pythia's to Laius, king of Thebes, setting off a series of tragic events that have echoed from the plays of Sophocles through the literature of Western civilisation; given a further dimension by Sigmund Freud they even influence the way we explain our lives today.

In *Oedipus the King* Sophocles tells the story of how Laius, when a son was finally born to him and his wife Jocasta, was so convinced of the prophecy that his son would kill him that he gave away the child to be exposed on Mount Kithairon. The baby was rescued by a shepherd and was adopted by the king and queen of Corinth, who were without children. When Oedipus grew up he was horrified to learn of the fate foreseen for him by the oracle, and to avoid killing the man he thought was his father and marrying the woman he thought was his mother, he left Corinth and went into permanent exile.

What happened next is described by Seferis with devastating simplicity: 'Laius was going to Delphi; Oedipus was returning. They met at this crossroads under the heavy mass of Parnassus. Neither of the two knew whom he was facing. They argued. Oedipus killed his father.'

Sophocles in his play tells us that the two men quarrelled over the right of way – neither Oedipus nor Laius, each in his chariot, would allow the other precedence on the narrow mountain road. Is this the first recorded incident of death from road rage?

Oedipus faced another serious obstacle on his way to Thebes: the dreaded Sphinx who murdered anyone who failed to give the correct answer to a riddle. The Sphinx had become such a menace to society that Creon, brother of Laius and now temporarily on the throne of Thebes, promised that anyone who could get rid of the monster would inherit the kingdom and marry Laius's widow, Jocasta.

The riddle of the Sphinx was: *Who has four legs in the morning, two in the afternoon, and three in the evening?* Many had set out to the Sphinx's lair, confident of providing the right answer, but none had returned. Oedipus was not afraid to try and in fact answered correctly: Man, who crawls on all fours as a baby, walks on two legs as an adult, and uses a stick when he is old. Stunned by the reply, the Sphinx was easily done away with and Oedipus, triumphant, continued on to Thebes where he became king and married ... Jocasta.

We like to believe that the truth will always come out in the end, and in this case it did, leading to misery and death, dramatically revealed in the next two plays of Sophocles's Theban trilogy, *Oedipus at Colonna* and *Antigone*.

In *Harry Mount's Odyssey*, the author, at the time travelling with other journalists, wrote:

One hot afternoon, on the way from Athens to Delphi, we stopped at a petrol station at a crossroads on the outskirts of Thebes. As I bought a chocolate bar from the kiosk, the man behind the till told me that this was the crossroads where Oedipus killed his father.

I stopped and stared through the plate-glass window as the petrol pump attendant filled up our minibus. Heavy trucks careered across the crossroads, leaving a trail of red dust. Low-rise, concrete flats and shops were sprinkled at random spots along the road. There wasn't a single sign – no stall selling Oedipus-related tourist tat; no Oedipus Complex shopping centre. And yet this was the spot that spawned not just one of the great Greek myths, but also a psychological condition – even if Dr Freud was not quite right in his analysis [...] For a few seconds before climbing back on the bus with the other hacks, I felt unaccountably moved by this distinctly unlovely place.

George Seferis, many years earlier, approached Delphi from the port of Itea, writing in his 1961 article:

It is nice to start from the seashore and enter among the olive trees under the silver leaves of the plain of Criseos, enumerating, as you pass by, the wrinkles on the dense gathering of trunks; and if by chance this shadow weighs heavily upon you and you raise your eyes, you suddenly see, in the perpetually moving blue, the twin peaks of Parnassus [...] Up there in Delphi, after you pass the village and reach the temple, you have the feeling that you have entered a place separate from the world [...] an amphitheatre nestling on the first steps of Parnassus.

[...] In the morning, at Marmaria, I went again to see the rocks that rolled down from Parnassus and destroyed the temple of Athena, as mentioned by Herodotus. In the beginning of our century, another storm detached three large rocks and completed the destruction. The rocks are there among the trampled works of men, still showing, motionless now, their initial force. I remembered Angelos Sikelianos as he was listening to the onset of such a wind: 'Not a sound is heard anywhere; and suddenly a horrendous roar, a strong and unbelievable roar breaks out as if from every direction. It is the great wind from Parnassus which starts up unexpectedly from the peaks towards the open spaces, with such force that you think it will shatter even the rocks to dust.' The poet of Delphi – if any of our contemporaries can be called the man of Delphi – was writing in his house high up near the Stadium, where I met him for the first time. His house is now in ruins; an ugly bust of him outside the door underlines the futility of glory.

Visitors to Delphi like to drink at the Castalian spring and it was in these running waters that pilgrims washed before praying at Apollo's shrine. Above the spring are great cliffs from which in ancient times the Delphians threw those guilty of sacrilege and other crimes. The famous Aesop, he of the fables, met his end in this way in about 570 BCE. Practically nothing is known for sure about Aesop, born in Asia Minor? a slave? excessively ugly? a great storyteller? That last at least is certain, and his stories – Achilles and the Tortoise, the Fox and the Grapes, and a hundred others – live on today. But it seems his fame and his skill in storytelling was not enough to save him. What could he have done to offend the Delphians so deeply? Osbert Lancaster in facetious vein feared that he 'had been so unwise as to make a few unfortunate though doubtless well-merited cracks about the local administration'.

Mary Renault wrote of her experience of Delphi in the spring of 1962:

We drove to Delphi, which although sublime in the daytime seems to distil its real mystery at night, with the mountain smells, huge spaces full of moonlight falling away to the sea below, and the soft-harsh tinkle of the donkey bells, sometimes across the mountains and sometimes right under your window [...] The donkeys themselves seem particularly vocal in Delphi, every so often even in the depth of the night one will suddenly give a bloodcurdling cry full of tragedy and defiance; perhaps they have discovered the cleft from which the vapours of madness and prophecy escape since the earthquake closed the one used by the Pythoness.

There a fewer donkeys today, their places taken by equally vociferous but more numerous motorbikes and motor scooters.

David Sweetman, in his *Mary Renault, a Biography* (1993), knew the importance of Delphi to the author:

> To Mary the most unexpected thing about the site was the dominant position of the theatre, its tiered hemisphere looking down over the ruins of Apollo's temple and beyond into the great sweep of the valley. As she followed the Sacred Way eastward toward the stadium, she looked back to take a photograph, already aware that this was one image she would need to recall in detail.

The Mask of Apollo, set in the fourth century BCE, was taking shape in Renault's mind. Published in 1966, the novel was an instant bestseller on both sides of the Atlantic. It includes authentic descriptions of the way ancient dramas were made and put on the stage, and tells the story of an Athenian actor caught up in the dangerous politics of Syracuse, in which the philosopher Plato is also involved. The actor Nikeratus says, 'Ask some poet to describe the awe of Delphi, and some philosopher to explain it. I work with the words of other men. I looked back down the valley, the olives winding and falling mile on mile to a rock-clipped blink of sea.' He describes the towering peaks, cliffs and mountains overlooking the site:

> Truly Apollo is the greatest of all chorus-masters. The town, with his temple in the midst, is tiny as a toy in all this vastness; yet all those titan heads seem to stand around that and look towards it. They are the chorus round his altar; if he raised his arm they would sing a dithyramb. I don't know any other deity who could bring off such a show. At Delphi, you don't ask how they know it is the centre of the earth.

In 362 CE, Emperor Julian, who was vainly attempting to ban Christianity and bring back the Olympian gods, sent his personal physician to Delphi, by then a rather desolate place, to offer the oracle his support. In return he received the last recorded prophecy of the priestess. It seems that the oracle still retained its powers, for although it was not for some 30 years that the Christian Emperor Theodosius finally clamped down on the Olympian cults, making it a crime even to enter a temple, to the oracle the end was clearly in sight. As Edith Hall, in *Introducing the Ancient Greeks* (2014), translates it:

> Tell the king that the hall with its sculptures has fallen to the
>   ground;
> Apollo has no chamber any more, and no prophetic bay-leaves,
> No speaking spring: the water that had so much to say has
>   dried up.

Contemplating the demise of Delphi, Seferis considers the meaning of time passing:

> What we know now is that the duration of this earth, as well as of this corner, within the loins of Parnassus, is relative – it may end tomorrow or after a million years; and when we say *eternity*, we do not have in mind something measured in years, but something like Pythia, who, when falling into a trance, saw the whole of time past and future as one thing. Or, to remember my friend E. M. Forster, *we must* call things *eternal*, in order to be able to struggle up to our last moment and enjoy life. This sacred temple would probably whisper something like that to us [...] No matter how much you resist, you cannot but have a feeling of sanctity about it. At least this: let us be true to ourselves.

The semi-circle of fortified harbour walls of Nafpaktos, not far from Delphi, makes it easy to imagine oneself back in Venetian times. The little port boasts a statue of Miguel de Cervantes Saavedra, right hand held high, in his fingers a feather quill. This was the hand, the sculptor is reminding us, that penned *Don Quixote*; his left arm, hanging stiffly at his side, was rendered lifeless from wounds received in the Battle of Lepanto.

Called Lepanto by the Venetians, it was from Nafpaktos in October 1571 that a fleet of 250 Ottoman war galleys gathered to repel the fleet of the Holy League that was approaching from the west. In command of the Christian fleet was the young Don Juan of Austria, illegitimate son of the Holy Roman Emperor Charles V, and it is this 'last knight of Europe' who is the hero of G. K. Chesterton's poem 'Lepanto'.

> Strong gongs groaning as the guns boom far,
> Don John of Austria is going to the war,
> Stiff flags straining in night-blasts cold
> In the gloom black-purple, in the glint old-gold.
> Torchlight crimson on the copper kettle-drums,
> Then the tuckets, then the trumpets, then the cannon, and
>   he comes.

Lepanto was the last great battle fought exclusively with galleys. About 150,000 men rowed, roared, shot at, hacked and stabbed each other that long afternoon and more than 20,000 of them died. Chesterton writes of the 12,000 'Christian captives, sick and sunless' who were freed from the captured Turkish galleys:

> Don John pounding from the slaughter-painted poop,
> Purpling all the ocean like a bloody pirate's sloop,
> Scarlet running over on the silvers and the golds,
> Breaking of the hatches up and bursting of the holds,
> Thronging of the thousands up that labour under sea
> White for bliss and blind for sun and stunned for liberty [...]

Many more, chained to their benches, drowned.

The victory over the Turks was celebrated throughout Europe as a first sign that the Ottoman Empire was not invincible. In fact, little changed; it was not for another two centuries that the threat of invasion and conquest from the east finally receded.

Chesterton ends his ballad imagining Cervantes thinking of his eventual return to his homeland, the first stirrings of an idea in his head ...

Cervantes on his galley sets the sword back in the sheath
(Don John of Austria rides homeward with a wreath.)
And he sees across a weary land a straggling road in Spain,
Up which a lean and foolish knight forever rides in vain,
And he smiles, but not as Sultans smile, and settles back the
    blade [...]
(But Don John of Austria rides home from the Crusade.)

Just over a century later, George Wheler was in Nafpaktos when it was visited by the pasha of the Morea (Peloponnese) – ostensibly to get rid of the many pirates who used the port as a base from which to rob merchant ships passing through the straits. He describes in *A Journey into Greece* what was probably the usual way Ottoman governors went about their business:

We came at a very ill time to see this place: because the next day, so soon as it was light, all the barques were seized upon, to bring over the Basha of Morea, who had received orders to come hither, and to Saint Mauro, to burn all the galliots, or small galleys, of the pirates he should find there. But they staid not to be so complimented by him. The whole town was in a consternation at his coming: none stirred abroad, none opened their shops or doors. However we had the opportunity to see his reception, without stirring out of our chamber, it overlooking the harbour. The whole of his train was near five hundred persons, of which fifty Sclavonians were his guard. He crossed over from Vostitsa, a town of the Morea, opposite to Lepanto. Before him in a boat came kettle-drums, others playing upon hautboys and another string'd instrument, played on by a Moor; between which we could conceive no manner of harmony. Before him also was carried upon a pole, two horse tails, the marks of his dignity.

At his arrival the port saluted him with five guns, and the *Veivode, Caddi,* and other chief officers of the town, came to the gate at his landing, to kiss his vest, and received him with all the respect they were capable to give him. So soon as he was landed, he mounted on horse-back, and was conducted to the *Veivode*'s house; the rest accompanying him on foot. The next day he clapped the Emir in prison, instead of his brother, who had murdered one of the town a great while ago. But he came off again for a sum of money; which was all the Basha desir'd. The next day after he demanded fifty horses of the Turks, fifty of the Hebrews, and thirty of the Christians; these being the least part of the town.

Having made this token gesture towards the maintenance of law and order, and after collecting enough in fines and horses to cover, and more, the costs of his expedition, the Pasha departed.

Passengers in a car crossing the beautiful Rio-Antirrio Bridge that today spans the Gulf of Corinth, the longest full suspension bridge in the world, have an extraordinary view (drivers: keep your eyes on the road). Hovering over the narrows separating the mountains of the mainland and the mountains of the Peloponnese, they can scan the seas that stretch on either side and consider that few other scenes encompass such a concentration of past violence and bloodshed. For here, until Greece was reclaimed for Europe in 1832, was the gateway between East and West, and on this coast, from Corfu to the Gulf of Corinth and south to Cape Matapan, are the sites of conflict whose names ring out – Actium, Lepanto, Navarino, and a hundred others long ago forgotten. Among those still remembered is a small town, now of little strategic importance and well off the main tourist track, Missolonghi (Mesolongi).

Here at the south-western extremity of Greece the land does not so much come to an end as fade away; amidst these reedy lagoons and mosquito-ridden swamps it is impossible to say with any certainty where exactly the coastline runs. Salt marsh and sandbank and mudflat stretch away in a heat-hazy perspective towards the west, where an occasional cottage raised on piles or an isolated patch of reeds lends an improbable, lake-like character to the open sea. Missolonghi, set in the midst of this desolate landscape, would seem to be the last town in the world; indeed I have never seen a place that wore a more final air. At first one feels very, very sorry for Byron but on reflection the subdued and muted character of this setting acquires a certain melancholy appropriateness. Even at midday beneath a blazing sun it has a twilight look, and it seems fitting enough that the final scene in a drama in which the main action had taken place against the architectural backdrop of Northern Italy, the stuccoed facades of Regency London, and the awful grandeur of the Pindus should be played out in the unaccented romanticism of this sad coast. For nowhere else possesses quite this atmosphere of absolute finality; as one watches the sun go down in the sea beyond Cephallonia, it is difficult to believe it will ever rise again.

(Osbert Lancaster, *Classical Landscape with Figures*, 1947)

Patrick Leigh Fermor, approaching Missolonghi by caique in the 1950s, had a similarly gloomy impression. He wrote in *Roumeli* that the town:

which soon floated towards us as though raft-borne on its rank lagoons, has a faint air of the Venetian approaches. The same amphibious feeling reigns. A spit of land appeared, and a lighthouse and we shouted back greetings to a russet Zakynthian caique with her bowsprit springing from a figurehead of Poseidon. To port lay salt-pans and wicker labyrinths for fish breeding. A channel meandered between two lighthouses, a fisherman mended his nets on a stinking dune. There were rush huts on the mud banks and flimsy pens of reed and bamboo; the breeze had a miasmal whiff. Half-naked men in enormous hats, up to their thighs in the hot and stagnant water, toiled at fishy tasks. The momentary air of Venice evaporated as the faded town grew bigger. A dome, a line of trees, a warehouse... The thought of those four strange winter months of Byron's sojourn here, his illness and death, only underlined the presiding atmosphere of melancholy. It is a sad place to die.

On 5 January 1824 Lord Byron, after narrowly escaping Turkish warships, landed in Missolonghi, for years a centre of Greek resistance which the Turks were determined to destroy. G. F. Abbott's *Songs of Modern Greece* (1900) celebrates its defiance in a siege not long before Byron's arrival when Markos Botsaris was its leader: 'They all swore by Ahmed Mohammed to enter Mesolonghi and feast there on Christmas day, before sunrise. "Allah! Allah!" they shouted and rushed forward. The Turks planted ladders to climb on the trenches, but the musket-shots and the sabre strokes made them fall as thick as frogs.'

Byron had been appointed by the London Greek Committee as its agent in support of the Greeks; he had waited several months in Kefalonia before making his move to the mainland. The Ionian Islands were under British rule and England refused to take sides in the conflict; Byron chose to stay in Kefalonia, rather than Zante or Corfu, because he had become a friend of the governor Charles Napier (later renowned as the conqueror of Sind), who was sympathetic to the Greek cause.

Lord Byron had felt an affinity with Greece from his first visit in 1809. He loved the beautiful and often dramatic scenery and was drawn to the mountain warriors of Souli, many of whom he took on as his private bodyguard; romantically, they were his kind of people. In Athens, he took the trouble to learn modern Greek. Foreigners at that time had a low opinion of the natives, deriding and looking down on them. Byron, however, found much to admire in the

Greeks, and perhaps because he was aware of the contradictions and failings in his own character, liked them despite their faults. In his notes to *Childe Harold's Pilgrimage* he rebutted the common accusation thrown at Greeks of ingratitude:

Now, in the name of Nemesis, for what are they to be grateful? Where is the human being who has ever conferred a benefit on Greece or Greeks? They are to be grateful to the Turks for their fetters, and the Franks for their broken promises and lying counsels. They are to be grateful for the artist who engraves their ruins and to the antiquary who carries them away: to the traveller whose janissary flogs them and to the scribbler whose journal abuses them! This is the amount of their obligations to foreigners.

Byron had arrived in a Greece at war yet divided by factions who feared each other as much as they hated their common enemy. Today there is a memorial garden on the site of the house where he stayed for the last months of his life, where he was welcomed ashore in triumph to the shouts of the crowd and the salute of cannon. The building was destroyed during World War II, but we know something about it thanks to several contemporary descriptions. It was a large two-storeyed house with wooden balconies on the shore of the lagoon, with rambling outhouses where Byron's rumbustious Souliotes were quartered. On the first floor was Colonel Stanhope (later Earl of Harrington), charged by the London Committee to educate and generally improve the Greeks by setting up a printing press and distributing a large supply of bibles. Byron called him 'the typographical colonel'. Byron's own rooms were on the top floor, furnished with Turkish sofas and decorated with every type of weapon, including 'carbines, fowling pieces, pistols, swords, sabres, a claymore', where he lived with Pietro Gamba, younger brother of his ex-mistress the countess Teresa Guiccioli, the page Lukas, some very large dogs and his two main servants, the long-suffering Fletcher, his valet for the last 20 years, and Tita Falcieri, a giant of a man who had been Byron's gondolier in Venice (and was later employed by Benjamin Disraeli). According to one visitor it was more like a busy inn than a private house.

For northerners accustomed to clouds and rain through much of the year, a wet spring is never a surprise, but in Greece something better is always expected; and yet how often, instead of blue skies and warming sun, day can follow day of drenching rain. It was Byron's misfortune to spend the last months of his life at Missolonghi during a long bout of such atrocious weather, when wet winds blew coldly from the south and continuous rain turned the marshy flatlands to a sea of mud. He wrote to his banker friend Hancock that 'if we are not taken off by the sword, we are like to march off with an ague in this mud-basket'; he added that he would probably die – apologising for 'a very bad pun' – 'not *mart*ially but *marsh*-ally.'

Fiona MacCarthy, in *Byron: Life and Legend* (2002), suggests that Byron's real heroism at Missolonghi was the sacrifice of his frequent need for quiet and solitary withdrawal. As soon as he arrived he was exposed to repeated visits by the chiefs and primates, each with his own large noisy following of undisciplined armed men, and since his presence and opinions were in continual demand his house was the meeting place of everyone concerned with planning the war. 'He, whose irritability was so intense, had to cope with the various military factions at Missolonghi, the constant sound of gunfire in the street. The writer disgusted by the brutal facts of war now had to endure the massacres and horrors of a primitive and savage confrontation in which prisoners were slaughtered without compunction.' Byron's days of self-indulgence were over. The romantic swing of this poem hardly conceals a reluctant acceptance that his life was changing:

> So we'll go no more a-roving
> So late into the night,
> Though the heart be still as loving
> And the moon be still as bright.

He wrote to Teresa Guiccioli, 'Of course you might suppose that this is not exactly the place to pass the carnival in.'

As representative of the London Greek Committee, which was raising a large loan to support the war, he had frequently to complain to its members about their unrealistic ideas – 'high-flown notions of the sixth form at Harrow or Eton'. He derided the often-irrelevant material sent to support the Greek cause, 'for instance the Mathematical instruments are thrown away – none of the Greeks know a problem from a poker [...] The use of trumpets too may be doubted – unless Constantinople were Jericho – for the Hellenists have no ear for Bugles – and you must send us somebody to listen to them.' Aided by his sardonic humour and acute sense of the ridiculous, the poet was finding his feet as man of action. Increasingly he was becoming the voice of practical common sense.

Much of Byron's time was spent trying to keep the peace between the three rival armed parties in different regions of Greece whose bitter feuds prevented united action against the Turks. A rich man, he had sold the remainder of his property in England and was now devoting his entire fortune to the Greek cause. While waiting for the loan from the London Committee, he used his own money to relaunch the Greek fleet lying at Hydra, and to plan an assault on the fortress port of Lepanto (Nafpaktos) using 500 Souliote warriors he now took on his payroll.

On 22 January 1824, the night before his thirty-sixth birthday, he had worked on a poem. Some of its verses proved to be prophetic.

> My days are in the yellow leaf:
> The flowers and fruits of love are gone;
> The worm, the canker and the grief
> Are mine alone!
> [...]
> The Sword, the Banner, and the Field,
> Glory and Greece, around me see!

> The Spartan, borne upon his shield,
> Was not more free.
> [...]
> If thou regret'st thy youth, why live?
> The land of honourable death
> Is here: – up to the Field, and give
> Away thy breath!
>
> Seek out – less often sought than found –
> A soldier's grave, for thee the best;
> Then look around, and chose thy ground,
> And take thy Rest.

Byron's health was deteriorating. He had a serious fit in February, following an earlier attack some months before. Depression and fears for his mental health led to dieting, purgatives and heavy drinking. 'I especially dread, in this world, two things [...] growing fat and growing mad.' He might have added, 'and growing old'. He was appalled at the signs of ageing, which were becoming all too apparent.

Byron was also in love – with his page-boy Lukas Chalandritsanos, feelings which were not returned. In the poem for his birthday he tried to overcome these emotions:

> Tread those reviving passions down,
> Unworthy manhood! – unto thee
> Indifferent should the smile or frown
> Of Beauty be.

Byron's main sexual energies were directed towards women, but his attraction to adolescent boys was never far below the surface. He and his friends made every effort to keep these feelings hidden: in Byron's day for the crime of sodomy you could be hanged. And yet he still wrote:

Thus much and more – and yet thou lov'st me not,
And never wilt – Love dwells not in our will –
Nor can I blame thee – though it be my lot
To strongly – wrongly – vainly love thee still.

These and other references to the love that dare not speak its name
were carefully removed by his friends after his death; and in a famous
fireside scene in the office of John Murray, his London publishers,
Byron's friends and executors consigned his memoirs to the flames.

Towards the end of March Byron agreed to attend a conference
at Salona (modern Amfissa) where it was hoped his presence would
unite the warring factions, but continuous heavy rainfall made travel
impossible. On 9 April, riding out with Pietro Gamba, Byron was
soaked through in a storm, fell ill, recovered, and fell ill again, enduring with his usual stoicism fits of shuddering, extreme headaches and
agonising pains throughout his body. His doctors prescribed bleeding,
the cure-all of the age, and set to with leeches and lancet. In the next
ten days they extracted some 2.5 litres, about 43 per cent of all his
blood, according to David Brewer in *The Flame of Freedom: The Greek
War of Independence* (2001) At the same time he was given a bizarre
assortment of medicines, including 'antimony, castor oil, Epsom salts,
henbane, cream of tartar, boracic, quinine, extract of tamarind, lau-
danum, ether and claret'. It is surprising that he lasted so long.

Chaos and grief surrounded Byron as his condition worsened.
English, Italian and Greek were the main languages spoken at
his bedside, where he was surrounded by his dogs and attended
by his two devoted servants, the ever-complaining Fletcher,
and the gigantic Tita Falcieri. Towards the end, in a moment of
consciousness and gripping tightly to Tita's hand, Byron could not
help seeing himself as usual the centre of a drama; half-smiling he
murmured to Tita, who was struggling with his emotions, 'Oh,
questa e una bella scena!'

In the evening of 18 April, while Missolonghi was battered by
thunder and violent storms of rain, he fell into a coma from which

he never recovered. His last words were, 'Now I must sleep.' Pietro wrote to Byron's half-sister Augusta, 'He died among strangers.'

The news took three weeks to reach London, where *The Times* announced the death of 'the most remarkable Englishman of his generation'. His coffin, soaked in 180 litres of spirits, arrived nearly a month later. But Byron was not buried in Westminster Abbey, as many believed he should have been. The government was embarrassed by his prominent participation in a conflict in which England claimed strict neutrality, while the establishment found it hard to forget the allegations of incest and infidelity that circled him, or forgive his years of self-imposed exile spent in dissipation rather than remorse. When Hobhouse requested the poet's internment in the abbey, the dean of Westminster advised him 'to carry away the body, & say as little about it as possible'.

For two days Byron lay in state in London, where police were called to control the emotional crowds, many of them women, determined to see his body. A long procession of coaches then escorted him through packed streets out of London to Nottinghamshire, where he was interned in the family vault at Hucknall Torkard.

Lord Byron has been called the first celebrity. His poetry and personality provoked what his wife called Byromania, and the ending of his life aroused an intensity of public grief that was not equalled until the deaths of President John F. Kennedy, and Diana, Princess of Wales. More passionately admired in France and the rest of Europe than in England, Byron and the 'Byronic' influenced Romantic literature, painting, music, opera, and even the way men dressed and behaved. In Greece streets and squares are named after him, and boys are still baptised *Veeron*. In the country where he died he remains a hero to this day.

More than a century later, partly because of rumours that the body had mysteriously disappeared, permission was granted to open the family tomb. The writer Cecil Roberts, present as the coffin lid was removed, remembered the moment he stood before 'all that remained of one who had been young, handsome, and the most famous man of genius of his age, a name throughout Europe'.

Statues of Byron and Botsaris can be seen in the town's Garden of Heroes close to the last remaining gate in the wall that Byron had helped to strengthen. In *Roumeli* Patrick Leigh Fermor writes of the poet and man of action:

> Thousands of children are baptized by his name, and his face is as familiar as any hero's in ancient or modern Greece. Every English traveller, however humble or unimpressive, and whether he knows or deserves or wants it or not, is the beneficiary of some reflected fragment of this glory. I wonder if any other figure in history has achieved such a place in a country not his own?

Two years after Byron's death Missolonghi was surrounded by a much larger Turkish army, and its supply route across the lagoon was cut off. On the night of 22 April 1826, 9,000 of the besieged – men, women and children – made a break for freedom. Some got through but most did not; those who remained blew themselves up. Ibrahim Pasha claimed his soldiers collected 3,000 heads and that ten barrels of salted ears were sent back to Constantinople for the sultan's approval.

The dramatic fall of Missolonghi resonated throughout Europe, not least because of its earlier associations with Byron. The most famous liberal writers, artists and musicians throughout Europe, admirers of Byron, voiced their dismay and public opinion began to put pressure on the governments of France and Britain to assist the Greeks. A year later British, French and Russian warships under the command of Admiral Codrington entered the bay of Navarino in the south-west of the Peloponnese where the Ottoman navy was at anchor. The battle that followed, unplanned but perhaps inevitable in the narrow confines of the bay, ended in the complete destruction of the Turkish fleet – perhaps an 'untoward event', as Britain's King George IV described it, but one that saved Greece from Turkish reconquest and moved it inevitably towards independence.

5

THE PELOPONNESE

Athletics must be one of the few sports the English cannot claim to have invented. Competition in racing, wrestling and jumping is as old as when humans first eyed each other across the mouth of a cave and soon became part of the life of every human settlement. Running and jumping featured in ancient Egyptian art, but as far as we know it was the Greeks who first organised athletic contests on a national and later international scale, and made the winners of the principal contests champions who were celebrated in their time and for generations after.

The most important of sporting competitions in ancient times was held at Olympia in the Peloponnese. Every fourth year for 1,000 years, from 776 BCE to 395 CE, the Olympic festival attracted citizens from all over the Greek world, in early years coming in their hundreds from neighbouring towns and city-states, and later in their thousands by land and sea from colonies in Italy and Sicily and as far away as Spain and Africa. The Games were held in honour of Zeus, the supreme god of Greek mythology, and a visit to Olympia was also a pilgrimage to his most sacred place. Judith Swaddling in *The Ancient Olympic Games* (1980) writes, 'There is no modern parallel for Olympia; it would have to be a site combining a sports complex and a centre for religious devotion, something like a combination of Wembley Stadium and Westminster Abbey.'

According to Pausanias, whose detailed travel guides to Greece were written around 175 CE, one of the first races held at Olympia was for women who wished to compete for the position of priestess of the goddess Hera, wife of Zeus. Candidates of either sex for

the priesthood of any religion today would be surprised to have
to line up for the 200 metres, and yet winning would certainly
demonstrate stamina and determination, qualities which might
be considered essential for the job. Over the next few centuries
almost every kind of athletic contest was included in the Games,
including horse and chariot racing, but the first race of all was the
running race over about 190 metres, called the *stadion* (hence the
word stadium).

Athletes competed naked (*gymnos* – our gymnastics) partly
because of the heat and also because the Games were a celebration
of the human body. For practical and aesthetic reasons, only the
young were allowed to compete. From the fifth century BCE the
Games were restricted to male participants. Married women were
forbidden to attend, though girls were allowed.

Pausanias tells us that the penalty for any woman detected
entering the Olympic assembly or even crossing the river Alpheios
during the forbidden days was to be hurled from the cliffs of
nearby Mount Typaion. Only one woman was ever caught. Her
husband was training their son for the Games, but he died before
the event. His wife Kallipateira disguised herself as a trainer and
took her son to Olympia; when he won, in her enthusiasm she
jumped over the fence enclosing the trainers, 'and as she leapt over
she showed herself'. Kallipateira was forgiven because her father,
her brothers and her son were all Olympic winners, 'but they
passed a law about trainers in the future, that they had to enter
the arena naked.'

Epictetus, writing in *Dissertations* in the first century CE,
captured what it must surely have been like in the extreme heat of
mid-August or the first rainstorms of September when the Games
were held:

There are enough irksome and troublesome things in life – aren't
things just as bad at the Olympic festival? Aren't you scorched there
by the fierce heat? Aren't you crushed in the crowd? Isn't it difficult

to freshen yourself up? Doesn't the rain soak you to the skin? Aren't you bothered by the noise, the din and other nuisances? But is seems to me you are well able to bear and indeed gladly endure all this, when you think of the gripping spectacles you will see.

And Lucian, in his *Anarcharsis* 100 years later, felt the same enthusiasm and excitement as those who attend the Olympic Games today:

No one can describe in mere words the extraordinary [...] pleasure derived from them and which you yourself would enjoy if you were seated among the spectators feasting your eyes on the prowess and stamina of the athletes, the beauty and power of their bodies, their incredible dexterity and skill, their invincible strength, their courage, ambition, endurance and tenacity. You will never stop [...] applauding them.

Pausanias in his *Guide to Greece* describes the colossal statue of Zeus, 13 metres (42 feet) tall and one of the Seven Wonders of the World, in the temple of Zeus. It was designed and constructed by Phidias, who had already made the famous chryselephantine statue of Athena for the Parthenon in Athens:

The god is sitting on a throne; he is made of gold and ivory. There is a wreath on his head like twigs and leaves of olive. In his right hand he is holding a figure of Victory, also of gold and ivory... in his left hand a staff in blossom with every kind of precious metal, and the bird perched on this staff is Zeus's eagle. The sandals of the god are of gold, so is his robe, which is decorated with animals and lilies. The throne is adorned with gold, precious stones, ebony and ivory.

Pausanias adds that although he had known the measurements and details of the statue before he saw it, the 'information falls far short of the impression the image makes on the spectator'.

Kazantzakis, who visited Olympia, felt that 'no other site in Greece incites a feeling of peace and concord in you, so gently, so compellingly.' Recalling in *Report to Greco* (translated by Peter Bien, 1965) how the 'garlanded heralds, the *spondophoroi*, set out from this sacred valley in summertime and ran to the farthest boundaries to the Greek world [...] proclaiming the *heiromenia*, the "sacred month" of the games' prompted his conviction that 'civilization begins the moment sport begins [...] the moment that life satisfies its primary needs and begins to enjoy a little leisure.'

With some relevance to sport and health today, Kazantzakis writes that the purpose of Greek athleticism was not simply to make bodies beautiful. 'The Greeks never served art for its own sake. Beauty always had a purpose: to be of service to life. The ancients wanted their bodies strong and beautiful so that these bodies might be receptacles of strong and beautiful minds,' an ultimate purpose being to defend the *polis*, their city:

Harmony of mind and body – that was the Greeks' supreme ideal [...] When Greece began to decline the athlete's body began at the same time to hypertrophy and kill his mind. Euripides was among the first to protest [...] the risks the spirit was running at the hands of athleticism. Later, Galen added his denunciation: 'They eat, drink, sleep, and evacuate their bellies, and roll in dust and mud – behold what life the athletes lead.' Heracles, the great martyr, who in the glorious years passed from exploit to exploit balancing mind and body to perfection, gradually degenerated into the huge-bodied, low-browed, 'wine-bibber and ox-eater.' And the artists, who in the great eras had created the ideal type of the youthful form, now took to representing the athletic bodies they saw around them with raw realism, heavy and barbaric.

Observing the sculptures from the western pediment of the temple of Zeus depicting the seizure of the Lapithae women by the centaurs, Kazantzakis was struck by the furious rage of the combatants, biting and stabbing one another. 'The beast has been let loose in a savage outburst of violent passion; age-old scenes somewhere between man and ape-man are revived before our eyes.' And yet the spirit of Olympia, of civilisation, dominates in the end. 'A mystic tranquility, however, extends over all this astonishing primitive passion, because standing with perfect composure in the midst of the frenzied people, invisible to all the combatants, is Apollo, his right arm, and only his right arm, stretched out horizontally.'

The Games not only became the most famous sporting event of the ancient Mediterranean world; they were also – besides a religious festival – a cultural event, attracting sculptors showing off their works and poets reading out their verses in the hope of finding wealthy patrons. Cities and states boasted of their athletes and often tried to lure the best to compete under their name (a practice not uncommon in our modern Games). Pausanias recounts the particularly blatant example of the Cretan Sotades at the ninety-ninth festival (384 BCE). He was victorious in the long-distance race, then four years later raced and won as a citizen of Ephesus. The Cretans took this very badly and exiled him. Pausanias tells us of several instances of diving, for example, in boxing. The use of performance-enhancing drugs is not recorded, though one wonders whether the highly recommended downing of a shot of fermented boar's excrement before a race would be classified as doping today.

The conquest of Greece by the Romans gradually changed the character of the Games, which became more of a glitzy extravaganza than a religious sporting festival. The Emperor Nero further lowered the bar when he changed the year of the Games to suit the date of his triumphal tour of Greece, and also insisted that a prize for poetry be included which, as expected, he won. He was also awarded victory in the chariot race – despite falling out of the chariot (and being seriously hurt) well before the finish.

The end came in the late fourth century CE when Theodosius, the first Christian Roman emperor, banned all pagan cults. The statue of Zeus was taken to Constantinople. As Judith Swaddling remarks, ironically this may have saved it from being burned with other pagan temples on the order of Theodosius II in 426 – only for it to be destroyed in a fire that swept the city less than 40 years later.

Over the following centuries a series of earthquakes and floods completely buried the ancient site under several metres of earth, and it was only rediscovered in 1766 thanks to Richard Chandler, an English antiquarian carrying out an exploratory mission on behalf of the Society of Dilettanti. French archaeologists dug at Olympia in 1829, but it is to the Germans whose excavations date from 1875 that we owe the splendid ruins now exposed to view.

The concept of the Olympic Games has kept a powerful hold on the European imagination, and the ideals which they represent have never been entirely forgotten. Athletic 'Olympic' contests were held in seventeenth-century England and nineteenth-century France, and there were numerous calls, especially from newly independent Greece, to revive the Games internationally. But it was because of the efforts of Baron de Coubertin, who had been so impressed by the Germans' work in Olympia, that the ancient four-year cycle was renewed. The first of the modern Olympics was held in Athens in 1896.

Corinth was always of fascination to me. In its time it had been the richest and most dissolute city of the ancient world; its rulers had included the tyrant Periander, one of the Seven Sages; it had given its name to the humble currant, which once it exported in huge quantities. As a young man visiting Greece for the first time, I was interested in a particular aspect of Corinth: the temple of Aphrodite high on Acrocorinth, the almost-impregnable fortress on the mountaintop overlooking the city. Here the goddess was worshipped in the form of the Syrian Astarte, and in its heyday hundreds of sacred prostitutes offered themselves to those of her pious devotees who felt strong enough after trudging the steep path to her temple at the summit, almost 600 metres above the distant sea. Nowadays you can drive up to the great gates of the acropolis, but I had to make the ascent on foot, which made me think that the position of these temples of Aphrodite – another famous site was the top of Mount Eryx in Sicily – was no accident: when the votaries finally reached the temple precincts they were so drained of energy that any religious coupling that followed must surely have been moderated by more spiritual thoughts.

Strabo, who travelled much of the known world during the reign of the Emperor Augustus, wrote in his *Geography* that the city was usually described as 'wealthy' because of its commerce, 'since it is situated on the Isthmus and is master of two harbours, of which the one leads straight to Asia, and the other to Italy; and it makes easy the exchange of merchandise from both countries that are so far distant from each other.'

He noted that 'the temple of Aphrodite was so rich that it owned more than a thousand temple slaves, courtesans, whom both men and women had dedicated to the goddess. And therefore it was also on account of these women that the city was crowded with people and grew rich; for instance, the ship captains freely squandered their money, and hence the proverb, 'Not for every man is the voyage to Corinth' (i.e. don't go there unless you have plenty to spend). A courtesan accused of not working (not touching or spinning wool), replied, 'Yet, such as I am, in this short time I have taken down three webs' (a web here meaning a mast and its rigging – three well-off sea captains had been her clients).

Corinth was captured by the Romans in 146 BCE and comprehensively looted and destroyed; it lay almost deserted for 100 years until Julius Caesar resettled the city. Its prosperity had been partially restored when Strabo visited, but when he climbed to the top of Acrocorinth he found the temple of Aphrodite in ruins. At least he was able to admire the spectacular view: 'From the summit, looking towards the north, one can see Parnassus and Helicon – lofty, snow-clad mountains – and the Crisaean Gulf, which lies at the foot of the two mountains and is surrounded by Phocis, Boeotia, and Megaris.'

F. L. Lucas and his wife Prudence stood here in 1933 and recorded in their *From Olympus to the Styx*, published the following year: 'from this height of Acrocorinth the landscape, its peaks and islands, even their names, are hardly altered since the days of Pericles and Alexander. Before such changelessness the solitary watcher has at moments the sense of confronting eternity – whether its reality, or its embodiment limned on some vast canvas stretching round the skies.'

The view, one of the finest in Greece, has changed little, as is confirmed by Robin Barber in the 2001 *Blue Guide*: on a smogless day in winter you can see as far as Aigina and the Parthenon ... much of the Saronic Gulf and all of the Gulf of Corinth. The ruins of the temple, however, can no longer be distinguished by the ordinary traveller, being overlaid by 'a small basilican church, a watch tower, a cloistered mosque, and a paved Venetian belvedere' – not a bad historical summary, in architectural terms, of 2,500 years.

Eighty years after Strabo was in Corinth, St Paul arrived from Athens. Paul had to earn his living while he preached and as he was a tent-maker he chose to stay with Aquila and his wife Priscilla of the same profession; they had recently arrived from Italy because the Emperor Claudius had expelled all Jews from Rome. When Silas and Timotheus joined him from Macedonia, as recounted in the King James Version of Acts of the Apostles, 'Paul was pressed in the spirit, and testified to the Jews that Jesus was Christ. And when they opposed themselves, and blasphemed, he shook his raiment, and said unto them, Your blood be upon your own heads; I am clean: from henceforth I will go unto the Gentiles.'

Paul had such success with his preaching that many of the Corinthians were baptised. 'And he continued there a year and six months, teaching the word of God among them.' Not, however, without the growing hostility of the Jews. The proconsul, a typically practical Roman, wisely steered clear of the religious argument:

And when Gallio was the deputy of Achaia, the Jews made insurrection with one accord against Paul, and brought him to the judgment seat, saying, This fellow persuadeth men to worship God contrary to the law. And when Paul was now about to open his mouth, Gallio said unto the Jews, If it were a matter of wrong or wicked lewdness, O ye Jews, reason would that I should bear with you: but if it be a question of words and names, and of your law, look ye to it; for I will be no judge of such matters. And he drave them from the judgment seat. Then all the Greeks took Sosthenes, the chief ruler of the synagogue, and beat *him* before the judgment seat. And Gallio cared for none of those things.

Paul had founded an important Christian community in Corinth and kept its sometimes unruly members close to his heart, writing to them two long letters of admonishment and encouragement. The Corinthians were known for their easy living. 'It is commonly reported that there is fornication among you' – and not only fornication. Paul did not hold modern Western views of tolerance, and the effeminate and homosexuals were firmly excluded from the kingdom of heaven. And yet in that first letter to the Corinthians, sent from Ephesus, he wrote that description of love that forms perhaps the most frequently quoted verses of the Bible – in the New King James Version:

Though I speak with the tongues of men and of angels, but have not love, I have become sounding brass or a clanging cymbal [...]

Love suffers long and is kind; love does not envy; love does not parade itself [...] hopes all things, endures all things [...]

When I was a child, I spoke as a child, I understood as a child, I thought as a child; but when I became a man, I put away childish things. For now we see in a mirror, dimly, but then face to face. Now I know in part, but then I shall know just as I also am known.

And now abide faith, hope, love, these three; but the greatest of these is love.

It is not known how the new Christian community in Corinth reacted to these words but it seems that Paul's reprimands were not always accepted without complaint. In his second letter to his brethren in Corinth he felt obliged to remind them, rather impatiently, that adhering to the faith was no easy choice – look what I have had to go through: 'Of the Jews five times received I forty stripes save one. Thrice was I beaten with rods, once was I stoned, thrice I suffered shipwreck.' Of all people, Paul had every reason occasionally to feel sorry for himself, listing among his tribulations the perils of the sea, false brethren, weariness and painfulness ... 'in hunger and thirst, in fastings often, in cold and nakedness'. And all this before his arrest and imprisonment, shipwreck on his voyage to Rome and subsequent violent end in that city.

The philosopher Diogenes, a founder of the school of Cynics in the fourth century BCE, lived his last years (we are told by his biographer Laertius) in Corinth. Cynics lived by example and Diogenes followed a lifelong profession of discipline and austerity (*askesis*, our asceticism) – though in his case carried to an ostentatious extreme.

'Diogenes became the real and only original Cynic, or "Dog"', writes Charles Seltman in *Riot in Ephesus* (1958),

> because he consistently practiced what he preached. Every call of nature was to be satisfied exactly as a dog satisfied it. If a vulgar public looked on, who cared? His possessions were limited to a stout staff – for his hard life had crippled his bones and he needed support – a bowl for food or drink, one cloak (which he used only in winter), and a great pottery vat, often misdescribed as a tub, which was his sole residence.

Several of his sayings have happily survived the centuries. Asked which wine he preferred, he answered, 'wine that someone else has paid for'. He was seen begging alms from a statue and when asked why he did so, replied, 'to get practice in being refused'. Criticised for masturbating in public, he said, 'I wish it was as easy to banish hunger by rubbing the belly.' Some of his sayings would strike a note today. When he saw temple officials leading away a man who had stolen a cup from one of the treasurers, Diogenes said, 'There go the big thieves leading away the little thief.' Asked why he was walking about in broad daylight with a lamp, he replied, 'I am looking for an honest man.'

Diogenes was born in Sinope, a city on the Black Sea. Later, asked where he came from, he said: 'I am a citizen of the world.' He was the first ever to use the term 'cosmopolitan' at a time when a person's city was an essential element of his identity.

He was a contemporary of Plato, but the two did not get on. He attended one of Plato's lectures in Athens when Plato proposed a description of Man: 'animal, biped, featherless', for which Plato was applauded. Diogenes went out, bought a chicken, plucked it and returned, holding it aloft: 'Here is Plato's man.' Plato had not much to say about Diogenes, except to describe him as 'Socrates gone mad'.

In 326 BCE there took place Diogenes' famous exchange with the young Alexander of Macedon who had just summoned a congress of reluctant Greek states to a meeting in Corinth to plan the invasion of Persia; he had been duly acclaimed general to command the Greek army. Tutored by Aristotle, Alexander was well educated and had heard of the famous, or rather, notorious philosopher and wanted to meet him. Diogenes at that time was living in his large clay vat just outside the city walls near the Kraneion market, where centuries later Pausanias saw his tomb. Alexander was brought to him accompanied by the great and good of the city-states of the League.

A marble relief preserved in the Villa Albani in Rome depicts the scene. Alexander, magnificently armed and caparisoned, stands looking down at the old, half-naked philosopher, who is sitting in his vat. To the embarrassment of Alexander's entourage, Diogenes seemed to have nothing to say to the young general. Surprised at this lack of reaction or even acknowledgement of his presence, Alexander is said to have begun what turned out to be only a brief conversation. Charles Seltman imagined the conversation in his *Riot in Ephesus*:

'Do you know who I am?'
'No'
'I am Alexander, the king.'
A grunt perhaps; then, 'I am Diogenes the Dog.'
Silence.
Then Alexander: 'Are you not afraid of me?'
'Why, what are you, a good thing or a bad?'
'Good,' said Alexander.
'Well,' said the sage, 'who's afraid of the good?'
Another long and awkward pause. Eventually Alexander said, 'Diogenes, I can give you anything. If there's something you want, just ask!'
'There is one thing,' the philosopher replied, looking up. 'Move aside. You're standing in my sunlight'.

Alexander's reaction to this response is not known, but later he is reported to have said, 'If I were not Alexander, I would be Diogenes.' According to Plutarch, Alexander and Diogenes died on the same day in the same year, 323 BCE, one aged 90, the other 33.

Let Charles Seltman, whom I remember had a sneaking respect for Diogenes, have the last word:

There is really very little to be said in favour of the crazed old man, obsessed with his theory of *paracharaxis*, which made him entirely destructive. Yet we may perhaps allow him one merit; for he succeeded in demonstrating the extreme tolerance of fourth-century Greeks. In scarcely any other age or country would such a man escape molestation from an outraged and indignant public,

even though Diogenes the Dog broke almost every rule and law
that the police are expected to enforce.

Those who have been caught in a violent storm in the mountains
of Greece will recognise Kazantzakis's description of his attempt
to climb Mount Taygetus, near the ruins of the Byzantine city of
Mistra. In *Report to Greco* he writes:

> the pine tree's balm, the fiery rocks, the hawks hovering above
> me, the impregnable solitude – all these fortified my heart. I
> climbed happily for many hours. Around noontime, however,
> black clouds gathered overhead. There were muffled thunderclaps.
> I started back down at a run, feeling the storm approaching
> behind me. I jumped from stone to stone, raced, competed
> with it so that it would not overtake me. But suddenly the pines
> quivered, the world grew dark, and I was belted by lightning
> flashes. The whirlwind had caught me. Plunging face downward
> on the ground so that I would not fall, I closed my eyes and
> waited. The whole mountain shook; next to me two pines split in
> half and thundered down the slope. I smelled the sulphur in the
> air. All at once the torrent let loose. The wind subsided and huge
> necklaces of water poured out of the sky. The thyme, savory, sage,
> and mint, battered by the downpour, threw forth their scents.
> The whole mountain began to steam [...]
>
> Getting up, I resumed the descent [...] Soon the sky cleared
> [...] Far in the distance below I spied the freshly bathed ruins of
> the Frankish citadel of the Villehardouins at the top of its hill,
> above Mistra. The entire sky had turned gold and green.

Robert Byron was at Mistra in May 1926. He wrote to his mother:
'Mistra, the only Byzantine town in existence, is about 1½ miles from
Sparta – the weirdest place – perched on a precipitous hill – all the
houses and a huge palace still ¾ standing and nearly uninhabited.

Wonderful frescoes open to wind and rain – cisterns, fireplaces, ovens – all the domestic life is apparent. We spent the most entrancing and tiring 2 days there, our shoes being cut to ribbons on the rock. In one little vaulted hole, seeing a piece of window moulding I took off my coat and crawling in on my stomach unearthed four whole skulls and three skeletons – how prosaic skulls are.'

In 1832 Alphonse de Lamartine, the French writer, poet, politician and historian, was travelling to the Levant with his English wife, their eight-year-old daughter Julia, and a few friends. Julia was ill from a serious lung condition, probably tuberculosis; it was hoped that she would benefit from the sea voyage and the milder climate of the Mediterranean. In *Travels in the East* (1839) he describes his arrival at Nauplia, the new capital of Greece.

> We enter a vast bay, that of Argos; we glide along with the wind aft, and with the velocity of a flight of swallows. The rocks, mountains, islands of the two shores, fly like dark clouds from before us. Night falls; we already perceive the head of the bay, though it is six leagues distant; the masts of three squadrons anchored before Nauplia are sketched out like a winter forest against a background of the sky and the plain of Argos. The darkness becomes soon complete; fires are lit on the mountain slopes, and in the woods where the Greek shepherds are tending their flocks; the ships are firing the evening gun. We see all the gunports of these sixty vessels at anchor gleaming successively, like the streets of a great town lighted by its lamps; we enter this labyrinth of ships, and are about to anchor in the middle of the night close to a little fort which protects the roadstead of Nauplia, in front of the town, and under the guns of the castle of Palamides.

When de Lamartine woke with the sun the next morning and went on deck, he was disappointed. The town was hardly more than a village, the houses in ruins and the streets littered with fragments of walls overturned by cannon in the recent war against the Turks.

We have passed two days at Nauplia. The state of Julia's health again distresses me. I shall remain a few days more, to wait till she is completely recovered. We are on shore, in the chamber of a wretched inn, opposite a barrack of Greek troops. The soldiers are all day stretched out under the shade of the fragments of ruined walls; their costumes are rich and picturesque; their features bear the impress of misery and despair, and of all those fierce passions which civil war kindles and foments in those savage souls. The most complete anarchy reigns at this moment over all the Morea [Peloponnese]. Each day one faction triumphs over the other, and we hear the musketry of the *klephtes*, of the Colocotroni faction, who are fighting on the other side of the gulf against the troops of the government. We are informed, by every courier that descends from the mountains, of the burning of a town, the pillage of a valley, or the massacre of a population, by one of the parties that are ravaging their native country. One cannot go beyond the gates of Nauplia without being exposed to musket shots. Prince Karadja had the goodness to propose to me an escort of his *palikars* to go and visit the tomb of Agamemnon; and general Corbet, who commands the French forces, politely offered to add to them a detachment of his soldiers. I refused, because I did not wish, for the gratification of a vain curiosity, to expose the lives of several men, for which I should eternally reproach myself.

De Lamartine's voyage continued to Athens and then to Lebanon and the Holy Land. His daughter Julia finally died of her illness in Beirut in December that year.

Some 20 years later Julia Ward Howe, the American women's rights activist and famous as the author of *The Battle Hymn of the Republic*, visited Greece. In *From the Oak to the Olive* (1868), she remarked on how habits change with the climate: 'we were now come to the regions in which men use the two ends of the day and throw away the middle.' When she stepped ashore at Nafplio (Nauplia), the town had been partly rebuilt. She described the narrow, irregular streets, many of the houses with balconies. Athens was now the capital of Greece, but although the civil war was over, brigandage was still a serious threat in the countryside. A crowd had gathered in one of the streets to see a bandit's head which had been brought in for collection of the reward:

> The evening of our sojourn in Argos saw an excitement much like that which blocked the street at Nauplia. The occasion was the same – the bringing home of a brigand's head, but this is the very head and fount of all the brigands, Kitzos himself, upon whose head had been set a price of several thousand drachmas. Our veteran with difficulty obtained a view of the same and reported accordingly. The robber chief of Edmond About's 'Hadji Stauros' had been shot while sighting at his gun. He had fallen with one eye shut and one open, and in this form of feature his dissevered head remained. The soldier who was its fortunate captor carried it concealed in a bag, with its long elf-locks lying loose about it. He showed it with some unwillingness, fearing to have the prize wrested from him. It was, however, taken on board our steamer, and carried to Athens, there to be identified and buried.

Just as civil war had prevented de Lamartine from seeing the tomb of Agamemnon, Kitzos's bandits had made it unsafe for Julia Ward Howe. 'But at this moment the band were closely besieged in the mountains. They wanted their head, and so did Kitzos. We, in consequence, were fully able to visit the treasure of Atreus and the ruins of Mycenae without fear or risk from those acephalous enemies.'

In 1876 Schliemann got his permit to excavate in the Peloponnese and despite the heat arrived at Tiryns with his Greek wife

Sophia at the beginning of August. Included in the supplies ordered for the dig were '120 bottles of the finest Bass Pale Ale, 50 tins of American peaches, 50 tins of corned beef and 10 of tongue.' Finding the inn too dirty, they soon moved to the Hotel des Etrangers in Nafplio.

In *Tiryns* (1885), his account of the excavations, Schliemann describes his daily routine:

> My habit was to rise at 3.45 a.m., swallow 4 grains of quinine as a preservative against fever, and then take a sea bath; a boatman, for 1 fr. daily, awaited me punctually at 4 o'clock, and took me from the quay to the open sea, where I swam for 5 or 10 minutes. I was obliged to climb into the boat again by the oar, but long practice had made this somewhat difficult operation easy and safe. I drank in the coffee house *Agamemnon*, which was always open at that hour, a cup of black coffee without sugar, still to be had for the old price of 10 Lepta (a penny) though everything had risen enormously in price. A good cob (at 6 frs. daily) stood ready and took me easily to Tiryns, where I always arrived before sunrise, and at once sent back the horse for Dr. Dörpfeld. Our breakfast was taken regularly at 8 a.m. during the first rest of the workmen, on the floor of the old palace at Tiryns. It consisted of Chicago corned beef... bread, fresh sheep-cheese, oranges, and white resined wine.

Excavations at nearby Mycenae started a week later. The size of the workforce had been agreed, but soon Schliemann, without consulting anyone, increased the number of workmen and intensified the pace of the dig. He also quarrelled with Panagiotis Stamatakis, a young archaeologist who had the unfortunate task of supervising the work on behalf of the Greek Archaeological Society and the government. An extract from one of Stamatakis's despairing reports back to the Greek Archaeological Society in Athens is typical of many:

The work proceeds in utter confusion [...] I have often spoken to Mr Schliemann about this lack of order but he does not listen to me at all. Mr Schliemann conducts the excavation as he wishes, paying no regard either to the law or to the instructions of the Ministry or to any official. Everywhere and at all times he prefers to look to his own advantage.

Stamatakis was probably referring to Schliemann's habit of secretly rewarding workmen who came directly to him with any interesting objects they found.

On 24 November 1876 Schliemann wrote to his friend Max Müller in Oxford:

There are in all 5 tombs, in the smallest of which I found yesterday the bones of a man and a woman covered by *at least* five kilograms of jewels of pure gold, with the most wonderful archaic, impressed ornaments [...] Today I emptied the tomb and gathered there 6 kg of beautifully ornamented gold leafs; also many earrings [...] one represents Hercules slaying the lion [...] There were also found two scepters with wonderfully chiseled crystal handles [...] I telegraphed today to the Times. I had hardly touched the second tomb when I found a beautiful ornamented gold cup & 4 large bronze vessels. This tomb is the largest and will probably give most gold.

In the next few days Schliemann's workmen, now increased to 114, dug down into two more shaft graves. Besides the remains of the dead, a huge quantity of gold ornaments were found, including the famous gold masks, the largest of which Schliemann believed covered the face of the entombed King of Mycenae who had led the Greeks to the walls of Troy. 'I have gazed on the face of Agamemnon,' he is reputed to have said. On 28 November he sent a telegram to King George of Greece: 'With great joy I announce to Your Majesty I have discovered the tombs which the tradition proclaimed by Pausanias indicates as the graves of Agamemnon,

Cassandra, Eurymedon, and their companions, all slain at a banquet by Clytemnestra and her lover.'

As David Traill writes in *Schliemann of Troy*, finally Schliemann had uncovered signs of a civilisation that seemed to match in grace and sophistication the world of the Homeric heroes.

Captain William Martin Leake was an artillery officer sent by the British government to advise the Ottoman Turks in their conflict with the French. In 1801 and 1802 he worked on a survey of Egypt with W. R. Hamilton, secretary to Lord Elgin, and together they sailed homewards from Athens with the Elgin Marbles on board. In *The Hill of Kronos*, Peter Levi continues: 'Their ship was wrecked off Kythera, and it was Leake, pistol in hand, who saved the lives of the crew by suppressing a panic. It was also Leake who sent down divers at once to rescue the marbles. His own Egyptian notes were lost, but Hamilton's were saved. He was twenty-five years old.'

Leake was later imprisoned by the Turks, escaped from Thessaloniki and was appointed British resident at the court of Ali Pasha in Ioannina. In his years in Greece Leake rode – with an armed escort, and Pausanias's *Guide to Greece* in his hand – all over the country. He was interested in everything about Greece, past and present. His assiduously noted observations were later published as *Travels in the Morea* (1830) and *Travels in Northern Greece* (1835). Here he is in the Mani in the south of the Peloponnese (or Morea as it was then known).

An affair, which happened two months since at Vathy, shows the state of society in Mani. The son of a priest had by accident killed a boy, a relation of another priest. The latter papas declared war against the former, which is done in Mani in a formal manner, by crying out in the streets. The first papas went to his church to say mass with pistols in his girdle, such being a common custom in Mani; but, as is usual in such cases, he laid them behind the altar, on assuming the robe in which the priest performs divine service. The other papas entered the church with some of his party, and the instant the office was concluded, walked up to his enemy, who was still in his robes, fired a pistol at him, which flashed in the pan: the latter, then running behind the altar, seized his arms, shot his enemy and one of his adherents, and drove all the rest out of the church. The affair was then settled by the interposition of the bey himself, in whose village it had happened. A composition in money, for the balance of blood, is the only efficient mode of making peace in these cases. When one of a family is slain, the person who takes upon him to revenge the injury often vows not to change his clothes or shave or eat meat till his revenge is satisfied.

Like many travellers to the Mani, before and after, Leake was fascinated by the towers that stood out like exclamation marks on the rocky and barren peninsula.

Each person of power and every head of a family of any influence has a pyrgo, which is used almost solely as a tower of defence: the ordinary habitation stands at the foot of it. The Bey's relations and a few of the kapitani maintain some soldiers in their towers, but in general these buildings are uninhabited, except in time of alarm. To overturn the pyrgo of the enemy and to slaughter as many of his relations as possible, are the objects of every war. The tower has loopholes in the different stories and battlements at top, and not easily subdued. Most of the ordinary dwellings are built with loopholes in the walls; nor are the villages, in which there is no inhabitant of sufficient opulence to build a pyrgo, the more peaceable on that account, but quarrel among themselves or with their neighbours, and endeavour to overturn one another's houses just like their betters. Every *pyrgo* has a cistern, which has an arched covering of stone, with a little wooden door kept constantly locked.

To those who know Greece, the Mani brings to mind the book by Patrick Leigh Fermor published in 1958, and followed eight years later by *Roumeli,* considered among the best travel books of the twentieth century. Leigh Fermor, who died in 2011 aged 96, was the last of those talented and inspired young men who came to Greece before the World War II, who lived there for a significant part of their lives and who left their mark in writing or art that has given pleasure to many and done much to shape our view of the country. The list includes Lawrence Durrell and his younger brother Gerald, Henry Miller, Robert Byron, Bernard Spencer, Peter Levi, Philip Sherrard, John Craxton and Edmund Keeley.

Patrick Michael Leigh Fermor (known to his friends as Paddy, in Crete as Mihali) set off on a long walk from London to Constantinople in 1933. He was 18 at the time. A rebel and failure at school in England, for him the adventure promised hope and a new start. The account of this journey appeared many years later in *A Time of Gifts* (1977), *Between the Woods and the Water* (1986) and *The Broken Road*, published in 2013, two years after his death. Already on this first visit in 1935 he had begun to show his fascination with language, and a passionate interest in the folklore and customs of the most remote areas of Greece. At the outbreak of war in 1939 he enlisted in the army. Making full use of his fluency in Greek, he was there when the Germans invaded, and in Crete when it fell in 1941. The following year he was assigned to what was later known as the Special Operations Executive (SOE) and spent most of the war in the Cretan mountains helping to lead the island's resistance to the German occupation.

In the 1950s Leigh Fermor explored the Peloponnese and especially its most southerly parts. In his book *Mani*, a long love-letter to Greece, he wrote about these journeys. Visiting Kalamata he was accompanied by Joan Rayner, a photographer, whom he would eventually marry, and Xan Fielding, a fellow officer in the Cretan resistance whose book *The Stronghold* (1955) tells his story of those years.

A heatwave had combined with a religious feast day:

and the waterfront was crowded with celebrating citizens in liquefaction [...] The stone flags of the water's edge, where Joan, Xan Fielding and I sat down to dinner, flung back the heat like a casserole with the lid off. On a sudden, silent, decision we stepped down fully dressed into the sea carrying the iron table a few yards out and then our three chairs, on which, up to our waists in cool water, we sat round the neatly laid table-top, which now seemed by magic to be levitated three inches above the water. The waiter, arriving a moment later, gazed with surprise at the empty space on the quay; then, observing us with a quickly-masked flicker of pleasure, he stepped unhesitatingly into the sea, advanced waist-deep with a butler's gravity, and, saying nothing more than 'Dinner-time', placed our meal before us – three beautifully grilled *kephali*, piping hot, and with their golden brown scales sparkling.

The other diners on the quayside, delighted at this spectacle, sent over numerous cans of retsina and the table was soon surrounded by fishing boats. 'Leaning from their gently rocking boats, the fishermen helped us out with this sudden influx of wine, and by the time the moon and the Dog-Star rose over this odd symposium, a mandoline had appeared.'

As the caique carrying Paddy and Joan chugged down the western coast of the peninsula, approaching Cape Matapan and Tartarus, the entrance to Hades, they saw how on half a dozen heights:

a hundred sombre towers, each cluster thrust aloft on a coil of terraces, sailed up into the morning to break the parallel slanting rays of the sun, every campanile shedding a long blade of shadow along the sun's advance.

As the caique sailed further east, village after village turned its sunlit walls to us. They seemed to be suspended in the air to glow and flash there like the lustres of chandeliers. A headland rose and hid them and as we sailed by the little gulf of Marmari the sun was already high in the limitless Greek sky: a sky which is higher and lighter and which surrounds one closer and stretches further into space than anywhere else in the world. It is neither daunting nor belittling but hospitable and welcoming to man and as much his element as the earth; as though a mere error in gravity pins him to the rocks or to the ship's deck and prevents him from being assumed into infinity.

Reflecting on the violent history of the Mani peninsula, he found peace among the ruined temples of Demeter and Aphrodite at Kyparissos, near Cape Matapan.

The slow fall of the evening among this smashed and scattered masonry, the decrescendo and then the silence of the cicadas, the wide unruffled gleam of the sea below and the nerve-stilling quietness of the air [...] A spell of peace lives in the ruins of ancient Greek temples. As the traveller leans back among the fallen capitals and allows the hours to pass, it empties the mind of troubling thoughts and anxieties and slowly refills it, like a vessel that has been drained and scoured, with a quiet ecstasy. Nearly all that has happened fades to a limbo of shadows and insignificance and is painlessly replaced by an imitation of radiance, simplicity and calm which unties all knots and solves all riddles and seems to murmur a benevolent and unimperious suggestion that the whole of life, if it were allowed to unfold without hindrance or compulsion or search for alien solutions, might be limitlessly happy.

Leigh Fermor admired and was attracted by the harsh but independent lives of the Maniots. Their warlike attitudes and the towers they built to defend their families from endless vendettas they themselves had initiated were the consequence of a long and lawless history fighting off any invader inclined to dominate the barren peninsula they called home. In the Mani Leigh Fermor found echoes of Crete and memories of the war, of those six years from the age of 24 that inevitably influenced his life; it was there, just north of the Mani peninsula, that in 1964 he and Joan bought some land and built the house near Kardamyli that was to be his main home for the remainder of his life.

One of the many talented visitors at Kardamyli was Bruce Chatwin, already the author of the acclaimed travel book *In Patagonia*. Chatwin had known the Leigh Fermors for years and stayed in the house in 1970 when he was drafting *The Nomadic Alternative*. He loved Kardamyli. 'The whole Taygetus range plunges straight down into the sea,' he wrote in a letter to his wife Elizabeth, 'and eagles float in thermals above the house.'

Fifteen years later, determined to complete the book that was eventually to be published as *Songlines*, he came to Kardamyli again, staying for the next seven months in the Hotel Theano, five minutes' walk away. After long mornings writing, he and Paddy would tramp the hills, engaged in endless conversations on 'abstruse art-forms and movements of thought, history, geology, anthropology and all their kindred sciences'. Slowly, the book took shape.

While Chatwin intensely admired Leigh Fermor, in literary style, as Artemis Cooper says in her *Patrick Leigh Fermor: An Adventure* (2012), 'they were aiming for opposite poles. While Paddy's prose was a rich and elaborate tapestry built up in layers, Chatwin was aiming for an austere simplicity that used as few words as possible for maximum effect.'

Nicholas Shakespeare, in his biography *Bruce Chatwin* (1999), calls Leigh Fermor Chatwin's 'last guru'. A wanderer like Chatwin, Leigh Fermor had lived a life of dramatic action and had the same wide interests. His *Time of Gifts* had come out the same year as *In Patagonia*. Despite the difference in age, they had much in common, and the admiration was mutual, Leigh Fermor describing Chatwin as a 'very extraordinary, highly gifted, rare person'. 'Paddy and Bruce are a very different type of creature,' wrote Sybille Bedford the novelist and biographer, 'but they are both grandees of style and erudition. In both a toughness goes with a certain sybaritic quality.'

Songlines was published in 1987 and became an immediate bestseller. Two years later Chatwin had died of AIDS. His widow Elizabeth brought his ashes to Kardamyli, where they were buried under an olive tree near a Byzantine chapel, a place that Chatwin had loved, on a promontory over the sea.

Joan died of a fall at Kardamyli in 2003. She was 91. In a letter to a friend, Leigh Fermor wrote: 'I constantly find myself saying "I must write – or tell – that to Joan"; then suddenly remember that one can't, and nothing seems to have any point. And then I remember all those happy years [...] and the tears shift a bit.'

Leigh Fermor lived on at the house, occasionally travelling and always writing, until succumbing to cancer in 2011. He died the day after arriving in England in the house Joan had inherited from her brother in Dumbleton, Gloucestershire, and was buried in the churchyard there with Joan. A sculpture of his head in bronze joins that of Wilfred Thessiger in the hall of London's Travellers Club where he had been a member for many years.

6

CRETE

In middle of the sable sea there lies
An isle call'd Crete, a ravisher of eyes,
Fruitful, and mann'd with many an infinite store;
Where ninety cities crown the famous shore,
Mix'd with all-languag'd men.

(Homer, *Odyssey*, trans George Chapman, 1615)

Chapman's translation of the *Odyssey* was published soon after William Lithgow, the author of his *Rare Adventures and Painefull Peregrinations*, reached Crete. He would not have agreed with Chapman's description as his hardships on the island were as unpleasant and dangerous as any in his travels.

Having already been attacked, robbed and beaten by a gang of 'three Greek murdering *renegadoes* and an Italian *bandido*' on a mountain road not far out of Grabusa, and after an exhausting day's travel, he:

at night attained to the unhappy village of Apockichorio, where I could have neither meat, drink, lodging nor any refreshment to my wearied body. These desperate Cretans thronged about me, gazing (as though astonished) to see me both want company, and their language, and by their cruel looks, they seemed to be a barbarous and uncivil people. For all these highlanders are tyrannical, bloodthirsty and deceitful. The consideration of which, and the appearance of my death, signed to me secretly by a pitiful woman, made me to shun their villainy in stealing forth from them in the dark night, and privately sought for a secure place of repose in a umbrageous cave by the sea side, where I lay till morning with a fearful heart, a erased body, a thirsty stomach, and a hungry belly.

Homer must have been referring to a Crete of a much earlier age.

Minoan ships are sleeping in the trees,
The tight-hipped men, frieze over stucco frieze,
With blue-scaled fish that swallow and exude
An ochre sea, bulls in steep solitude.

At the King's festival – red petals blown
Across a wide court's emptiness,
How silent the libations of distress,
And soft the brush of wrinkled feet on stone […]

All round, the climbing waste of broom,
The flower-cups swollen with the royal gold,
The buried jars that niggardly hold
Their hollow gloom.

King Minos' justice! feather-tilted scales
To weigh the thistledown that swirling sails
Out through the night, where neither tears nor gold
Can bribe the brooding gods when all is told.
(C. A. Trypanis, 'Cnossus', from *The Cocks of Hades*, 1958)

In Mary Renault's *The King Must Die*, Theseus, one of the ten young men and women carried off from Athens for sacrifice to the Minotaur, approaches the 'House of the Axe' for the first time:

It was a palace within whose bounds you could have set a town. It crowned the ridge and clung to its downward slopes, terrace after terrace, tier after tier of painted columns, deep glowing red, tapering in toward the base, and ringed at head and foot with that dark brilliant blue the Cretans love. Behind them in the noonday shadow were porticoes and balconies gay with pictured walls, which glowed in the shade like beds of flowers. The tops of tall cypresses hardly showed above the roofs of the courts they grew in. Over the highest roof-edge, sharp cut against the deep blue Cretan sky, a mighty pair of horns reared towards heaven.

This description of ancient Knossos owes almost everything to the work of the English archaeologist Arthur Evans, who excavated and dramatically restored the ruins which he believed were the palace of the legendary King Minos. Evans had followed Schliemann's dramatic discoveries at Troy and later at Mycenae and Tiryns with intense admiration. In 1883 he and his wife visited the German and his young wife Sophia in their magnificent house in Athens and were shown some of his extraordinary finds. Evans could not believe that a culture with such high standards of craftsmanship could have had existed without writing and was intrigued by Schliemann's interest in excavating a site, possibly of the same civilisation, in Crete. The Cretans were in the middle of one of their bloody attempts to free themselves from Turkish rule and at a time of war and mutual massacre little in the way of archaeology could be achieved. In 1900, however, ten years after Schliemann's death and when the last Turkish forces had withdrawn from the island, Evans managed to buy the site of Knossos. With assistants and 32 local diggers (eventually there were 180) he set to work. Almost immediately he uncovered part of an ancient city.

'Evans', wrote Margalit Fox in *The Riddle of the Labyrinth* (2013), 'had come upon the ruins of a sophisticated Bronze Age civilization, previously unknown, that had flowered on Crete from about 1850 to 1450 B.C. Predating the Classical Age by a thousand years, it was the oldest European civilization ever discovered.' Together with the spectacular antiquities brought to light were a huge number of clay tablets mysteriously inscribed with hieroglyphs and figures in a language unknown to living man. Some tablets found with a similar but earlier script Evans named Linear A; the writing on the much larger treasure trove, which held such high promise of unlocking the secrets of this prehistoric civilisation, he called Linear B.

Evans was 48 years old, keeper of the Ashmolean Museum in Oxford and already a distinguished archaeologist. His discoveries at Knossos, especially the cache of tablets with the incomprehensible script, made him immediately famous. The tablets had been wet clay when written on: the fire that had destroyed the palace in about 1450 BCE had baked them hard and preserved them for posterity. Evans guessed that they held detailed administrative records of daily life and knew that to read them would dramatically illuminate the past; it was a challenge that few archaeologists or historians could resist.

So began a search to decipher Linear B that was to occupy several hundred brilliant minds for the next 50 years, a search as gripping as a detective story. As an intellectual feat, the unravelling of Linear B has been compared to mapping the structure of DNA. 'The decipherment was done entirely by hand,' writes Margalit Fox, 'without the aid of computers or a single bilingual inscription. It was accomplished, crumb by crumb, in the only way possible: by finding, interpreting, and meticulously following a series of tiny clues hidden within the script itself. And in the end, the answer to the riddle defied everyone's expectations.'

Though he lived until 1941, Sir Arthur Evans (he was knighted in 1911) failed to decipher the script and, like many who attempted the task, becoming addicts in the process, believed it to be related to some ancient language such as Hittite, Sumerian or Etruscan. Though mistaking its origin, those who over the years tried to unlock the code came up with a number of important clues. Foremost among these scholars, and the only woman, was a modest American classics teacher in New York, Alice Kober, whose significant role has only recently been recognised.

In the end it was a young architect with a remarkable mind who had been obsessed with the mysterious script since a teenager, who solved the riddle. Using many of Alice Kober's carefully assembled clues, his own intuition and exceptional intelligence, Michael Ventris deciphered the code, finally realising that Linear B was not related to another Near Eastern language, as he himself had thought, but was in fact an early form of Greek.

Alice Kober did not live to see the solution; she died aged 48, two years before Ventris achieved his breakthrough. She never saw Knossos, source of the puzzle that absorbed so much of her life, and was able to travel to Greece only once, in the summer of 1939, years later remembering nostalgically her 'scrambles up and down the north slope of the Acropolis'. Michael Ventris visited Crete in 1951, staying at the Villa Ariadne, and like some after him, was disappointed at the way the palace and the frescoes had been restored; Mycenae, he said, which remained a magnificent ruin, affected him more deeply.

He did not enjoy the triumph and fame of his discovery for long. Always a complex character, in 1956 he became estranged from his wife and children and deeply depressed. He died in a car accident, aged 34. Suicide was suspected by some, but as Margalit Fox writes, 'Perhaps it does not matter. Ventris's achievement' was 'startling, monumental and incontrovertible.'

Meanwhile, more tablets inscribed with Linear B were discovered on the mainland, notably at Pylos, site of Nestor's palace in Homer's *Iliad*. It became clear that this was not a 'Minoan' civilisation, as Evans described it, but Mycenaean. The accounts, including tax records, detail every aspect of life – from agriculture and livestock to the making of perfumes, inventories of furniture to the construction of war chariots and the cost of horses and weapons, including arrows, spears and swords, some inlaid with gold and silver ... In these records, meticulously kept, was born Europe's first bureaucracy.

Also revealed were requirements for banquets, some of which must have been considerable events. John Chadwick, in *The*

Decipherment of Linear B (1958), cites one that includes '1,574 litres of barley [...] 115 litres of flour, 307 litres of olives, 19 litres of honey, 96 litres of figs, 1 ox, 26 rams, 6 ewes, 2 he-goats, 1 fattened pig and 585 litres of wine' – the barley alone being enough to feed more than forty people for a month.

Other tablets list the names of men, including archers and rowers, assigned to military duty on land and sea both in Crete and at Pylos, including 'the watchers guarding the coastal regions'. Yet, however well organised the defences of this ancient empire, in the end they failed, though it is not known whether the enemy came by land or by sea, or struck from deep below the earth's surface. Knossos was burned and destroyed some time after 1450 BCE; on the mainland Pylos survived for another 200 years. 'What actually happened remains a tantalizing mystery,' wrote Chadwick. 'All we know is that the palace was looted and burnt. The absence of human remains suggests that no resistance took place there; [...] the archaeological picture suggests that the population was reduced to something like a tenth of its earlier numbers.'

'So ended the first flush of Greek civilization,' concludes Margalit Fox,

> and from then till the coming of the Greek alphabet centuries later, the art of writing was at best a dimly remembered dream. Before long, the Mycenaean archives – describing a world of monarchs and slaves, gods and goddesses, spinners and weavers, men who made art and men who made war – had passed from readability into darkness, where they would languish for three thousand years.

In the summer of 1955 three undergraduates in their second year at Cambridge set off from Canea on the north coast of Crete to cross the White Mountains on foot; they aimed to come down to the sea on the southern shore of the island through the gorge of Samaria. World War II had finished only ten years earlier and the wounds of the savage civil war that followed were still raw. But these young men knew little of the fierce complications of modern Greek history. They had been impressed by the wartime adventures of Xan Fielding and Patrick Leigh Fermor (including the capture of a German general!); and they had heard of the magnificent range of mountains that bisected the island and of the lawless inhabitants of their wild and inaccessible slopes, the black-clad and black-booted warriors of Sfakia.

Though all three travellers were fit and healthy, they nevertheless baulked at the prospect of trudging up rough mountain tracks with heavy rucksacks on their backs in the heat of a Greek August. As it happened there was a solution, and one of them had tried it in Spain the previous spring: he had bought a donkey, loaded his possessions on its back and set off from Cordoba to Granada. Buy at the start of the journey, sell at the end – how can you lose? In this case he did lose: the donkey died of old age two days short of Granada. But such a misfortune would not be allowed to happen in Greece.

'Michael, I think you can tell a donkey's age by its teeth. In Spain, did you look at its teeth?'

'No.'

'There you are.'

The risks involved in buying secondhand vehicles, whether donkeys or cars, might differ in detail but in general are similar. In this case the qualities or faults of every animal offered for sale would be assessed by all three of them: the possibility of fraud could be safely excluded.

A few days later two donkeys with haversacks and primitive camping equipment strapped to their backs, and accompanied by their new owners, started up into the foothills of the White Mountains. The purchase price had been agreeable to the buyers and highly satisfactory to the sellers. The donkeys had passed the carrot test, designed to exclude candidates unfit for the gruelling expedition that lay ahead: both animals chewed rapidly and well, the older using particularly large and yellow teeth. One donkey was grey, a large and powerful beast, the other was younger, a smaller and more delicate creature with a soft brown coat. Perhaps inevitably, they were named Daedalus and Icarus.

A difficulty faced by the party, as it wended its way upwards past clusters of cottages and dry olive groves into the hills, was the extreme slowness of their progress. This realisation was underscored by the way they were constantly overtaken by streams of heavily loaded mules and donkeys piled high with produce with their owners sitting happily on top. Greeting them politely, the passing Greeks could not hide bemused expressions at the contrast between the rapid gait of their own burdened beasts and the leisurely pace of the foreigners' animals carrying practically nothing.

'They need the occasional whack,' John suggested, referring to the donkeys. But neither he nor his companions were willing to beat their animals into action. A discovery that night turned out to be helpful: Daedalus evinced a powerful attraction for Icarus. Whether Daedalus was a homosexual donkey, or merely bisexual, was of little concern to his owners: the next day the speed of the little caravan was increased simply by putting Icarus in the lead.

But it was still too slow in the eyes of the locals. That afternoon they were asked to deliver some urgently needed penicillin to a sick child in Lakkoi, a village on the Omalos plateau, which they were expected to reach before nightfall. Hours later the moon rose, lighting the white dirt track still winding ahead upwards into the hills; they were late, with possible consequences too serious to contemplate. Two of the young men pressed on to deliver the medicine; the third made camp and waited with the donkeys. An hour later the penicillin reached its destination – a house-to-house search for 'Stavros' in the sleeping village, a darkened doorway under an oil lamp held high, a woman's whispered thanks.

To reach the head of the gorge of Samaria and descend to the southern coast, it was necessary to cross the high plateau of the Omalos. Dust devils danced in the broad street of Lakkoi dividing a row of low houses, one of which was a small general store almost bare of provisions. The Englishmen had run out of food: all they could buy was olive oil and a few potatoes and onions, which they loaded onto Daedalus's broad back. They then proceeded down the street.

Women in long dresses were sweeping outside their houses, children played in the dust; men lounged or sat back on chairs propped against the walls. As they passed, the women gathered their children close to them; the men, in embroidered waistcoats over baggy breeches and high boots, heavily moustached and with the famous black *sarikis* tied rakishly around their heads, stared at the travellers in silence. Michael, who had been working on his Greek phrasebook, essayed a smile and a hesitant, 'Please, the road to Samaria?' No word in reply, simply an outstretched arm, pointing one way, out of the village.

Unnerved by this chilling reception, so unusual in Greece, it was some time before the travellers found their voices.

'Blimey.'

'Like the American Wild West ...'

'Can't blame them really ...'

'Why not?'

'Think of the foreigners who came by before us ... the last lot probably machine-gunned half the village. And before them the Venetians, and the Turks ... I don't think foreigners walking down that street ever brought them anything good.'

Silence.

'But we're English.'

'How would they know that?'

As they discovered later, David was right. As Antony Beevor recounts in *Crete: The Battle and the Resistance* (1991), in September 1941, not long after the German airborne invasion of Crete and the evacuation of the defeated Allied forces, the Omalos plateau was overrun by some 2,000 mountain troops and forced to submit to special tribunals: 110 men, including 39 civilians and 6 British military personnel, were found guilty of attempting resistance and executed.

But in 1955 the Englishmen and their donkeys had other important things to think about, food being one. They had eaten practically nothing for two days, expecting to find tavernas where none existed. A feast of potatoes and onions was planned for the evening. That midday they stopped exhausted under a carob tree to which they tied Daedalus, letting Icarus graze free. They ate the last biscuits, drank some water, took off all their clothes and stretched out on sleeping bags in the shade, drowsed by the zinging of the cicadas.

Late afternoon and a cry startled them awake. Daedalus, overcome with lust, had broken free and launched himself on Icarus, who, having failed to dodge his advances, set off at a gallop, ears flat back, across the plain, Daedalus pounding at his heels.

The young men did not hesitate. Wasting no more than seconds to put on their shoes, they took off after the escaping animals, determined to recapture their property and save Icarus from a fate worse than death.

Earlier that morning, when they had stopped under the carob tree, the parched and barren fields around them had been deserted, not a living creature in sight. Now, as they ran stark naked down the track, eyes fixed on the donkeys disappearing into the distance, they noted with alarm that the countryside was no longer empty. Scattered about them were the dark shapes of shawled women, bent almost double, working in the fields. As the two donkeys raced past them, pursued by a naked, white-skinned young man, followed seconds later by a second, then a third, the women unbent themselves and stood, hands shading their eyes, scarcely believing the apparitions passing swiftly by ...

Three days later, the party debouched through the towering cliff gates of the gorge of Samaria onto the beach near Ayia Roumeli and the blessedly cool blue welcome of the sea. To reach the gorge they had descended a steep valley through dense pine forest to a stream that provided water for themselves and for the donkeys, which had proved themselves brave but unsuitable for the steep and narrow paths that only mules could negotiate. They had fought a forest fire. John, exhausted by the heat and hours of beating at flames, had fainted while blowing up his mattress and fell, cutting his head on a boulder. Now, bandaged with a strip of black shirt, he looked as dangerous as any Cretan. They had finished the potatoes and onions, but a family living in a cliff-side cottage at the head of the gorge, learning that they were English, took pity on them and after shots of *tsikoudia*, the raki of the Cretan mountains, fed them on eggs and vegetables, washed down with resin-sharp red wine.

At the time, perhaps fortunately, they had little idea of whom they might meet on their trek across the White Mountains. During the three years of civil war until 1949 the Communists in Crete had much less support than on the mainland and were defeated earlier, the *andartes* finally retiring to their last stronghold on the island – the gorge of Samaria. The National Army, convinced it could now annihilate them, approached the gorge from both ends: instead, most *andartes* escaped by scaling the cliffs. Many lived on in the White Mountains as outlaws, surviving on stolen sheep; the last two came down in 1974 after the collapse of the Colonels' regime.

They had reached their destination – Ayia Roumeli, the prosperous mart where they would sell Daedalus and Icarus, probably at a handsome profit, and then take the weekly caique to the little port of Sfakia, eastward along the coast. Except that Ayia Roumeli was no prosperous mart, far from it.

Part of it was less like a village than a collection of small houses threaded together like beads on a short string of dusty track. But first things first: they were desperate to throw themselves into the sea. Making camp under the cliffs half a mile from the village, they swam, dug a hole in the sand and found water, and collected driftwood from the beach in readiness for a fire. What would they cook on it? It was a pleasure to plan the menu. Steaks, of course; baked potatoes, green salad?

Returning to the village, they were quickly disillusioned. The front room of the house that served as the only shop had even less to offer than the one on the Omalos. There was no taverna, of course no butcher. They bought eggs and bread, and asked, tentatively, for a chicken. A bird was caught, and paid for, but to their surprise and some alarm, was handed over fully feathered and very much alive.

An easy question in retrospect: why not ask the shopkeeper to execute the bird? He would have done so willingly and without hesitation; translation would not have been necessary, a simple gesture sufficient. Some kind of shame held them back. As they walked back to their camp, their dinner dangling upside down and making the occasional despairing cluck, it was discussed who would do the job. David, the most practical of the three, reluctantly agreed to try his hand. But the shameful truth was that despite being in Crete, a land of recent vicious war and bloody reprisal, of vendetta and violence, hardship and bravery ... they themselves were too feeble to even wring a chicken's neck.

Dinner was not to be simply achieved. The chicken escaped and only after a chase in circles on the beach, all three trying to throw themselves on the wildly squawking bird, was she finally recaptured, and killed. They then set about gutting and plucking, tasks which presented difficulties none of them had ever encountered before.

The shortage of food at Ayia Roumeli was no different in May 1941 when the king of Greece and his party escaped across the mountains and emerged through the gorge of Samaria at the shore, hoping to be taken off by the Royal Navy to safety in Egypt. They were met by a boy who handed them a note from Sir Michael Palairet, who was waiting for them at Ayia Roumeli. As Beevor describes it, 'The young messenger returned at top speed to the Legation party, clearly relishing his role in the drama. "The King is coming! The King is coming!" he cried out. *Lady Palairet promptly organized a meal of potatoes*' (my italics).

Antony Beevor describes the evacuation of the royals from the rudimentary jetty at Ayia Roumeli, an event not without its accompaniment of farce. The British army and Royal Navy officers present bickered as to who should be in charge of the royals; incredibly, the admiral only had a torch with which to signal their arrival on the beach. 'The tantalizing lights far out in the Libyan Sea ignored his stream of Morse, and tempers became strained.' In the darkness, and no doubt looking anxiously over their shoulders at the sky above the mountains lit by flashes from the battle on the other side of the island, they eventually succeeded in getting aboard the destroyer, HMS *Decoy,* sent to collect them. 'Next morning, 23 May, the royal evacuees, with emotions straight out of Hornblower, looked through portholes to see the battle-fleet including the *Valiant* with Prince Philip of Greece on board [...] Unknown to them, another relative, Prince Philip's "Uncle Dicky" [Lord Louis Mountbatten], was at that time following on behind, his three destroyers under heavy air attack.'

From their first day on the coast, the three undergraduates had been befriended by a gentle, half-witted deaf-mute called Yanni, whom the villagers treated with amused but kindly tolerance. Yanni was happy to run simple errands for the Englishmen. Their affection for him cooled temporarily when, returning from a swim, they found him masturbating into their water hole, obliging them to dig again further along the beach.

Time was running out. The caique for Sfakia was due in three days. But first, the donkeys had to be sold, the invested capital recouped. The villagers of Ayia Roumeli were friendly and interested, but they had their own problems and, not unlike the Englishmen, they were short of cash. Frustrating enquiries and failed negotiations followed. Finally an offer was made by a shepherd to purchase Daedalus. He was ready to pay – not with money, but with cheese: 80 kilograms of *graviera*, the best in Crete, as he reminded them. While the Englishmen struggled to imagine how they could carry, let alone dispose of such a quantity of cheese the shepherd added that of course it was not ready yet: he would deliver it down to the village, without fail, in October.

This was the last straw and the travellers decided to cut their losses; Michael's business scheme had failed, for the second (and sadly not the last) time. Daedalus was handed over in exchange for a few drachma and, more importantly, food and wine. Icarus was presented, with some ceremony, to Yanni, a gift of ownership witnessed by the shopkeeper and others. Leaner and poorer, but rich in memories, the three embarked at dawn on the caique for Sfakia; from there they would head for Gortyna and Knossos – by bus. (The above draws on David Gaunt's unpublished account, 'A Walk in the White Mountains', 1955).

The defence of Crete in 1941 was hardly a triumph of British arms. Evelyn Waugh was an officer in intelligence who landed on the island just as the decision had been made to surrender it. Beevor writes that Waugh's 'depiction of the debacle on Crete, both in his diaries and in his novel, *Officers and Gentlemen* (1955), the second book of his Sword of Honour trilogy, is more vivid than anything else written about those last days, but the novel in particular must be seen more as a projection of a personal sense of disillusionment'. This was because Waugh saw the collapse in Crete as the collapse of the British ruling class. In a letter to Diana Cooper some months afterwards, he wrote: 'The English are a very base people. I did not know this, living as I did. Now I know this through and through and they disgust me.'

Waugh might have offered a more appealing picture of his fellow countrymen if he had known of their involvement in the Cretan resistance during the next four years. With the apparently imminent defeat of the British in North Africa by Rommel's advancing army and the likely loss of Egypt, the island became an important intelligence outpost for British Headquarters in Cairo as it tried to assess and foresee the movement of arms and men sent against them. Then, as the war turned in the Allies' favour, Crete became a possible launching pad for the invasion of Europe (to the disgust of the Cretans, Sicily was finally chosen). As a consequence a number of brave and hardy British officers, a mixture of academics and adventurers and sometimes both, were clandestinely shipped in or parachuted on to the island to assist the Cretans, who needed little encouragement since armed opposition to invaders was an ancient and popular tradition. Some of the British who spent dangerous months and even years in the mountains have written memorably about the island, notably Xan Fielding and Patrick Leigh Fermor, while C. M. Woodhouse later wrote several distinguished books on modern Greek history. Less well known are Greek authors, the most interesting perhaps being George Psychoundakis, whose book *The Cretan Runner* (1955) was translated into English by Leigh Fermor.

'The job of a war-time runner in the Resistance Movement', Leigh Fermor writes in his introduction to that book:

> was the most exhausting and one of the most consistently dangerous of all. It entailed immense journeys on foot at full speed over some of the most precipitous country in Europe, carrying messages between the towns and the large villages and the secret wireless stations in the mountains; humping batteries and driving camouflaged explosives and arms, and occasionally a British straggler in disguise, on the backs of mules, through heavily garrisoned areas [...] Three of the other early starters – of whom, in the early days, there were less than a dozen – were captured and shot, two after long imprisonment and appalling tortures in Ayia Jail. None of them was paid and there was no incentive but a sense of duty to their country and their allies.

'They were all mountain boys,' Leigh Fermor continues. 'Most of them had pastured their families' flocks since they could walk. All were poor, and George's family was the poorest of all.' The most unusual thing about George Psychoundakis, however, was not his poverty, loyalty or physical stamina, but that he was a self-educated writer who composed 'homespun patriotic poems, theoretical verses about love or satires on local life'. The manuscript in five thick exercise books that after the war he thrust into Leigh Fermor's hands was of a different character. *Pictures of our Life During the Occupation* provided that rare view of a conflict seen through the eyes of the humblest of participants, and a Cretan, with unflinching descriptions of the curious foreigners who had arrived bringing gold sovereigns, weapons and the promise of freedom. It told a story of daring escapes, friendships and betrayals between men always on the move from one remote and primitive mountain hideout to another.

For them the longed-for end of the fearsome Cretan winter and the coming of spring is best described by Leigh Fermor:

> Cavemen released, free to leave the mountains at last, and bound for some faraway meeting or gathering of guerillas, we would descend to the foothills and lose height down glimmering staircases of olive and vineyard. The villages through which we stalked with our guns cocked were silent and unreal as fictions of snow and ivory. We tiptoed under their arches and down lanes that twisted round corners in paper fans of steps. Sometimes we stopped with circumspection at the shutter of a friend's house, and after a brief entry and whispered confabulation, continued on our way. Metallic chestnut woods gleamed; the oleanders and poplars were doubly silver by the beds of shrunken streams. The water had dwindled to a net of quicksilver in a waste of boulders that Venetian or Turkish bridge-builders had spanned with pale arcs of masonry. At a loop in the valley, hundreds of frogs drowned the nightingales, the drilling of crickets and the little owl's hesitant note. We heard dogs in the villages and brief jangles as flocks woke and fell asleep in folds half-way to the sky. These sounds strung a thread of urgency and collusion through the peace of the night. Sometimes we would lie flat with held breath in a cactus clump or among the rocks or flattened against a wall under an archway till the footfalls of an enemy patrol died away.

Leigh Fermor accepted that his passionate devotion to Crete and the Cretans was subjective, that the 'circumstances of war and the exhilaration of youth had much to do with it'. But not his admiration for the islanders' courage. When they warmly welcomed and cared for straggling Allied soldiers, when the punishment for harbouring them was death and the destruction of their villages, he writes in *Roumeli*, 'they not only risked everything to help their solitary allies; they made them members of the Cretan family. Best of all, they forgave our mistakes.' Better than most, he knew what this meant, though in the land of honour and vendetta there were some things that could never be forgiven.

In May 1944 he and a group of resistance fighters and two other British officers were about to move off from a mountain sheepfold where they had been hiding when Leigh Fermor picked up his rifle, which a short time earlier had been used by others for arms practice, and not noticing that a bullet was still in the magazine, accidentally fired off a round. Tragically the bullet hit and seriously wounded Yanni Tsangarakis, a trusted fighter and old friend; he died an hour later.

His companions knew that this had been a terrible accident but Leigh Fermor could not forgive himself. 'No amount of writing about it will bring Yanni back to life, nor excuse my not examining the magazine before closing the bolt.' In view of the sensitive relationships between Cretan families the group persuaded Leigh Fermor to keep the cause of Yanni's death secret until the war ended. Late in 1945 he and Xan Fielding returned to Crete; besides lectures, and a triumphant tour of their old haunts in the White Mountains, an important objective for Leigh Fermor was to visit the Tsangarakis family and ask for their forgiveness.

Artemis Cooper writes in *Patrick Leigh Fermor*:

The story that he had died in a German ambush had not lasted beyond the end of the war, and now Paddy felt honour bound to visit the village of Photineou and tell Yanni's brother Kanaki exactly what happened.

Kanaki came down from his house to see Paddy, who was waiting for him by the old fountain. Without any preamble he said, 'Mihali, is it true that you killed my brother?' Paddy replied, 'Yes, Kanaki, it was a terrible accident, it was me …' – 'That's all I wanted to know,' said Kanaki, who turned on his heel without shaking hands.

A year later he tried once again:

Asking the taxi to wait on the Rethymno road, Paddy walked up to Photineou and Kanaki's house, which was high on the mountainside. Paddy knocked and went in […] 'He stood up, saying, "What do you seek here, Mihali? We are not friends," laying his two fingers on the butt of the pistol in his sash. It was no good, so I left, very sad.'

When Leigh Fermor broached his plan to capture a German general in Crete and whisk him off by submarine to Egypt, opinions at HQ in Cairo were divided and it was not until April 1944 that the go-ahead was finally given. Leigh Fermor had wanted Xan Fielding to be his second-in-command, but Fielding was short and dark and would make an unlikely German officer. Instead it was William Stanley Moss who was chosen and on the night of 26 April Leigh Fermor, Moss and a group of trusted Cretan resistance fighters waited at a spot chosen on the road not far from General Kreipe's HQ in the Villa Ariadne, where Sir Arthur Evans had lived while excavating Knossos. The story is told by Artemis Cooper in *Patrick Leigh Fermor*, by Leigh Fermor in his unpublished 'Abducting a General' and in *A Time of Gifts* and by W. S. Moss in *Ill Met By Moonlight* (1950): 'During the hour and a half of our vigil a few German trucks and cars drove past at intervals […] very close to us, all coming from the south and heading for Heraklion […] time seemed to pass with exasperating slowness [...] On the tick of 9.30 Mitzo's torch flashed clearly three times.'

The two British officers, dressed in German field army grey, stepped out into the road. Some details of their uniforms were out of date and in daylight would have given them away, but in the darkness escaped notice. Leigh Fermor recounted:

> Billy waved his disc and I moved my red torch to and fro and shouted 'Halt!' The car came to a standstill and we stepped right and left out of the beam of the headlights, which, inspite of being partly blacked out, were still very bright, and walked slowly, each to his appointed door [...] I saluted and said '*Papier, bitte schön*.' The General, with an officer-to-man smile, reached for his breast-pocket, and I opened the door with a jerk – this was the cue for the rest of the party to break cover.

In a moment General Kreipe, shouting and swearing, had been handcuffed and forced into the back of the car, the driver had been coshed and his place taken by Moss, with Leigh Fermor, wearing the General's hat, beside him:

> In the car, Paddy addressed the General in German. 'Herr General, I am a British major. Beside me is a British captain. These men [referring to the three Cretans with him in the back of the car] are Greek patriots. I am in command of this unit, and you are an honourable prisoner of war. We are taking you to Egypt.'

The general's reaction to this announcement must have been mixed: he was deeply humiliated and angry, and yet at least it seemed he would not be immediately killed by the Cretans. He was concerned at the lack of his hat. He was promised it back, but not yet.

To reach the mountains to the south it was first necessary to drive through Heraklion:

Billy drove through no less than twenty-two checkpoints. Two factors tipped the odds in their favour. General Kreipe did not like checkpoints and used to growl at sentries who kept him waiting, so when they saw his car with its two unmistakable metal pennants they tended to wave him through. The blackout also came in handy. Although the streets were crowded with Germans, everyone looked like shadows; only odd chinks of light escaped from doors and windows. Billy 'calmly and methodically hooted his way through the mob [...] collecting many salutes as the soldiers cleared out of the way.' To anyone peering in, the back of the car would have been impenetrably dark. In the front, Paddy made sure that the General's hat with its gold braid was visible, and not his face. The last checkpoint at the Chania Gate was heavily defended, and it looked as if the sentry with the red torch meant business. Billy slowed down smoothly, giving the guards enough time to recognize the Opel. The barrier was still down; but as Paddy barked, 'Generals Wagen!' Billy began to accelerate, and the barrier came up just in time.

[...]

No-one slept well that night, and as dawn broke and the sun illuminated the snow-streaked hump of Mount Ida, the General murmured a line in Latin: 'Video ut alta nive candidum Soracte ...'

It was one of the few Odes of Horace that Paddy knew by heart, and which he had translated at school. Taking up where the General had left off, he went on to the end of the poem.

Leigh Fermor finishes the tale:

The General's blue eyes swivelled away from the mountain-top to mine – and when I'd finished, after a long silence, he said, 'Ach so, Herr Major!' It was very strange. 'Ja, Herr General.' As though, for a long moment, the war had ceased to exist. We had both drunk at the same fountains long before, and things were different between us for the rest of the time we were together.'

Two weeks of arduous climbing followed in which the general, who had hurt his leg when dragged out of his car, fell several times. The party was forced to sleep in caves in the extreme cold and with little food, constantly in fear of detection by increasing numbers of German troops who had thrown a ring round Mount Ida. With good luck, and despite farcical errors, the general and his abductors were finally taken off a secluded beach by a motor launch on 15 May and spirited away to Egypt.

After the war Leigh Fermor encouraged Moss to write an account of the adventure. *Ill Met By Moonlight* was published in 1950, and later made into film with Dirk Bogarde in the lead. Artemis Cooper writes:

> That year Moss published *Gold is Where You Hide It*, an investigation into what the Nazis had done with the treasures of the Reichsbank. But something in Billy seemed unable to adjust to the post-war world. Leaving Sophie and his two young daughters in London, he travelled to Antarctica, and after that sailed round the islands of the Pacific. By the time he settled in Kingston, Jamaica, he was drinking heavily. Despite the urgings of his friends he refused to seek help, and died there in August 1965, aged only forty-four.

'The islanders' passion for their country turns the island itself into the heroine of most of their songs,' writes Leigh Fermor in *Roumeli*.

> 'Crete, my beautiful island, crown of the Levant,' runs one of the couplets they often sing, 'your earth is silver and your rocks are diamonds.' This is more than a flowery trope: the metamorphic limestone mass, especially when it soars above the tree-line in a wilderness where nothing can grow, does shine like silver and lends to the great peaks, even in August, an illusion of eternal snow; and the sharp-edged and many-faceted rocks throw back the light with a dazzling and adamantine flash. In ravines and hollows at midday,

when the sun has drained every shadow, a hint of fear is present. There are no trees for the cicadas, no goat-bells to be heard across the stagnant air; the far-off ricochets of an invisible shepherd practicing against a boulder, stop. Sound expires with a gasp; the only hint of life is a horned skeleton lying among the rocks, as though an ogre had lived not far off. The world becomes a hushed and blinding wilderness. Colour ebbs from the sky; the hot mineral shudders; all is haggard and aghast. It is the hour of meridian fright and an invisible finger runs up the nape of the lonely traveller there and sets his hair on end. At moments like these the island stands in the sea like an anvil for the inaudible strokes of the sun.

The heavy silences of summer noons give way soon enough to evenings when the hardships of life are forgotten, glasses of *tsikoudia* and wine surround plates of steaming *mezes*, the *lyra or bouzouki* is taken down from its hook on the wall and the dancing begins. In *The Stronghold*, Xan Fielding describes evenings in one of his favourite tavernas watching the *rebetiko*:

One man at a time would take the floor [...] and stand there for a moment with arms outstretched, waiting to be possessed by the music. The rhythm seemed to invade his body first by way of his fingers, which would begin snapping impatiently as though to summon the other limbs into action. An answering shuffle from his feet, two or three stealthy steps forward, and the dancer was then launched into the long series of complicated movements, flicking his ankles, stamping his feet, slapping his heels. Then came the sinister swoops and dips, the drunken, off-balance lurches and miraculous recoveries – all executed as though in a trance, with the performer's head thrown back and smiling at the ceiling or else bent forward in dreamy contemplation of his own shoes.

The kind of dancing Fielding was writing about, when a single dancer gets to his feet when the mood demanded, was observed at that time only by the relatively few foreign travellers in Greece. Ten years later Greek music and dancing suddenly became familiar throughout much of the Western world – Kazantzakis has a lot to answer for:

I first met him in Piraeus. I wanted to take the boat to Crete and I had gone down to the port. It was almost daybreak and raining. A strong sirocco was blowing the spray from the waves as far as the little café, whose glass doors were shut. The café reeked of brewing sage and human beings whose breath steamed the windows because of the cold outside. Five or six seamen, who had spent the night there, muffled in their brown goatskin reefer-jackets, were drinking coffee or sage and gazing out of the misty windows at the sea.

[...]

A stranger of about sixty, very tall and lean, with staring eyes, had pressed his nose against the pane and was staring at me. He was holding a little flattened bundle under his arm [...] As soon as our eyes had met – he seemed to be making sure I was really the person he was looking for – the stranger opened the door with a determined thrust of his arm. He passed between the tables with a rapid, springy step, and stopped in front of me.

'Travelling?' he asked, 'Where to? Trusting to providence?'

'I'm making for Crete. Why do you ask?'

'Take me with you?'

I looked at him carefully. He had hollow cheeks, a strong jaw, prominent cheek bones, curly grey hair, bright piercing eyes.

'Why? What could I do with you?'

'Why! Why!' he exclaimed with disdain. 'Can't a man do anything without a why? Just like that, because he wants to? Well, take me, shall we say as cook [...]'

I started to laugh. His bluff ways and trenchant words pleased me.

'What are you thinking about?' he asked me familiarly, shaking his great head. 'You keep a pair of scales, too, do you? You weight everything to the nearest gram, don't you? Come on, friend, make up your mind. Take the plunge!'

The great lanky lubber was standing over me, and it tired me to have to look up at him. I closed my Dante. 'Sit down,' I said to him. 'Have a glass of sage?'

'Sage?' he exclaimed with contempt. 'Here! Waiter! A rum!'

He drank his rum in little sips, keeping it a long time in his mouth to get the taste, then letting it slip slowly down and warm his insides. 'A sensualist,' I thought. 'A connoisseur ...'

'What kind of work do you do?' I asked.

'All kinds. With feet, hands or head. All of them [...]'

'Where were you working last?'

'In a mine. I'm a good miner. I know a thing or two about metals, I know how to find the veins and open up galleries. I go down pits; I'm not afraid [...]'

'And what have you got in your bundle? Food? Clothes? Or tools?'

My companion shrugged his shoulders and laughed. 'You seem a very sensible sort,' he said. 'Begging your pardon.'

He stroked his bundle with his long, hard fingers.

'No,' he added, 'it's a santuri.'

'A santuri? Do you play the santuri?'

'When I'm hard up, I go round the inns playing the santuri. I sing old klephtic tunes from Macedonia. Then I take my hat round – this beret here! – and it fills up with money.'

'What's your name?'

'Alexis Zorba.'

After some further conversation, the narrator asks Zorba whether he is married.

'Aren't I a man?' he said angrily. 'Aren't I a man? I mean blind. Like everyone else before me, I fell headlong into the ditch. I married. I took the road down-hill – catastrophe! I became head of a family, I built a house, I had children – trouble. But thank God for the santuri.'

[…]

'Zorba, it's agreed. You come with me. I have some lignite in Crete. You can superintend the workmen. In the evening we'll stretch out on the sand […] we'll eat and drink together. Then you'll play the santuri.'

'If I'm in the mood, d'you hear? […] I'll work for you as much as you like. I'm your man there. But the santuri, that's different. It's a wild animal, it needs freedom. If I'm in the mood, I'll play. I'll even sing. And I'll dance the Zeimbekiko, the Hassapiko, the Pentozali – but I'll tell you plainly from the start, I must be in the mood […] As regards those things, you must realize, I'm a man.'

'A man? What d'you mean?'

'Well, free!'

I called for another rum.

Nikos Kazantzakis was born in Crete in 1883 when the island was still under Turkish rule. He studied law in Athens and philosophy in Paris. A philosopher as well as a writer, he was passionately concerned with the meaning of life, and man's place in it. He was also profoundly religious, and fascinated by the character of Jesus: his novels include *Christ Recrucified* (1948) and *The Last Temptation of Christ* (1955), in which Jesus appears as less than infallible, a human being struggling with the fears and desires of a normal man. As a result Kazantzakis fell foul of both the Greek Orthodox Church, which anathematized him, and the Roman Catholic Church, which listed *The Last Temptation of Christ* in its *Index Librorum Prohibitorum*; when Martin Scorsese's film of the book was released in 1988 many cinemas refused to show it.

Kazantzakis was nominated for the Nobel Prize four times; when he failed to secure the prize by one vote in 1957, Albert Camus, who won, said that Kazantzakis deserved it 'a hundred times' more than he did. Despite suffering from leukaemia, Kazantzakis spent the last few years of his life travelling the world and writing about his travels. He died in Germany on the way back from China in 1957. The Greek Orthodox Church refused to allow him burial in a cemetery; instead his tomb is on one of the bastions of the great Venetian wall surrounding the city of Heraklion where he was born. He wrote his own epitaph which in English reads: 'I hope for nothing. I fear nothing. I am free.'

The inevitably small readership in Greek has always meant that earnings for Greek writers depended largely on their work being translated. *The Life and Times of Alexis Zorba* had been written in the 1940s but was first published in English, as *Zorba the Greek,* in 1952. Kazantzakis only became famous on the release of Michael Cacoyannis's film, starring Anthony Quinn, with music by Mikis Theodorakis, in 1964. In 1960 *Never on Sunday* had filled the cinemas of Europe and America, and *Zorba* had the same wild success. Those years saw Greece suddenly in the cultural limelight. Higher incomes and lower air fares encouraged a flood of visitors to Greece.

I'm off again in a day to an island where lemons grow & oranges melt in the mouth & goats snatch the last fig leaves off small trees the corn is yellow and russles & the sea is harplike on volcanic shores saw the marx brothers in an open air cinema and the walls were made of honeysuckle.
(John Craxton, 1948)

Writing to Ben Nicholson from Poros in 1948, Craxton wrote:

I hope to come back to London in April, May to make a new exhibition but I dread town life, this place spoils me & I suffer a million nerves when I have to face the proposition of no more mountain water or clear air, sea & my friends in the local tavern or this quiet house with no telephone or traffic outside.

John Craxton was not only a painter but a designer of sets for ballet and opera, becoming a close friend of Margot Fonteyn and a group of artists and writers including Graham Sutherland and Lucian Freud; he designed the covers of almost all of his friend Patrick Leigh Fermor's books.

David Attenborough spoke at John Craxton's memorial service at St James's, Piccadilly, London, on 4 February 2010. An old friend of Craxton's, he told how when the young artist, aged 23, was able to leave England after the war he went to Greece: to Poros, Hydra and eventually Crete.

Suddenly the melancholic young man disappears from his pictures. And his landscapes become positively joyous – the sparkle of the Mediterranean Sea, the shaft of sunshine stabbing through the darkness of the rocky gorge, the wonder of asphodels apparently sprouting from barren rock.

[...]

Line was, from the beginning, crucially important in his painting. He didn't care for the smudgings of other styles. He liked to know where an object began and ended. The lines in his early drawings, which he drew with both brush and pen, already had an extraordinary incisiveness and eloquence. But now in Crete they became positively exultant and magically coloured [...]

It was in Crete, he declared, that he learned what he described as a very salutary lesson for a painter – that life is more important than art. Those are his words. And he certainly relished life to the full. He enjoyed riding across Europe between Crete and London on his Triumph Tiger motorcycle. He loved parties, enjoying them in both embassies and village bars with equal gusto. He loved food – particularly eccentric, unusual food. One of my great pleasures in life was to be taken by John to his favourite harbour-side restaurant in Hania and be given a dish of boiled sea creatures which even I, who am supposed to have some knowledge of the animal kingdom, found hard to identify.

In 1948, in a letter to a friend whose husband had been killed in a gliding accident, Craxton wrote:

> Sadness is as much a part of the summer as happiness & the great Greek sun makes deep shadows around the streets and houses & in the evening the sky goes bright yellow & mauve & then scarlet & then the moon hangs over the plopping sea around & gazes down & watches very indifferently. I paint a picture the size of my wall of girl on the shoulders of a boy reaching into a fig tree at the saddest yellow cat I've ever painted – it will be your cat [...]
>
> I will go to the monastery and light you a large yellow candle – when I watch the candles & the dark ikons of the Virgin & the dark saints I become very religious & there exists in the atmosphere a strange other world of something that's very comforting. I think we have all become too materialistic and that a return to face objects & places that have a spiritual existence of their own is inevitable. There's a great human grandeur about the Greek church & a spirit of optimism that I find heaven sent.

Craxton was not enthusiastic about Kazantzakis's novel *Zorba the Greek* but he helped the director Michael Cacoyannis find locations for the film when he came to Canea in 1964. In his biography *John Craxton* (2011), Ian Collins writes:

> He watched the tearful eviction of Simone Signoret from the rôle of Madame Hortense, the hotelier and ex-courtesan, and drove her Oscar-winning replacement, Lila Kedrova, to the site on his motorbike. Zorba himself – Anthony Quinn – appeared at the Hania house to show the artist his paintings. 'They look like occupational therapy,' Craxton said helpfully. Quinn then said he fancied sculpting, and was told that the best shop for materials was in Rome – whence his private jet was duly despatched.

Craxton's favourite taverna in the harbour rose to the occasion and hosted nightly parties for the large and famished cast. 'Irene Papas came escorted by her mother. Alan Bates considered buying a house nearby; although he left, hordes came in his wake on the Zorba trail: the tranquil harbour would be noisily developed and Crete ultimately transformed for tourism.'

'There's very little mist in the atmosphere in Greece,' Craxton told Martin Gayford in 1992:

> It's very clear; one can see very far and very close with the same amount of clarity. One doesn't get a tonal perspective, one gets a structural perspective. The Byzantine painters were terribly clever at that. The good ones invented perspective – exactly what the Cubists thought they had invented. There's a lot of invention in Byzantine painting. Landscapes are abstracted, rocks are abstracted, and yet they manage to convey in that abstracted shape the essence of rock. It's a very unnaturalistic way of painting but it has a strong feeling of reality about it [...] One of my objects in life is to try and find a way of expressing something real by unreal means. As Picasso says, art is a lie – but a lie that helps you make a truth.

In a letter to the curator Bryan Robertson in 1967, Craxton wrote that he enjoyed the reality of modern Greek life and 'perhaps in a romantic way I get absorbed by the elements of myth, if they exist, in everyday existence.' Craxton became the great portraitist of goats – demonic, wilful, undisciplined – 'caught in colour and held in the angular geometry of rocky terrain', clear elements of myth in everyday existence: 'Zeus, hidden from a murderous father in a cave on Mount Ida, was raised by a goat to be king of gods. And the agrimi (actually introduced to Crete in Minoan times) also gave a glimpse of horny Pan, himself half-goat, god of flocks and shepherds, hunting and rustic music – a divine Craxton patron.'

In 1960 Margot Fonteyn and other VIPs were on board Onassis's yacht *Christina O* where the guest of honour was Winston Churchill.

Collins recounts that Margot Fonteyn ensured that her old friend Craxton was invited to dinner when the yacht put into Souda Bay, where Churchill was to be presented with a Cretan dagger:

> Seated opposite Sir Winston, Craxton feared the guest of honour was 'close to gaga'. Questions of world affairs drew little response, but he perked up on learning that he faced a fellow painter. As a drunken Craxton was near to fixing a painting trip for the next day, he was removed to the far end of the table by jealous politicians eager to get back into the picture. There he quizzed Lady Churchill on the portrait of her husband by Graham Sutherland, which had been commissioned by both houses of Parliament and which she and the sitter were known to hate [...] 'Why not arrange a little accident?' asked Craxton, ever the joker. 'Oh, Mr Craxton! Really!' giggled Lady Churchill. When hearing later that the painting had indeed been destroyed, he was horrified that he might have supplied an incendiary idea – then relieved to learn that the picture was ashes (on Lady Churchill's orders) before that dinner.

In that year Craxton rented an old house, which he later bought, on the Venetian waterfront of Canea. Here was his base for many years, except for the time the Colonels were in power. Craxton died aged 87 in 2009. His ashes were scattered in the harbour he loved so much by his companion Richard Riley.

William Lithgow spent his last days on Crete at a monastery in Canea, the guest of four friars; he left with mixed feelings:

> in regard of their great cheer and deep draughts of malmsey I received hourly, and oftentimes against my will. Every night after supper, the friars forced me to dance with them, either one galliard or another. Their music in the end was sound drunkenness, and

their syncopa turned to spew up all; and their bed converted to a board, or else the hard floor, for these beastly swine were nightly so full, that they had never power to go to their own chambers, but where they fell, there they lay till the morn. For the space of twenty-one days of my being there, I never saw any one truly sober.

From Canea this often complaining but always entertaining traveller took ship through the islands to Constantinople.

7

THE AEGEAN ISLANDS

The stripping by foreigners of Greece's ancient artefacts was in full swing when Charles Robert Cockerell, in the company of two Germans and another Englishman, sailed from Piraeus to the island of Aigina to study and excavate the ruins of the temple of Zeus (now known as the temple of Aphaia) on a highpoint of Aigina's north coast. In *Travels in Southern Europe and the Levant* (1810), Cockerell recorded:

> As we were sailing out of the port in our open boat we overtook the ship with Lord Byron on board. Passing under her stern we sang a favourite song of his, on which he looked out of the windows and invited us in. There we drank a glass of port with him, Colonel Travers, and two of the English officers, and talked of the three English frigates that had attacked five Turkish ones and a sloop of war off Corfu, and had taken and burnt three of them. We did not stay long, but bade them 'bon voyage' and slipped over the side. We slept very well in the boat and next morning reached Aigina.

They had barely settled into their camp, hired workmen and begun measuring and drawing when:

> one of the excavators, working in the interior portico, struck on a piece of Parian marble which, as the building is of stone, arrested his attention. It turned out to be the head of a helmeted warrior, perfect in every feature. It lay with the face turned upwards, and as the features came out by degrees you can imagine nothing like

the state of rapture and excitement to which we were wrought […] Soon another head was turned up, then a leg and a foot, and finally, to make a long story short, we found […] no less than sixteen statues and thirteen heads, legs, arms, etc […] all in the highest preservation, not three feet below the surface of the ground. It seems incredible, considering the number of travellers who have visited the temple, that they should have remained so long undisturbed. It is evident that they were brought down with the pediment on the top of them by an earthquake, and all got broken in the fall.

Despite opposition from the primates of the island, Cockerell and his friends managed to ship the statuary by night to Piraeus, and having rented a large house in Athens set about joining the broken pieces:

Some of the figures are already restored, and have a magnificent effect. Our council of artists here considers them as not inferior to the remains of the Parthenon […] We conduct all our affairs with respect to them in the utmost secrecy, for fear the Turk should either reclaim them or put difficulties in the way of our exporting them. The few friends we have and consult are dying of jealousy.

The jealousy between the foreigners in Athens extended to national level and there was acute rivalry as to which country should become the owners of such magnificent sculptures. As usual the English were slow in parting with money for anything to do with art, and the statues were finally bought by Prince Ludwig of Bavaria. Cockerell made up for this loss to his country by his digging in Arcadia at the temple of Apollo at Bassae. Twenty-three pieces of the frieze he discovered there were sold to the British Museum, where they can be seen today. Cockerell, who had trained as an architect, went on to a distinguished career in England, designing a number of important buildings including the Ashmolean Museum in Oxford.

> Lone from the summit of a lofty isle,
> The columns of a ruined temple lift
> Their shattered fronts, each with its diadem
> Of crumbling architrave and withered weeds.

So wrote the American poet George Hill on seeing the temple of Aphaia on Aigina in 1820. When another American poet and writer, Patricia Storace, visited the temple she was moved to consider the attributes of ancient Greek temples that made them unforgettable. In *Dinner with Persephone* (1996) she wrote:

> Height is important – you must have the sense of revelation height gives to the religious, the sense that you have arrived as a pilgrim at a place where many perspectives meet, where you can come close to seeing everything. Sound is equally important, at every temple site I have visited. A rarefied silence, broken by the powerful secret language of the winds in the pine trees, as there is here, or the grand recitations of the waters, as at the site on Thasos. The gods must always speak at a temple site, in sounds we can hear but not understand, sounds we can only interpret. And finally there must be a sense not only of revelation in the site, but of mystery, of continuation into places you can't see, into unknown worlds. Here the waters of the narrow Saronic Gulf move beyond the mountains of Aigina, between them and the Greek mainland to a destination you can't see; blue water and light stretch to infinity, as soundless boats sail past, backed by immovable cliffs that look like temples themselves, pieces of divine design.

Samuel Gridley Howe, the husband of the author of the *Battle Hymn of the Republic*, took part in the Greek war of independence and found employment for the hungry in building a mole on the island, which is still in use. When Howe's project was finished in 1828, he wrote in his diary, 'I have enriched the island of Aigina by a beautiful, commodious, and permanent quay, and given support to seven hundred poor.'

Henry A. V. Post was a member of the New York Greek Committee supporting the Greeks in the war of independence. While on Hydra in 1827–8 Post was able to compare Greek sailors with those of other nationalities who had come to help Greece fight for freedom. Writing in his *Visit to Greece and Constantinople* (1830), he found that:

> Greek sailors are a much superior class of men to those of either England or America. They are not mere hirelings, who ship for a single voyage, and squander away their earnings, the first opportunity, in low and degrading debaucheries; they are frequently men of families, who have an interest in the vessel in which they sail, and to which they are permanently attached. There are many towns, such as Hydra, Spetzin, Tenos, Mykone, etc., inhabited almost entirely by seafaring men. Though they are a good deal addicted to their light wines and raki, as their common strong beverage is called, they rarely roll into that excessive indulgence which disgraces the seamen of other countries. An English or American sailor is a mere animal; he makes himself such by his vices, and is treated as such by his officers [...] spoken to like a dog, and fed like pig.

Post also preferred the Greek sailors' diet, showing himself to be one of the earliest proponents of the Mediterranean diet: mainly 'bread, cheese and olives, seasoned with an onion, and varied occasionally by a piece of salt fish, or plate of bean porridge'. He compared 'the Greek crew sitting cross-legged round their meagre table' to 'the American mess, crowded into a dirty forecastle, and devouring their more substantial beef and port like swine out of a common trough'. Furthermore:

the American sailor is notorious for his profanity and contempt for things sacred; the Greek is devout or at least reverent in the observance of his religion, such as it is. Every Greek vessel is hallowed by a little picture of the Panagia, or Virgin, and sometimes of some saint, with a lighted lamp suspended before them; and a pot of burning incense is every evening carried round by the cabin boy, who officiates as priest, and smokes in turn every one of the ship's company, who all hold their caps over the purifying vapour, and piously cross themselves, while they pray the Panagia or St Nicholas for a prosperous voyage.

In case any of his readers might be led to think otherwise, Post adds: 'In point of skill and dexterity in the management of a vessel, the Greeks sailors will bear a comparison with any in the world.'

Perched on a rock among pine trees high on a ridge of Mount Dirphis on the island of Skopelos, you are presented on a bright clear day with a breathtaking panorama coloured by the beauty of the present, loaded with omens from the past. Sixty nautical miles to the north-east a grey-blue triangle hovers above the sea – Athos, the Holy Mountain, whose monasteries for 1,000 years have kept safe the art and traditions of Christian Byzantium. Far below, the rocky, forested shores of Skopelos descend to the sunrise over the shoulders of the Sporades, a chain of green-grey islands lifting their heads above the sea. Closer, in the other direction to the west, across the channel lies the island of Skiathos and behind it the mountains of mainland Greece: Mount Pelion, speckled with the white houses of villages on its slopes, too far, however, to see the centaurs, as Matthew Arnold saw them in 'The Strayed Reveller' (1849):

> In the upper glens
> Of Pelion, in the streams,
> Where red-berried ashes fringe

The clear-brown shallow pools;
With streaming flanks, and heads
Rear'd proudly, snuffing
The mountain wind.

And beyond Pelion, northwards up the coast to Mount Ossa, in the furthest distance brooding, its summit masked in cloud, Olympus.

The views from high on the mountainsides of Skopelos, looking north and west, perfectly encompass the scenes of approaching violence and tragedy that played out in the late summer of 480 BCE and changed the course of European history.

As Xerxes marched with the army through the passes of Mount Olympus his fleet sailed south from what is today Thessaloniki. Leonidas waited with his Spartans at Thermopylae; the Greek fleet, equally outnumbered, watched from Artemision, its cape clearly visible from Skopelos.

The Persians sent ten of their fastest ships, almost certainly Phoenician, ahead. They surprised the three Greek triremes patrolling as lookouts in the channel between Skiathos and Skopelos. Herodotus describes what happened: 'The Persians gave chase; the ship from Troezen [...] fell into their hands at once, and her captors, picking out the best-looking of the fighters on board, took him up forward and cut his throat, thinking, no doubt, that the sacrifice of their first handsome Greek prisoner would benefit their cause.'

'The trireme from Aigina', the historian continues, 'gave the Persians some trouble. One of the soldiers on board, Pytheas [...] distinguished himself that day, for after the ship was captured he continued to fight until he was nearly cut to pieces.' When finally he lost consciousness the Persians saw he was still breathing and, 'wishing to do all they could to save the life of so brave a man, they dressed his wounds with myrrh and linen bandages.' Later, they showed him off to the rest of the fleet, 'and treated him with much kindness. The other prisoners from the ship were enslaved.'

The crew of the third trireme, Athenian, rowing for their lives, ran their ship aground north of Pelion and, leaping out, managed to make their way back overland through Thessaly to Athens.

Today's traveller, on board hydrofoil, ferryboat or yacht, will cross the same waters, probably in fine weather. But the Aegean even in summer is not always calm, as the invading Persians soon found. As the great fleet rowed and sailed southwards it was obliged to anchor at night along the steep mainland coast under Olympus, Ossa and Pelion. Here there are no harbours and only short stretches of beach, not nearly enough to accommodate the several thousand war galleys and cargo vessels of this great armada. Herodotus tells us:

> the ships of the first row were moored to the land, while the remainder swung at anchor further off [...] row upon row, eight deep. In this manner they passed the night. But at dawn of day calm and stillness gave place to a raging sea, and a violent storm, which fell upon them with a strong gale from the northeast – a wind which the people of those parts call a Hellesponter.

As the storm increased in violence the crews of those ships moored closest to shore 'forestalled the tempest by dragging their ships up on the beach, and in this way saved both themselves and their vessels. But the ships which the storm caught out at sea were driven ashore.' Herodotus reckons some 400 ships were wrecked along the coast, thousands were drowned and huge quantities of treasure and provisions were lost.

A Greek who farmed land near Cape Sepias (on the mainland opposite Skiathos) did well from the catastrophe. 'Many were the gold and silver drinking cups, cast up long afterwards by the surf, which he gathered [...] and treasure-boxes and gold articles of all kinds and beyond count came into his possession. Ameinocles', says Herodotus, 'grew to be a man of great wealth in this way; but in other respects things did not go too well for him: he too, like other men, had his own grief – the calamity of losing his offspring.' (How the children died is not mentioned, but the comment is typical of Herodotus, whose stories often pointed to the dangers of *hubris*, the fall from prosperity to misfortune as a result of divine envy.)

The storm lasted three days. Finally the magi, the Zoroastrian priests who accompanied the fleet, got to work. Herodotus says that by sacrificing victims and chanting spells against the wind they calmed the gale. 'Or', he could not resist adding, 'perhaps it stopped by itself.'

When news came that Leonidas and his Spartans were dead, the Greek fleet abandoned its station at Artemision and fled south, gathering at the island of Salamis. The Persians followed, and as their ships rounded Cape Sounion the marines on deck and the thousands of rowers toiling at their benches below must have observed with satisfaction smoke rising from the burning Acropolis. Their destination too was Salamis where, they thought, final victory awaited them.

Old Hadoula, sometimes known as Jannis Frankissa, lay beside the hearth, with her eyes closed and her head resting on the step of the fireplace, the cinder-step as it is known. She had not dozed off, she was giving up her sleep at the cradle of her sick grand-daughter. As for the new mother, who had given birth to the sick child, she had been sound asleep for a little while now in her unhappy nest on the floor.

The little hanging lamp guttered under the canopy of the fireplace. It threw shadows instead of light on the few miserable sticks of furniture, which looked cleaner and grander at night than in the daytime. The three half-burnt logs and the big upright balk of timber in the hearth made a lot of ash, a few glowing cinders and a flame that crackled quietly and reminded the old woman through her drowsiness of her absent young daughter Krinio.

So begins *The Murderess* (1903) by Alexandros Papadiamantis, translated from the Greek by Peter Levi.

'What happens', Levi writes in his introduction, 'with the whole weight of what leads to it, is like a wild scream of protest' – against the poverty and backwardness of a Greek island only gradually and painfully being drawn into the modern world; a protest above all against the dowry system which, until very recently, obliged 'the poorest women and the poorest families to scrape together marriage settlements for every girl born'. Set on the island of Skiathos, *The Murderess* tells how the old woman Hadoula becomes obsessed with the misery and despair of poor families burdened with too many daughters, and feels obliged to remedy the situation in her own way. A haunting and tragic story, it is also a thriller, with a chase across the wild hills of the island that ends 'on the neck of sand that links the Hermitage rock with dry land, half-way across, midway between divine and human justice'.

Alexandros Papadiamantis was born on Skiathos in 1851. His father was a priest and the family was not well off. Largely self-taught, he went to school in Chalkis, for a short time in Mount Athos and finally in Athens, where lack of money prevented him from completing his studies. He began to write for newspapers and became well known, especially for his many short stories, most of which were set on Skiathos where he had roamed as a boy and knew every angle of mountain and shore.

Papadiamantis deeply disapproved of the corruption and hypocrisies of modern life. He was ascetic and religious, but wrote about the ordinary people of the island without judging them and always with sympathy. Although considered by many the greatest writer of modern Greek prose, he has been difficult to translate and his work has only recently made its mark on European literature.

He never married and was known as a *kosmokalogeros*, a 'monk in the world'; he shunned publicity, and few people who met the tall man with the bristly black beard and shabby overcoat knew who he was. Overwork, heavy smoking and drinking undermined his health and in 1908 he returned to the island he had always loved; he lived in the house his father had built and which had been his home since he was nine. There, three years later, he died of pneumonia. The house, only a few narrow streets from the harbour front, is now a museum dedicated to the writer. Its simple rooms and furniture powerfully evoke the atmosphere of nineteenth-century island Greece.

> *Sea-sound floods my veins,*
> *Above me the sun*
> *Like a mill-wheel grinds,*
> *The wind beats wide wings;*
> *Unseen the axle throbs;*
> *My deep breath is not heard,*
> *And the sea, as on the sand,*
> *Calms and spreads within me.*
> (Angelos Sikelianos, 'The Return', 1996, translated
> by Edmund Keeley and Philip Sherrard)

Looking south from Skopelos, from the roadside above the southern cliffs of the island, you can see like a shadow on the horizon the blue-grey shape of Skyros, 65 kilometres (40 miles) away.

Skyros has a call upon the English, and on all who speak English, because it is the island where the poet Rupert Brooke died and is buried. In April 1915 he was on a troopship steaming north from Alexandria, headed for the Dardanelles, part of the ill-fated attack on the Turks which ended in the disaster of Gallipoli. He was 27 years old and, like many of his companions on board, had never fired a shot in anger.

Brooke was already famous. He was admired for his personal charm and youthful good looks; his lyrical poems were known and loved by many. As the country braced itself for the coming conflict, his 1914 war sonnets, reflecting the surge of idealism and patriotism throughout the country, were published to popular acclaim. On Easter Sunday 1915, the last of the sonnets, 'The Soldier', was read out by the dean from the pulpit of St Paul's Cathedral.

> If I should die, think only this of me:
> That there's some corner of a foreign field
> That is forever England.

Three weeks later he was dead.

Letters he wrote while on board ship to Gallipoli hinted at a premonition of death and also a sense of resignation, as did this fragment of the last poem he wrote:

> I strayed about the deck, an hour, tonight
> Under a cloudy, moonless sky, and peeped
> In at the windows, watched my friends at table,
> Or playing cards, or standing in the doorway,
> Or coming out into the darkness. Still
> No-one could see me.
>   I would have thought of them
> Heedless, within a week of battle – in pity,
> Pride in their strength and in the weight and firmness
> And link'd beauty of bodies, and pity that
> This gay machine of splendour'ld soon be broken,
> Thought little of, pashed, scattered ...
>   Only, always,
> I could but see them – against the lamplight – pass
> Like coloured shadows, thinner than filmy glass,
> That broke to phosphorus out in the night,
> Perishing things, and strange ghosts – soon to die
> To other ghosts – this one, or that, or I.

'There are moments,' he wrote in his journal, 'there have been several, especially in the Aegean – when through some beauty of sky and air and earth, and some harmony with the mind, peace is complete and completely satisfying. One is at rest from the world, and with it, entirely content [...] Every second seems divine and sufficient.' If only he could 'store up reservoirs of this calm and content, fill and seal great jars or pitchers during these half-hours, and draw on them at later moments, when the source isn't there, but the need is very great'.

Because Mudros Bay in Lemnos was overcrowded, his transport and several other ships were redirected to Tres Boukes Bay in Skyros. During the next few days he went ashore with his fellow officers. Arthur Asquith wrote to his sister describing the abundant wildflowers and the powerful scents of thyme, sage and mint, and how his men who had come ashore in the daytime had shot at adders and played with the tortoises. 'The water near the shore, where the bottom is white marble, is more beautifully green and blue than I have ever seen it anywhere.'

Brooke was not well. We know now that he had contracted septicaemia in Egypt, probably from a mosquito bite. His condition suddenly worsened and on 23 April he was transferred to a French hospital ship, but there was little the doctors could do for him.

His friend and fellow officer Denis Browne was with him:

At 4.46 he died, with the sun shining all round his cabin, with the cool sea-breeze blowing through the door and the shaded windows. No one could have wished a quieter or a calmer end than in that lovely bay, shielded by the mountains and fragrant with sage and thyme [...]

We buried him the same evening in an olive grove where he had sat with us on Tuesday – one of the loveliest places on this earth, with grey-green olives round him, one weeping over his head.

Nigel Jones, in *Rupert Brooke: Life, Death and Myth* (1999) takes up the story:

A party of a dozen burly Australian pallbearers waited on the dark shore [...] As clouds moved across the moon, they inched their way by lamplight up the stony river course towards the olive grove. It took the cortege nearly two hours to negotiate the difficult path in the darkness, with sentries posted every twenty yards to light their way. The procession was led by a stoker with a lantern, followed by Brooke's platoon sergeant, Saunders, holding a large wooden cross that had been made by the men of the platoon for their departed officer. Shaw-Stuart came next, with a group of men bearing rifles to form a firing party, followed by the coffin, which was accompanied by Paris and Quilter.

The grave was dug and ready when the grave-digging party spied the bobbing lights of the cortege approaching up the valley just before 11 p.m. Seeing the size of the coffin, Oc leapt into the grave with a spade and hastily lengthened it. The earth walls were lined with olive branches and sprigs of pungent sage. Chaplain Failes recited the burial service of the Church of England and the coffin was lowered into its resting place.

Those present remembered most the flaring lamps, the clouds scudding across the moon's face, the insistent smell of island herbs. Three volleys were fired over the grave. The shots rolled around the surrounding hills, sending the goats running with a wild jingle of bells.

The men of Brooke's platoon had made a wooden cross which they had carried up with the coffin. On it, the Greek interpreter wrote in pencil an inscription in Greek: 'Here lies the servant of God, Sub-Lieutenant in the English Navy, who died for the deliverance of Constantinople from the Turks.'

The fleet sailed at six that morning. Denis Browne never saw the grave again: he was killed at Gallipoli a few weeks later; few of the officers and men of the burial party survived the war.

News of the poet's death prompted Winston Churchill, then first lord of the Admiralty, to write emotionally in *The Times*: 'Rupert Brooke is dead. A telegram from the Admiral at Lemnos tells us that his life has closed at the moment when it seemed to have reached its springtime.'

In the decades after the war, in anger at the tragic suffering and waste of human life, the idealistic patriotism of Rupert

Brooke was accounted naive and sentimental; literary opinion came down heavily in favour of poets such as Wilfred Owen, Siegfried Sassoon and Robert Graves, who described the futility of war from their own personal experience, stressing its horror and squalid brutality.

Those who at the outbreak of war found it *dulce et decorum* to die for their country might well have felt differently had they struggled through the mud and blood of Flanders. Rupert Brooke did not live to fight in the trenches and it will never be known how his poetry might have developed if he had. Yet Brooke was a poet of his time: his war sonnets captured perfectly the mood and convictions of millions of English men and women in 1914, including, it should be added, the poets who later wrote of the war from a very different point of view. Some of his poems, such as 'The Soldier' and 'Grantchester', which have already stood the test of a century, will always remain among the treasures of English poetry.

In the early 1960s I was on a sailing boat in the Aegean and with a friend visited Skyros to see the poet's grave, important to me as his poems, first read as a ten-year-old, had inspired me to follow him to the same college at Cambridge. In those days there was no road to the grave, and none but the vaguest of directions were to be had from the little town. Barren and uninhabited hills, broken by rocky inlets scattered with olive trees, surrounded Tres Boukes; when *Astarte* dropped anchor the bay was empty and there was not a soul to be seen.

We spent two days in the search, clambering up and down the stony slopes, cutting our shoes to pieces, and stumbling over the many tortoises that thrive in this deserted corner of the island. We were lucky not to meet any adders, but the tortoises were there and the water still brilliantly clear. But which was Brooke's valley?

After two attempts we gambled on one that seemed the most likely. Leaving *Astarte* at anchor in the cove and the dinghy drawn up on the beach in the company of our new tortoise friends, we started up the stony track. We soon understood why it had taken the burial party so long to negotiate, at night, that narrow, rocky streambed. As I recounted the story in *Gates of the Wind* (1965, republished as *An Island in Greece,* 2007):

> Nearly a mile from the sea, where the sides of the ravine closed in and the light was a pale green filtered through olive leaves, we found it: an incongruously Victorian marble tomb, wrought iron trespass rails round the Pentelic slab. A fine olive tree grew at the head of the grave, spreading its branches over the marble. It is unusual in rough country like this to hear birds, but in this olive grove the air was full of them; in Greece I had never heard so many sing together. We rested a long time by the grave, listening to the birds, and cicadas, and the distant jangle of a goat-bell. It was afternoon and the sky had become suddenly overcast. Experimental gusts of warm, sage-scented wind sighed down the valley, shaking down black olives over the tomb.

That night, as we lay anchored off a beach at the entrance to Brooke's valley, an exceptionally dramatic storm burst on the island. We should have moved to a more protected cove but stayed where we were,

> partly paralyzed by the sight and sound of this prolonged and apparently cosmic detonation. It lasted all night, and it was impossible to sleep. We smoked, shivered and drank coffee; deafened with thunder, we kept our faces pressed to the closed portholes. Gusts of wind tore across the sea, buffeting *Astarte* and heeling her over with the violence of their impact, as blue lightning slashed down at the mountains around. We had the doubtful privilege of observing, less than a hundred yards away on the beach, a stunted tree struck by lightning burn and smoke in the rain. *Astarte*'s mast, thirty-five feet above the water, was twice as high as that poor trunk of scorched wood.

On 23 April 2015, the centenary of the poet's death and burial, I stood at the grave again. This time among the olive trees gold braid glittered on the cuffs of naval officers of Greece, the USA and Great Britain, and with them around the grave stood the British ambassador, the mayor of Skyros, Greek regional representatives, and the Anglican canon of all Greece, assisted by a few bemused tourists.

After speeches, and a recital of 'The Soldier', Greek soldiers presented arms and a bugler sounded the Last Post; the cast of this brief theatre dispersed as swiftly as it had gathered, in military trucks and a cavalcade of motor vehicles by the road that now links the north of the island with this distant and lonely spot.

As the sound of the last car died away and the place reverted to its usual peace and silence I thought it extraordinary that I had first been here 47 years after Brooke's death, and again 53 years later. Those 100 years seemed suddenly comprehensible: a century was not so long, after all. What had changed? Not the surroundings. These were the same olive trees that had overseen the grave-diggers toiling by lamplight on that spring night 100 years ago. Only the tomb, now maintained by the British War Graves Commission, had changed, its railings bright with paint. The interpreter's inscription in Greek, first written in pencil on a wooden cross, is now carved in marble round the base of the tomb.

The Greeks have never forgotten Lord Byron who died at Missolonghi in the cause of Greek freedom, and now there was Rupert Brooke, his statue in bronze standing in Skyros town. Both these English poets who lost their lives in Greece retain a symbolic value separate from the qualities of their poetry. The river Cam was far away, but as the American author and critic Paul Delany wrote, 'Now another Cambridge poet, who had loved to swim in Byron's Pool, had shared Byron's fate.'

Two days before his own death in action at Gallipoli, Denis Browne wrote: 'Coming from Alexandria yesterday, we passed Rupert's island at sunset. The sea and sky in the East were grey and misty; but it stood out in the west, black and immense, with a crimson glowing halo around it. Every colour had come into the sea and sky to do him honour.'

A few hours' sail south from Skyros are the Cyclades. When one thinks of Greek islands it is usually the Cyclades that swim into one's mind – that scattering of magnificent, half-barren mountains, their heads raised above blue sea. Together with every educated person in nineteenth-century Britain, the Romantic poets were steeped in ancient Greek culture and history. Though neither Shelley nor Keats ever visited Greece they felt as if they knew it well. Shelley wrote of its 'nodding promontories, and blue isles, / And cloud-like mountains', and when Keats first read Chapman's translation of Homer his sense of revelation was so intense that he felt like the Spaniard Cortez who, 'silent, on a peak in Darien', caught his first sight of the Pacific Ocean. I like to think that if Keats had not died so young he would have followed the desire expressed in his 'Sonnet to Homer' and crossed the sea from Italy to the country that meant so much to him.

> Standing aloof in giant ignorance
> Of thee I hear and of the Cyclades,
> As one who sits ashore and longs perchance
> To visit dolphin-coral in deep seas.

Lord Byron's hero Juan, wrecked in the Cyclades, makes it ashore on an island where he is cared for by the beautiful Haidee and her maid who hide him in a cave by the beach:

> They look upon each other, and their eyes
>   Gleam in the moonlight; and her white arm clasps
> Round Juan's head, and his around her lies
>   Half buried in the tresses which it grasps;

> She sits upon his knee, and drinks his sighs,
>> He hers, until they end in broken gasps;
> And thus they form a group that's quite unique,
>> Half naked, loving, natural and Greek.

Robert Byron, his distant relative, writing in the 1920s succumbed like many before him and many after to the magic of Greek seas. In *The Byzantine Achievement* (first published 1929) he wrote:

> Sail from Italy or Egypt. And as the rose-tinted shores of islands and promontories rise incarnate from the sea, a door shuts the world behind [...]
>
> What magnet of our stifled love holds this blue, these tawny cliffs and always the mountains framing the distance? Why does the breeze blow with the scent of baking herbs which the misty shores echo in their colours? What is this element, hybrid of air and water, physical as a kiss, with which the night enfolds us? The islands float past, forming and reforming in good-bye, gleaming golden white against the sharp blues, or veiled in the odorous haze of evening.

The following lines by Odysseus Elytis (translated by Edmund Keeley and George Savidis) perfectly catch the glitter of sunlight on an Aegean swept by summer wind. The poem is part of 'Axion Esti' ('It is Worthy') which, when set to music by Theodorakis, became a passionate call to Greeks fighting repression. Elytis, together with his much older friend George Seferis, are the two poets of modern Greece whose poems sung to music by Theodorakis have become patriotic hymns to freedom:

> The islands with all their minium and lampblack
> The islands like the verterbrae of some Zeus
> The islands with their boatyards so deserted
> The islands with their drinkable blue volcanoes

Facing the meltemi with jib close-hauled
Riding the southwester on a reach
The full length of them covered in foam
With dark blue pebbles and heliotropes

Sifnos, Amorgos, Alonnisos
Thasos, Ithaca, Santorini
Kos, Ios, Sikinos

Since 1873 the French School of Archaeology has been excavating on Delos, the little island in the centre of the Cyclades, sacred to Apollo. Despite their efforts it is still difficult to imagine the immense wealth concentrated in this restricted space. For centuries a focus of religious and political power, Delos was famous for its magnificent temples of Apollo, Artemis and numerous foreign gods, a bursting population of merchants, with docks and warehouses, and markets selling everything from silk to slaves.

As power shifted through the centuries, a number of catastrophes befell the island. Pausanias tells us of one. In 88 BCE Mithridates, king of Pontus, sent his admiral Menophanes to attack the island. Delos, birthplace of Apollo, was unfortified and the people were without weapons since 'it was believed that the presence of the god made it safe to do business there.' In the massacre that followed, foreigners and islanders were slaughtered together. Menophanes 'looted an enormous wealth from the merchants, and the entire mass of consecrated treasures, he sold the women and children into slavery and demolished Delos to its foundations.'

Pausanias adds with satisfaction that this outrageous sacrilege did not go unpunished. Menophanes was ambushed at sea and went down with his ship, while Mithridates finally lost his empire to the Romans: 'the god forced him to take his own life, though some say that he begged his own murder as a favour from one of his mercenaries.'

Marble, much of it from Naxos, had been brought to Delos to build its monuments and carve its statues; later it was broken up and carted away for use elsewhere. Travellers to the island in the seventeenth century had noted the continuous looting and destruction of the island's antiquities. Travelling with his friend George Wheler in 1756, Jacob Spon (*Voyage d'Italie, de Dalmatie, de Grece et du Levant*, 1678) described the 10-foot statue of Apollo which he found 'lying on the ground and reduced to little more than a shapeless trunk – the inevitable consequence of his great age and the maltreatment he has suffered from the various people who have landed on Delos. Some took foot, others a hand, showing him none of the respect and reverence that had been shown him in ancient times.' The Venetian governor of Tinos, Spon added, had recently sawn off part of the god's face 'since the whole head was too heavy to take away by boat'.

Spon and Wheler were stormbound on the island, a fairly common fate of travellers in that age of sail. Today popular and tourist-rich Mykonos, only a few miles across the sea, is the gateway to Delos; in summer the two islands stand in arresting contrast, one crowded and vibrating with modern life, the other deserted, the silent relics of the distant past scattered over its barren slopes.

In the 1960s *Astarte* sailed into the Sacred Harbour, dropped a stern anchor and nosed in among the caiques and motorboats crowded at the old quay. The hundreds of visitors shipped over from Mykonos, led by their guides, were scrambling over the ruins; in the afternoon they began to return to the quay and by sunset the last caique had gone, the sound of its engine failing in the still evening air. *Astarte* was the only boat left: we were alone on the island. That night a full moon rose over the ruins. Unforgettable, the ghostly streets climbing between broken houses; a magical silence; deep shadows of the ancient stone lions crouching by the Sacred Lake; and on a block of shining marble, a large scorpion, motionless in the moonlight, tail raised in fear and warning.

The island of Paros is famous for its marble. It is also the birthplace of my favourite poet of ancient Greece, Archilochus, who lived between 680 and 645 BCE. Said to have been the son of a Parian aristocrat and a slave woman, he was a combination, rare at that time, of poet and soldier; his short life probably ended in battle. Some of his verses are translated in Richmond Lattimore's *Greek Lyrics* (1960): 'I am two things: a fighter who follows the Master of Battles, and one who understands the gift of the Muses' love.' He was not ashamed to admit that he lived by being a soldier: 'By spear is kneaded the bread I eat, by spear my Ismaric wine is won, which I drink, leaning upon my spear.'

One gets the impression that he knew what he was talking about, when it came to fighting:

> I don't like the captain with the spraddly length of leg,
> One who swaggers in his lovelocks and cleanshaves beneath the
>   chin.
> Give me a man short and squarely set upon his legs, a man
> Full of heart, not to be shaken from the place he plants his feet.

Archilochus was also unconventional. At a time when to abandon your shield in battle was considered the ultimate disgrace, and when Spartan mothers said goodbye to their sons going to war with 'Come back – with your shield, or on it!' his approach was refreshing:

> Some barbarian is waving my shield, since I was obliged
>   to leave that perfectly good piece of equipment behind
> under a bush. But I got away, so what does it matter?
> Let the shield go; I can buy another one equally good.

No wonder Sparta banned his poetry, which was considered subversive and bad for the young, an opinion shared by the poet Pindar. Most Greek and Roman writers, however, greatly admired Archilochus and rated him with Homer and Hesiod.

By all accounts Archilochus was a difficult man. He was the first of the Greek poets to write personally about his feelings, and perhaps the earliest recorded stereotype of the Greek who loves and hates with equal intensity – most loyal of friends but worst of enemies: 'One main thing I understand – to come back with deadly evil at the man who does me wrong.' One feels that the concept of forgiveness was just not in his mind's vocabulary. 'My lord Apollo, single out the guilty ones; Destroy them, O destroyer god!'

Here a former friend has been shipwrecked and captured by Thracians. Archilochus has little sympathy for him, in fact delights in his misery:

> slammed by the surf on the beach
> naked at Salmydessos, where the screw-haired men
> of Thrace, taking him in
> will entertain him (he will have much to undergo,
> chewing on slavery's bread)
> stiffened with cold, and loops of seaweed from the slime
> tangling his body about,
> teeth chattering as he lies in abject helplessness
> flat on his face like a dog
> beside the beach-break where the waves come shattering in.
> And let me be there to watch;
> for he did me wrong and set his heel on our good faith,
> he who had once been my friend.

Archilochus fought in the colonisation of the island of Thasos. He clearly did not think much of this deeply forested island, where he was unsuccessful in love:

> Here the island stands
> stiff with wild timber like a donkey's bristling back.
> This is no place of beauty, not desirable
> nor lovely like the plains where the River Siris runs.

While on Thasos he is said to have reacted violently when his suit of a Thracian princess, Neoboule, was rejected.

> Here I lie mournful with desire,
> feeble in bitterness of the pain gods inflicted on me,
> stuck through the bones with love.

> Luxurious in a spray of myrtle, she wore too
> The glory of the rose upon her, and her hair
> Was all a darkness on her shoulder and her back.

> If it only were my fortune just to touch Neoboule's hand.

> Such is the passion of love that has twisted its way beneath my
>   heartstrings
> And closed deep mist across my eyes
> Stealing the soft heart from inside my body.

Like many of the poets of those distant times, his work comes down to us mainly in fragments: 'Glaucus, look! The open sea is churning to a wash of waves deep within. A cloud stands upright over the Gyrean cape, signal of a storm, and terror rises from the unforeseen.'

On drowned bodies:

> Hide we away these painful gifts of the lord Poseidon.
> Say goodbye to Paros, and the figs, and the seafaring life.

And here is one of his epigrams:

> The fox knows many tricks, the hedgehog only one.
> One good one.

The islands of the eastern Aegean – Lesbos, Samos, Chios, Rhodes, and also little Patmos, scene of St John's revelations ('I, John, both your brother and companion in tribulation [...] was on the island that is called Patmos for the word of God and for the testimony of Jesus Christ') – have produced more than their fair share of poetry of lasting quality, and their poets still speak to us from the long-distant past. In *Don Juan*, Byron wrote:

> The Isles of Greece! The isles of Greece,
> Where burning Sappho loved and sung.

Sappho, born towards the end of the seventh century BCE, came from a privileged aristocratic family on the island of Lesbos. Her family was involved in the island's political conflicts and for a time she was exiled to Sicily, where Cicero later saw a statue of her in Syracuse. In the ancient world she was greatly admired for her poetry and songs, many of which were written for accompaniment on the lyre. Strabo in his *Geography* says that in all history there was no woman who could seriously rival her as a poet, while to Plato there were not just nine muses but ten, Sappho being the tenth.

She was one of the first poets to write in the first person, describing frankly her own feelings of love and loss. Best known for her erotic poetry, she wrote of love for women and men, at a time when homosexual love, whether male or female, did not strike anyone as unusual or noteworthy. Only in the last 150 years have 'sapphic' and 'lesbian' acquired their present meanings; the poet would have been surprised and I think disappointed that it was this aspect of her poetry that had made her and her island famous.

We know little about Sappho's life except that she had two brothers and was married to a wealthy trader. This fragment, translated by Willis Barnstone, is evidence that she had a daughter:

> I have a small daughter who
> Is beautiful like a gold flower.

> I would not trade my darling Kleis
> For all Lydia or even for
> The beautiful island Lesbos.

Despite her popularity only one complete poem has come down to us; the rest are in fragments. This is partly due to luck and the inevitable losses suffered by all classical authors from the destruction of libraries and the devastation caused by barbarian invasion. In the case of Sappho it is also likely that as Christianity intensified its grip across Europe her erotic and 'lesbian' poetry met with increasing intolerance. Joseph Addison in the *Spectator* of 15 November 1711 wrote that her poems were 'filled with such tenderness and rapture, that it might have been dangerous to give them a reading'. Indeed, in 1073, in both Rome and Constantinople, her poems were publicly burned.

Sexual passion had never been expressed so openly:

> Like a windstorm
> Punishing the oaktrees,
> Love shakes my heart.

Or:

> For Brocheo
> When I look at you my voice fails,
> My tongue is broken and thin fire
> Runs like a thief through my body.
> My eyes are dead to light, my ears
> Pound, and sweat pours down over me.
> I shudder, I am paler than grass.

In Sappho's life of privileged leisure the discussion of poetry and music were important, and it is said that she taught or mentored a number of young women, daughters of the island's aristocracy, among whom were Anaktoria and Atthis; this is a poem she dedicated to the latter, who had just left to get married, translated by W. Barnstone:

So I shall never see Atthis again,
And really I long to be dead,
Although she too cried bitterly

When she left, and she said to me,
'Ah, what a nightmare we've suffered,
Sappho I swear I go unwillingly.'

And I answered, 'Go, and be happy.
But remember me, for surely you
Know how I worshipped you. If not
Then I want you to remember all
The exquisite ways we two shared;
How when near me you would adorn

Your hanging locks with violets and
Tiny roses and your sapling throat
With necklets of a hundred blossoms;

How your young flesh was rich with kingly
Myrrh as you leaned near my breasts on
The soft couch where delicate girls

Served us all an Ionian could desire;
How we went to every hill, brook,
And holy place, and when early spring

Filled the woods with noises of birds
And a choir of nightingales – we two
In solitude were wandering there.

And here is part of a poem to Anaktoria, now a soldier's wife in Lydia, (my translation):

> Some say a troop of cavalry,
> others infantry on the march or a fleet of ships under sail
> are the finest sights in this dark world.
> I say it is the girl you love the most.
>
> And I would prefer to hear your soft step
> And be warmed by your radiant smile
> Than witness all the racing chariots of Lydia ...

There are more than 200 fragments of Sappho's poems surviving, many on scraps of papyrus found in ancient Egyptian rubbish pits, and they are still being discovered, some in the last few years, even on material used to wrap mummies. Here are some of my favourites, translated by Willis Barnstone in *Greek Lyric Poetry* (1962):

> The moon has gone down
> The Pleiades have set.
> Night is half gone,
> And life speeds by.
> I lie in bed, alone.
>
> In gold sandals
> Dawn like a thief
> Fell upon me.
>
> Mother darling, I cannot work the loom
> For the Cyprian has almost crushed me,
> Broken me with love for a slender boy.

(Aphrodite, goddess of love, was often known as the Cyprian as it is said she was born from the foam on the beach at Paphos, Cyprus

– alternatively on the island of Cythera.) I like this sad epitaph for a young man lost at sea:

> Pelagon the fisherman. His father
> Meniskos placed here a fishbasket
> And oar: relics of a miserable life.

Sappho died in 570 BCE, though it is not known for sure how or where. According to an early myth, she fell in love with a ferryman, Phaedon, and when rejected by him threw herself off Cape Leucatas (see Chapter 1). Most scholars believe she died on Lesbos, and in support of this we have part of a poem to her daughter written when she was dying: 'It is not right for mourning to enter a house of poetry.' The story of the suicide jump may have been invented some centuries later to emphasise her heterosexuality.

Mytilene, the main city of Lesbos, was the home of the poet and aristocrat Alcaeus, a contemporary of Sappho. According to Richmond Lattimore, translator of many Greek poets, Alcaeus lived a stormy youth, first fighting tyranny and then resisting social change. Brave and opinionated, he wrote much political poetry but the poems that have come down to us 'showed no constructive political sense whatsoever'. And yet as a craftsman in verse he rivals Sappho. In this translation from Lattimore's *Greek Lyrics* he speaks politics in the language of the sea – both familiar to every Greek of his time and for centuries after.

> I cannot understand how the winds are set
> against each other. Now from this side and now
> from that the waves roll. We between them
> run with the wind in our black ship driven,
>
> hard pressed and laboring under the giant storm.
> All round the mast-step washes the sea we shipped.

> You can see through the sail already
>> where there are opening rents within it.
>
> The forestays slacken

Alcaeus also wrote:

> Hebros, loveliest of rivers, you issue
> Hard by Ainos into the dark blue waters
> Of the sea where, passing by Thrace you end your turbulent
>   passage;
> There, where young girls come in their crowds and, bathing
> With light hands their ravishing thighs, enjoy you
> as if some magical salve were in your
> wonderful waters.

And surely we recognise the season conjured by the poet as he invites us to drink wine:

> for the dog star, wheeling up the sky,
> brings back summer, the time all things are parched under the
>   searing heat.
> Now the cicada's cry, sweet in the leaves, shrills from beneath his
>   wings.
> Now the artichoke flowers, women are lush, ask too much of their
>   men,
> who grow lank, for the star burning above withers their brains
>   and knees.

The island of Lesbos is also said to be where the poet Arion was born, in about 660 BCE. Praised for perfecting the Dionysiac dithyramb and for inventing the seven-string lyre or *kithairon*, he is chiefly remembered for his miraculous escape from pirates on the back of a dolphin. The story goes that Arion was returning on a ship from Sicily rich with prizes he had won in poetry competitions when the crew decided to kill him and steal what he had. He asked permission to sing for the last time and, taking up his lyre, sang a hymn to Apollo, the god of poetry. The music attracted a school of dolphins which began to accompany the ship. When Arion finished his song he threw himself into the sea. As he sank a dolphin came up under him and let him cling to its back, finally setting him ashore at Cape Matapan, the southernmost point of the Peloponnese.

Arion is the first to signal the warm relationship humans claim to have with dolphins. The poet Pindar wrote, 'I am like a sea-dolphin, whom the lovely melody of flutes moves on the surface of the waveless sea.'

Samos, within sight of Lesbos, is the island where Anakreon lived, having been born on Teos (in about 575 BCE). He was a refugee from the Asian coast, having fled from there when the Persians invaded. On Samos he was an honoured guest of the island's ruler (tyrant) Polycrates, and when Polycrates died, Anakreon was summoned to Athens by Hipparchos. Good poets were greatly respected, always in demand and well looked after. Things were done differently in those days. Peter Levi in *History of Greek Literature* translates some of his lines: 'Gold-haired Eros hits me with a purple ball, provoking me to play with a pretty-sandal girl; but she comes from well-built Lesbos, doesn't like my hair for being white, gapes at an another girl.'

And:

> O boy with the girlish look,
> I follow you, you don't listen,
> And you do not know you hold
> The horses of my soul.

Peter Levi calls the Greek cities of the Ionian coast the seed-bed of European intellectual life. Samos, within sight of this coast, has the honour of being the birthplace of Pythagoras, though he lived much of his life in southern Italy and died there.

Among the philosophers who flourished in this part of the Aegean were Anaximander and Thales in Miletus, who inspired our thinking about physics and astronomy. Xenophanes of Kolophon strikes a few modern chords by ridiculing the common human conception of making god in his own image: 'Ethiopians have black, snub-nosed gods, and Thracians have blue-eyed, red-haired gods.' If cattle, or wild animals could draw and write, they would make their gods just like themselves. Xenophanes blamed Homer and Hesiod for making the Olympian gods all too human – lecherous, vengeful, cheats. There was only one god, he believed, and in mind and body this god was totally unlike mankind: all-seeing, all-thinking, all-hearing, he controlled everything with his mind.

A contemporary of Xenophanes was the philosopher and writer Heraclitus, who lived in Ephesus, another rich and flourishing Ionian city on the coast of Asia Minor looking out onto the Aegean Sea. It was Heraclitus who pointed out that we could never step into the same river twice. Everything runs, he said, everything flows. Only short pieces of his powerful and original writings have survived. He believed that fire in its many forms was the basic element of life. And he was a realist: 'War is common to all things, and justice is strife, and everything exists as a consequence of strife and necessity.' It was war that decided who were to be slaves, or who free – sadly, a belief as valid today as it was 3,000 years ago.

Lines written about Heraclitus by Callimachus of Alexandria have been translated into a much-loved poem by William Johnson Cory:

> They told me, Heraclitus, they told me you were dead,
> They brought me bitter news to hear and bitter tears to shed.
> I wept as I remembered how often you and I
> Had tired the sun with talking and sent him down the sky.

And now that thou art lying, my dear old Carian guest,
A handful of grey ashes long, long ago at rest
Still are thy pleasant voices, thy nightingales, awake,
For Death he taketh all away, but them he cannot take.

William Johnson was a master at Eton, a brilliant scholar and teacher, highly thought of by colleagues and boys alike. He remained in close and affectionate contact with many of his pupils after they had left school, several of whom became distinguished statesmen, including three prime ministers. But in 1872 'an indiscreet letter' he had written to a boy was intercepted by the parents and sent to the headmaster: he was forced to resign. The *Dictionary of National Biography* admits that 'No one can be quite sure of the exact circumstances of his resignation [...] There is no question, however, that he was dangerously fond of a number of boys. Although he probably did not allow his affections to take any physical form, he permitted intimacies between the boys.'

The American scholar William Lubenow, author of *The Cambridge Apostles* (1999), believes Johnson was fired because he was against the school's extreme authoritarianism: he committed the crime of Socrates, corrupting youth 'by creating a world of multiple loyalties'. In any case Johnson was deeply scarred by the event: he changed his surname to Cory and emigrated to Madeira, where he married and had a son. He later returned to England, dying there in 1892 aged 69.

The state of lawlessness in the Aegean in the centuries before 1800 is why so many island villages are still found perched high up on hilltops. William Lithgow certainly knew about the dangers of pirates. Not long after leaving Mykonos on his way across the Aegean to Constantinople he once more only just escaped capture:

In general of these Isles Cyclades, because they are so near one to the other, there are many Corsairs and Turkish galleots, that still afflict these islanders: Insomuch that the inhabitants are constrained to keep watch day and night, upon the tops of the most commodious mountains, to discover these pirates; which they easily discern from others, both because of their sails and oars. And whensoever discovered, according to the number of cursary boats, they make as many fires, which giveth warning to all the ports to be on guard.

On his way to Chios Lithgow had again almost drowned, struck by:

a deadly storm, which split our mast, carrying sails and all overboard [...] The sorrowful Master, seeing nothing but shipwreck, took the helm in hand, directing his course to rush upon the face of a low rock, whereupon the sea most fearfully broke. As we touched, the mariners contending who should first leap out, some fell over-board, and those who got to land were pulled back by the reciprocating waves.

Lithgow was warned by the crew not to try to escape before the others, and if he did they would throw him 'headlong into the sea. So being two ways in danger of death, I patiently offered up my prayers to God.'

'At our first encounter with the rocks, (our fore-decks, and boats gallery being broke, and a great lake made) the recoiling waves brought us back from the shelves a great way.' With seven drowned, the 11 left alive tried to row ashore, Lithgow being the last man into the boat, which then sank. Lithgow was only saved from drowning by clinging onto his 'coffino', which seems to have been a large box made of reed or cane in which he kept his 'papers and linen', and which, above all, floated.

The survivors sheltered in a cave until 'the fourth day at morn, the tempest ceasing, there came fisher-boats to relieve us, who found the ten Greeks almost famished for lack of food, but I in that hunger-starving fear, fed upon the expectation of my doubtful relief.'

Chios, where Lithgow finally arrived safely, was relatively prosperous in the seventeenth century compared with the rest of Greece, thanks mainly to its production of mastic, a precious commodity valued throughout the Ottoman Empire as well as in Europe, and partly because of the special privileges it had obtained from the Turks. At the same time, many visitors attested to the beauty of the island's women, prompting the thought that the wealthier the society the more free and independent are its women (think also of Sappho's time).

Lithgow is one who maintained that 'the women of the citty of Scio are the most beautiful dames (or rather angelical creatures) of all the Greekes, upon the face of the earth, and greatly given to Venery.' Surely he was writing from personal experience:

> They are the most part exceeding proud, and sumptuous in apparel, and commonly go (even artificers wives) in gownes of satin and taffety; yea, in cloth of silver and gold, and are adorned with precious stones, and gemmes, and jewels about their necks, and hands, with rings, chaines, & bracelets. Their husbands are their pandoors, and when they see any stranger arrive, they presently demand of him if he would have a mistress: and so they make whoores of their owne wives, and are contented with a little gaine, to weare hornes: such are the base minds of ignominious cuckolds. If a straunger be desirous to stay all night with any of them, their price is a chicken [sequin] of gold, nine shillings English, out of which this companion receiveth his supper, and for his paines, a bellyfull of sinfull content.

Lithgow had done his research well.

Lithgow was nearing the end of his journeys in Greece. He reached Jerusalem on Palm Sunday 1612 and continued to Egypt. Though he returned to Scotland it was never for long; the call of the unknown was too strong. Travels in North Africa followed, and in 1619–21 a journey to Spain, where he was imprisoned as a spy and tortured. He had some success as a writer and fame as a traveller. He is believed to have died where he was born, in Lanark, in about 1645.

In 1822 Chios was drawn unwillingly into rebellion against the Turks and in revenge many thousands of the island's population were slaughtered. Eugène Delacroix's dramatic painting *The Massacre at Chios* drew the attention of Europeans to the plight of the Greeks. In 1826 he painted *Greece on the Ruins of Missolonghi*, which showed the Greek survivors of the Turkish siege about to kill themselves rather than surrender. The subject was of particular interest to Delacroix, who was an ardent follower of Lord Byron, who had died there two years earlier.

William Thackeray visited Rhodes on his journey across the Aegean in 1844 when it was still under Turkish rule; he recorded his experiences in *Notes of a Journey from Cornhill to Grand Cairo* (1846):

Some of the huge artillery with which the place was defended still lies in the bastions; and the touch-holes of the guns are preserved by being covered with rusty old corselets, worn by defenders of the fort three hundred years ago. The Turks, who battered down chivalry, seem to be waiting their turn of destruction now. In walking through Rhodes one is strangely affected by witnessing the signs of this double decay. For instance, in the streets of the knights, you see noble houses, surmounted by noble escutcheons of superb knights, who lived there, and prayed, and quarrelled, and murdered the Turks; and were the most gallant pirates of the inland seas; and made vows of chastity, and robbed and ravished; and, professing humility, would admit none but nobility into their order; and died recommending themselves to sweet St. John, and calmly hoping for heaven in consideration of all the heathen they had slain. When this superb fraternity was obliged to yield to courage as great as theirs, faith as sincere, and to robbers more dexterous and audacious than the noblest knight that ever sang a canticle to the Virgin, these halls were filled by magnificent *Pashas* and *Agas*, who lived here in the intervals of war, and having conquered its best champions, despised Christendom and chivalry [...] Now the famous house is let to a shabby merchant, who has his little beggarly shop in the bazaar; to a small officer, who ekes out his wretched pension by swindling, and who gets his pay in bad coin.

Thackeray added:

In the Crusades my sympathies have always been with the Turks. They seem to be the best Christians of the two; more humane, less brutally presumptuous about their own merits, and more generous in esteeming their neighbours... Saladin is a pearl of refinement compared to the brutal beef-eating Richard – about whom Sir Walter Scott has led all the world astray.

Alphonse de Lamartine, continuing his voyage eastwards to Jerusalem, noted for 27 August 1833 in his *Travels in the East* (1850):

We set sail from Rhodes to Cyprus on a splendid afternoon. I have my eyes turned upon Rhodes, which sinks at last into the sea. I regret this beautiful island as an apparition one wishes to recall; I could have settled there, if it were less separated from the moving world in which destiny and duty compel us to live! What delicious retreats on the sides of the high mountains, and on the declivities, shaded by all the trees of Asia. I was shown a magnificent house, belonging to the former pacha, surrounded by three extensive and abundant gardens, bathed by numerous fountains, and adorned with ravishing kiosks. They asked 16,000 piastres for the purchase, that is to say 4000 francs (£150) – happiness at a cheap rate!

Lawrence Durrell was appointed press officer for the Dodecanese Islands in 1945, just before the British handed them over to Greece.

He lived in Rhodes at his beloved Villa Cleobulus, where he entertained visiting friends, including Patrick Leigh Fermor, Xan Fielding and John Craxton.

In *Reflections on a Marine Venus* (1953), pondering the epic sieges that Rhodes has sustained in the past 600 years, Durrell is standing on the section of the city's walls which the knights of England were responsible for defending:

> medieval walls – so broad that six horsemen could gallop abreast upon them [...] We can overlook the whole town from here, as well as the shrill private lives of a dozen families who live directly under the towering walls, in gardens picked out with palms and bushes of red hibiscus. A windmill turns, creaking, and from the invisible market-place rises the surf of human bartering – the vibration of business. On the wall itself two armies are fighting with wooden swords – a dozen children in paper hats against half a dozen bareheaded ones. They are not Knights and Saracens, as one might think, but British and Germans. The battle sways backwards and forwards. Nobody dies or is hurt, though one of the shock-troops has started crying. Their shouts marry the thin keening of the swifts by the walls, darting against the blue. High up against the sun an eagle planes above us, watching history plagiarising itself once more upon these sun-mellowed walls.

It seems appropriate in this chapter on the islands, and to end this book, to think of one of the great delights of Greece: its fleets of small fishing boats, caiques, moored at the quay of every harbour, their hulls bright with colours thrown as if randomly from a collection of tins of paint left over from more important work, thick timbers daubed not only the 'mid-sea blue or shore-sea green' of James Elroy Flecker's poem 'The Old Ships' but in crimson and in yellow ochre, astonishing combinations which to a northern eye are at first outrageous and yet within minutes cast a spell of acceptance.

Soon, the graceful low curves of the boats themselves, their lines well tested by centuries of wind and wave, spilling their reflections in the water, are seen to be in perfect harmony with the glittering seas and sunlight of the Aegean.

The old wooden passenger and cargo caiques have long gone from Greek waters, replaced by steel ferryboats and hydrofoils, so much faster and more fitting to modern times when passengers are always in a hurry. Those who remember the past try to control an irrational nostalgia for those big, slow, diesel-chugging ships, decks piled with sacks of flour, chickens, brightly shawled, long-skirted women planted amid heaps of baggage, anxiously adjusting their long skirts as they contemplate the first waves of nausea, many of them already seasick as soon as they step onto the crowded, pine-planked deck.

How superior is today's smooth and rapid transit across seas that barely remember the ships that sailed these waters in the past: Jason's *Argo*, and the oared vessels that carried the Hellenes to the walls of Troy; those long warships with three banks of oars, the triremes with their deadly rams; the slow-sailing, round-bellied merchant ships; the galleys and galleons of more recent times; the trading caiques, now rarely seen, their masts and yardarms no longer shrouded with sail but bare, used only to support an awning.

James Elroy Flecker, poet and playwright, who wrote 'The Old Ships' in 1914, was a friend of Rupert Brooke at Cambridge, and died, aged 30, a few months before Brooke. Only half jokingly, he called himself 'the dark and swarthy poet of despair'. Sick from tuberculosis from an early age, he struggled with the disease that finally killed him, in Davos, Switzerland in January 1915, his death judged by one critic as 'the greatest premature loss that English literature has suffered since the death of Keats'. Flecker worked in the British Consular Service mainly in the Lebanon, but he loved Greece and married a Greek, honeymooning in Corfu in 1911. He carries the unusual distinction for a poet of being admired by soldiers, his poetry called upon to express the aspirations of those elite warriors of modern times, the Special Air Service (SAS). Over the regiment's barracks in England's Hereford, a quotation shared with the NZSAS in New Zealand, are inscribed lines from his play *Hassan* (1922), the words of the pilgrims setting out on the Golden Journey to Samarkand:

> ... we shall go
> Always a little further; it may be
> Beyond that last blue mountain barred with snow
> Across that angry or that glimmering sea.

'The Old Ships' is set in the seas off Cyprus, but is equally about the wooden ships of every Aegean shore and harbour. Their final resting place is usually a beach, drawn up perhaps under a plane tree, their ancient timbers disintegrating with dignity, before time at last robs them of even the memory of what they were, and they are finally axed for firewood to warm some fisherman's winter stove. But Flecker's ship 'of some yet older day' has not yet reached its graveyard and is still, in his imagination, afloat.

> I have seen old ships sail like swans asleep
> Beyond the village that men still call Tyre,
> With leaden age o'ercargoed, dipping deep
> For Famagusta and the hidden sun
> That rings black Cyprus with a lake of fire;
> And all those ships were certainly so old
> Who knows how oft with squat and noisy gun,
> Questing brown slaves or Syrian oranges,
> The pirate Genoese hell-raked them till they rolled
> Blood, water, fruit and corpses up the hold.
> But now through friendly seas they softly run,
> Painted the mid-sea blue or shore-sea green,
> Still patterned with the vine and grapes in gold.

But I have seen,
Pointing her shapely shadows from the dawn
An image tumbled on a rose-swept bay,
A drowsy ship of some yet older day;
And, wonder's breath indrawn,
Thought I – who knows – who knows – but in that same
(Fished up beyond Aeaa, patched up new
– Stern painted brighter blue –)
That talkative, bald-headed seaman came
(Twelve patient comrades sweating at the oar)
And with great lies about his wooden horse
Set the crew laughing, and forgot his course.

It was so old a ship – who know, who knows?
– And yet so beautiful, I watched in vain
To see the mast burst open with a rose,
And the whole deck put on its leaves again.

AUTHOR PROFILES

Aeschylus (525–456 BCE)
The 'father of tragedy', the first and most influential of the Greek tragic dramatists. Only seven of his 90 plays survive, the *Oresteia* trilogy being the best known. *The Persians* provides valuable historical detail of the Battle of Salamis (479 BCE). For Aeschylus the most important achievement was that he fought at Marathon; only this proud fact appears on his epitaph, not his success as a playwright.

Alcaeus of Mytilene (c.620 BCE)
Lyric poet of Lesbos, slightly older contemporary of Sappho. Wrote on themes of love, drinking – and the politics of his island, from which he was exiled for part of his life. Only fragments of his verse remain but they were highly praised by Greek and Hellenic writers and also by the Romans, including Horace and Ovid.

Anakreon (582–c.485 BCE)
Popular lyric poet born on the island of Teos off the coast of Asia Minor. His elegant and light-hearted verses, written in his native Ionic, covered the universal themes of love and its disappointments, drinking, festivals and aspects of everyday life. Only fragments of his poetry remain.

Apollonius of Rhodes (first half of the third century BCE)
Prominent Homeric scholar but best known for his epic poem *Argonautica*, the story of Jason's search for the Golden Fleece, which influenced other poets, including Virgil. He became head of the Library at Alexandria.

Archilochus (680–645 BCE)
Born on the island of Paros, one of the earliest Greek lyric poets and the first whose verse frankly expressed feelings and emotions both of love and

of hate. The first warrior-poet, though with unconventional ideals – survival being his priority (understandably his poems were banned in Sparta). Most Greeks rated him with Hesiod and Homer.

Aristophanes (*c.*446– *c.*386 BCE)

Satirist and playwright of comic drama in Athens, his plays won many prizes at the annual festivals of the Lenaia and Dionysia. Of the 40 he wrote, 11 have survived intact, providing a rare insight into the daily lives and opinions of Athenians during the Peloponnesian War and after.

Mary Beard (1955–)

Professor of Classics at Cambridge University, 'Britain's best-known classicist'. Her TV historical documentaries on Pompeii and Rome bring the distant past vividly alive to an enthusiastic viewing public. A writer and lecturer (also in the USA), she is also a popular media personality.

Antony Beevor (1946–)

Writer and highly respected military historian. His books on the great battles of the twentieth century – for example *Stalingrad* (1998), *Berlin: The Downfall 1945* (2002) and *The Second World War* (2012) – have led to a much clearer understanding of these calamitous events and of the fate of ordinary citizens caught up in them.

Rupert Brooke (1887–1915)

Poet, graduate of King's College, Cambridge. Poems such as 'Grantchester' (1912) expressed a deep love of the English countryside while his war sonnets, especially 'The Soldier' (1914), reflected the patriotic idealism of most British people at the outbreak of World War I. A naval officer headed for the Dardanelles, he died of septicaemia and was buried on the island of Skyros.

Elizabeth Barrett Browning (1806–61)

Poet whose work was widely read in the Victorian era. A rival of Tennyson for poet laureate. Fought against slavery and for legislation against child labour. In ill health for most of her life, she died in Florence, where she lived with her husband the poet Robert Browning.

Lord Byron, George Gordon Byron (1788–1824)

Romantic poet. His debts and love affairs, with both sexes, shocked and fascinated English public opinion and led to self-imposed exile mainly in Italy. Known for his narrative poems *Childe Harold's Pilgrimage* (1812) and *Don Juan* (1819–24) and numerous shorter poems. His support of the liberation of Greece and his death at Missolonghi inspired international support for Greek independence.

Robert Byron (1905–41)

Distant relative of Lord Byron. Expelled from Oxford for hedonism. Became passionately interested in architecture, one of the first art critics to appreciate Byzantine culture. His best-known travel books are *The Station* (1928) about Mount Athos, and *The Road to Oxiana* (1937).

Callimachus of Cyrene (310–240 BCE)

From Cyrene in Libya. A noted scholar, poet and critic, known for his short poems and epigrams – including the saying 'big book, big evil' (*mega biblion, mega kakon*). Educated in Athens, he moved to Alexandria, where he thrived under the patronage of the Ptolemies. Called the 'father of librarians' thanks to his cataloguing of the great library at Alexandria.

Constantine Cavafy (1863–1933)

Born in Alexandria, Egypt, spent his childhood in England and most of his later life in Alexandria. Completed about 150 poems. Friend of E. M. Forster, who together with T. S. Eliot, Arnold Toynbee and others promoted Cavafy's work in the English-speaking world.

John Chadwick (1920–98)

Famous for decoding, with Michael Ventris, Linear B, a mysterious script unearthed in the ruins of Knossos. Chadwick was a linguist and classical scholar, a naval code-breaker during World War II. After Ventris's death he wrote *The Decipherment of Linear B* (1958).

Richard Chandler (1737–1810)

Antiquarian and writer. A member of an expedition in 1764 funded by the Society of Dilettanti, with the architect Nicholas Revett and the painter William Paris, to explore the antiquities of Ionia and Greece. He later wrote several books on his travels and on Greek antiquities.

François-René de Chateaubriand (1768–1848)
French aristocrat, writer and politician. His novels based on journeys among the Indian tribes of North America initiated a Romantic style influential both in France and abroad. Wounded in battle, he went into exile in England, at first supported and then criticised Napoleon; later a diplomat.

G. K. Chesterton (1874–1936)
Prolific writer, art and literary critic, acclaimed novelist, author of the Father Brown stories, journalist, philosopher and poet. Bernard Shaw called him a man of 'colossal genius'.

Maryse Choisy (1903–79)
French writer and philosopher who believed in psychoanalysis, which became an important tool in her novels. To learn more about the monks of Mount Athos, where women are forbidden, she disguised herself as a man, one of the few women to visit the monasteries.

Charles Robert Cockerell (1788–1863)
Architect. Travelled to Greece visiting ancient sites, excavating where possible and making detailed drawings of what he found. After doing the same in Italy, he returned to England, where he had a long and successful career; buildings he designed are still admired today.

Artemis Cooper (1953–)
Writer and biographer whose books include edited letters of some of her distinguished literary family. Her biographies include *The Kitchen Table* (2004) about the life of Elizabeth David and *Patrick Leigh Fermor: An Adventure* (2012).

John Craxton (1922–2009)
Painter who studied art in London and Paris. A romantic, he was influenced by his friend and mentor Graham Sutherland. After travelling in Europe he based himself in Canea, Crete, where he lived and painted until his death at 87. He was also a designer of ballet sets for Sadler's Wells.

Robert Curzon (1810–73)
Diplomat, traveller and author. Known for his collection of ancient Christian manuscripts – many of which are now in the British Library –

which he bought from Greek Orthodox monasteries in Meteora, Mount Athos and Palestine. Author of *Visits to Monasteries in the Levant* (1849).

Thomas Dallam (1575–1622)
Organ-builder employed by Queen Elizabeth I in 1599 to deliver a clockwork organ as a present to the Sultan Mehmet II. The diary of his journey to Constantinople and installation of the instrument at the Ottoman Court, first published by the Hakluyt Society, can now be read in today's English thanks to John Mole's *The Sultan's Organ* (2012).

Dante Alighieri (1265–1321)
Poet known chiefly for his *Divina Commedia*, divided into *Inferno*, *Purgatorio* and *Paradiso*, which influenced the work of writers and poets worldwide. One of the first Italians to write in the vernacular, a Tuscan dialect, rather than in Latin, and inspired Petrarch and Boccaccio to do the same, so playing an important role in founding the modern Italian language.

Diodorus Siculus (first century BCE)
Greek historian. Author of the 40-volume *Bibliotheca historica*. He covered the history of the known world from mythical times to the death of Alexander the Great and continued to about 60 BCE (when, it was said, he stopped out of exhaustion).

Diogenes (*c.*412–323 bce)
The most important, and most unconventional, of the early Cynic philosophers, born in the Ionian colony of Sinop on the Black Sea (modern Turkey). He moved to Athens but spent his last years in Corinth, in ostentatious poverty, living in an urn where he was visited by Alexander the Great. His teachings later developed into the philosophy of Stoicism.

Edward Dodwell (1767–1832)
Irish painter, travelled extensively in Greece (then part of the Ottoman Empire) between 1801 and 1806. His book *A Classical and Topographical Tour through Greece* (1819) was well received; still appreciated today are his paintings which appeared in *Views of Greece* (1821). He later lived in Italy, dying in Rome.

Gerald Durrell (1925–95)

Naturalist, animal conservationist and writer. During a boyhood on Corfu with his family that included his elder brother Lawrence, developed a passion for nature and wildlife, later bringing back and caring for endangered species from Africa and Latin America. Author of *My Family and Other Animals* (1956). Founder of the Durrell Wildlife Conservation Trust on Jersey.

Lawrence Durrell (1912–90)

Poet, novelist and travel-writer. Born in India, his youngest brother was Gerald Durrell the zoologist. In 1935 Lawrence lived and wrote in Corfu. During World War II he was in Egypt, later working for the British Foreign Service in Rhodes and Cyprus, Yugoslavia and Argentina. Travel books on Greece were followed by a series of novels, including the Alexandria Quartet (1957–60) and the Avignon Quintet (1974–85).

Odysseus Elytis (1911–66)

Poet and 1979 Nobel Prize-winner. Born in Heraklion, Crete, his family was from Lesbos; educated in Athens. After World War II he lived in Paris and returned there as voluntary exile during the Colonels' regime. Known especially for his *Axion Esti* (1959); set to music by Mikis Theodorakis, it became a much-loved patriotic hymn against injustice.

Epictetus (*c.*50–135 CE)

Stoic philosopher, born a slave in what is now Asia Minor, lived in Rome, studied philosophy and eventually gained his freedom, moving to Greece. He taught individual responsibility, acceptance of what could not be changed, and that every opinion must be carefully tested. His teachings are known only from what was written down by his pupil, the historian Arrian.

Euripides (*c.*480–406 BCE)

Athenian tragic dramatist who wrote some 95 plays, of which 18 or 19 have survived. Much younger than Aeschylus and Sophocles, Euripides was less a favourite with the Athenians, perhaps because of his more enlightened attitude, for example to women. His innovations as a playwright have influenced drama down to modern times.

William Falconer (1732–69)

Scottish poet and sailor who wrote from firsthand experience about ships, shipwrecks and the sea. Known mainly for his epic poem *The Shipwreck* (1762) and also for his marine dictionary, which was used not only by seamen but later by novelists such as Patrick O'Brian in his Aubrey–Maturin stories.

Xan Fielding (1918–91)

Born in India, educated in France and at Charterhouse School. Had a distinguished career in the SOE during World War II, especially in Greece. Of his several books and translations, *The Stronghold* (1955) is an account of his wartime experiences in Crete.

James Elroy Flecker (1884–1915)

English poet and dramatist educated at Oxford and at Cambridge. From 1910 he worked in the Consular Service in the Eastern Mediterranean. Died from tuberculosis in Switzerland at the age of 31. Lines from his verse drama *Hassan: The Story of Hassan of Baghdad and How he Came to Make the Golden Journey to Samarkand* (1922) are used by both the British and New Zealand SAS.

Margalit Fox (1963–)

American writer, student of linguistics, journalist and obituary writer for the *New York Times*, is the author of *Talking Hands* (2007) about sign language and *The Riddle of the Labyrinth* (2013), about decoding Linear B.

John Freely (1926–2017)

American writer and teacher born in Brooklyn, New York, with degrees from New York University and Oxford. Author of more than 40 travel, history and guide books, mainly about Greece and the islands, Turkey and the Ottoman Empire, as well as on the growth of science in Greece, Islam and medieval Europe.

Nikos Gatsos (1911–92)

Poet, critic and translator, a lifelong friend of Odysseus Elytis and part of the literary scene in Athens before World War II. Translated foreign plays and wrote lyrics for the music of Manos Hadjidakis and other Greek composers. His poem 'Amorgos' (1943) contributed to the development of modern Greek poetry.

William Golding (1911–93)

Educated at Marlborough and at Oxford. After an active war service he taught English literature until publication of his first book *Lord of the Flies* in 1954. Author of many novels and winner of numerous awards, including the Nobel Prize. His last novel, *The Double Tongue*, about the Delphic oracle, was published posthumously.

Robert Graves (1895–1985)

Prolific writer – poet, novelist, critic, classicist and translator – influential literary figure of the twentieth century. Among his best-known books are *Good-Bye to All That* (1929), his memoir of World War I, *The White Goddess* (1948), *The Greeks Myths* (1955) and historical novels including *I, Claudius* (1934) and *Claudius the God* (1935).

Herodotus (*c.*484–425 BCE)

The 'father of history', born at Halicarnassus (modern Bodrum), then part of the Persian Empire. Wrote the 'inquiries' (*Historia*), an account of the wars between Persia and the Greeks, with descriptions of the peoples of much of the known world: the first investigative history – and the first complete work of Greek prose. Spent part of his life in Athens and is believed to have died in Thurium in Italy.

John Cam Hobhouse (1786–1869)

Politician, educated at Trinity College, Cambridge, where he became a close friend of Lord Byron, accompanying him on his travels in Greece and Turkey; Byron dedicated the fourth canto of *Childe Harold* to him. An MP from 1830. The first to use the phrase 'His Majesty's (Loyal) Opposition'.

Homer (eighth or ninth century BCE)

Believed to have been the author of the epic poems the *Iliad* (an account of part of the siege of Troy) and the *Odyssey* (the journey home of Odysseus, one of the Greek leaders at Troy). It is thought that the poems were originally sung by travelling bards and were written down only in the seventh century. They have remained among the most highly regarded poems in European literature and have had a profound influence on Western culture.

A. E. Housman (1859–1936)

Poet, foremost a classical scholar, best known for the 63-poem cycle of *A Shropshire Lad* (1896). His poems, many of which have been set to music, captured the emotions of young men who loved the English countryside, many of whom were soon to die in World War I.

Samuel Gridley Howe (1801–76)
Philanthropist, born in Boston and graduate of Harvard Medical School. An enthusiastic supporter of the Greeks and admirer of Lord Byron, he joined the rebels and, though a surgeon, fought in the war, also raising funds from America. On his return to the US Howe became an effective social reformer.

Nigel Jones (1961–)
Historian, journalist and biographer, author of books on World War I and contributor to most British newspapers and magazines such as the *Spectator*. His *Rupert Brooke: Life, Death and Myth,* serialised in the *Sunday Times*, was published in 2003.

James Joyce (1882–1941)
Irish novelist and poet, whose avant-garde 'stream of consciousness' method made him one of the most influential writers of the twentieth century. His novel *Ulysses* (1922) parodies Homer's *Odyssey*, with story and characters set in modern Dublin.

Nikos Kazantzakis (1883–1957)
Major prose writer of modern Greek literature, born in Crete when the island was still under Turkish rule. Those of his novels translated into English, notably *Zorba the Greek* (1946) and *The Last Temptation of Christ* (1955), made him famous internationally. Much of his life was spent travelling and he died in Germany. His memorial carries the inscription in Greek: 'I hope for nothing. I fear nothing. I am free.'

Edmund Keeley (1928–)
Poet, novelist, essayist and translator, educated at Princeton and Oxford universities, with a special interest in Greek poets and modern Greek history. Winner of many prizes and awards for his novels and also his translations of Greek poets such as Cavafy, Seferis, Elytis and Ritsos.

Alphonse de Lamartine (1790–1869)
Distinguished French politician and influential writer, helped establish the Second Republic and ensured that the tricolour remained the flag of

France. One of the first French Romantic poets, he became a diplomat and politician, and worked to abolish slavery and the death penalty.

Osbert Lancaster (1908–86)
Cartoonist and satirist, writer, architectural critic and stage designer for theatre, ballet and opera. Studied art at the Slade. Over 40 years he drew some 10,000 cartoons for the front page of the *Daily Express*, gently mocking the English upper classes. Two of his books were on Greece, *Classical Landscape with Figures* (1947) and *Sailing to Byzantium* (1969).

Robin Lane Fox (1946–)
Classicist, writer, historian, gardener. Emeritus scholar of New College and Reader of Ancient History at Oxford. Awarded numerous prestigious literary prizes, notably for his studies of Alexander the Great. His latest book is on St Augustine.

Edward Lear (1812–88)
Famous for his nonsense verse, he was foremost an artist and illustrator specialising in drawing and painting birds. Born in London, the second youngest of 21 children, he had serious health problems all his life, including epilepsy, and bouts of depression which he called the 'morbids'. Lear travelled widely, sketching as he went, in Italy, Greece and as far as India.

Patrick Leigh Fermor (1915–2011)
Distinguished travel-writer who at 18 walked across Europe to Constantinople (*A Time of Gifts*, 1977). Spent most of World War II with the resistance in the mountains of Crete. His books include *A Traveller's Tree* (1950) about the Caribbean, and *Mani* (1958) and *Roumeli* (1966), both about Greece, where he built a house and lived until his death aged 96.

William Lithgow (1585–1645)
Adventurer and traveller born in Lanark, Scotland whose journeys, mostly on foot, took him across Europe to Greece, Egypt and the Middle East (1614–18) and later to North Africa and Spain (1627–9). He recorded his travels in *The Total Discourse of the Rare Adventures and Painefull Perigrinations of Long Nineteen Years Travayles* (1632, reprinted 1906).

Michael Llewellyn Smith (1939–)
Writer and diplomat. Author of books, among others, on Crete, Greece in Asia Minor, the modern Olympic Games, and Athens. Concluded his diplomatic career as British ambassador in Greece (1996–9) and was knighted.

Elizabeth Longford (1906–2002)
Elizabeth Pakenham, Countess of Longford, historian and author of numerous biographies of leading personalities of the nineteenth century, including *Queen Victoria* (1964), the *Duke of Wellington* (1969) and *Lord Byron* (1976).

F. L. Lucas (1894–1967)
Classical scholar, poet and literary critic, Fellow of King's College, Cambridge, known for his books on Aristotle and the Jacobean dramatist John Webster, and for his wartime intelligence work at Bletchley Park.

Lucian (120–180 CE)
Satirist and rhetorician, born in Syria, educated in Greek Asia Minor, where he became a master of the Attic Greek language and a skilled public speaker. He eventually settled in Athens. His fiction *A True Story* is known as one of the earliest novels in Western literature.

Justin Marozzi (1970–)
Historian, travel-writer, journalist and Fellow of the Royal Geographical Society. His books include *South from Barbary* (2001), an account of his travels in Libya, a biography of Tamurlane, and *The Man Who Invented History: Travels with Herodotus* (2008). *Baghdad: City of Peace, City of Blood* was published in 2014.

Menander (c.342–c.292 BCE)
Admired dramatist of Athenian new comedy. Only one of his 100 or more plays have survived intact, but many are known from adaptations by Roman writers such as Plautus and Terence, who developed his 'comedy of manners' style which has influenced drama to this day. Is said to have drowned while swimming in the port of Piraeus.

Henry Miller (1891–1980)
Original and innovative American writer, born in Manhattan, New York.
His semi-autobiographical novels, including *Tropic of Cancer* (1934) and
Tropic of Capricorn (1936) based on his life in New York and Paris, were
banned in the USA until 1961. Invited by Lawrence Durrell to Corfu in
1939, he wrote up his travels in Greece in *The Colossus of Maroussi* (1941).

John Mole (1945–)
Writer, born in Birmingham, author of many books of humour, memoirs
and fiction including *It's All Greek To Me* (2004) and *The Sultan's Organ*
(2012).

Harry Mount (1971–)
Author and journalist, educated at Westminster and Oxford University,
has written books on British architecture and on the English character and
landscape. *Harry Mount's Odyssey: Ancient Greece in the Footsteps of Odysseus*
was published in 2015.

Kostis Palamas (1859–1943)
Considered the 'national poet' of Greece, born in Patras, studied and later
taught at Athens University. His first poems, *Songs of My Fatherland,* were
published in 1886. His funeral in Athens in 1943 was the occasion of a
popular demonstration against the Nazi occupation. Author of the Olympic
Anthem, written for the first of the modern Olympic Games in 1896.

Alexandros Papadiamandis (1851–1911)
Novelist and short-story writer, the most influential of modern Greek prose
writers. Born on the island of Skiathos, he enrolled at Athens University but
could not afford to complete his studies. An unworldly recluse, he wrote
always about the poor and the difficulties and tragedies in their lives.

Pausanias (110– *c.*180 BCE)
Greek geographer and traveller, best known for his *Description of Greece,*
a detailed topographical and cultural picture of a country with a glorious
past and then a mere province of the Roman Empire. Invaluable to modern
historians and archaeologists.

Pindar (*c.*552 –*c.*443 BCE)
Greek lyric poet from Thebes, a near contemporary of Simonides of Ceos. Studied the art of lyric poetry in Athens and won his first commission to write a victory ode for the ruling family of Thessaly. Was probably in Aegina during the Persian invasion when Thebes was occupied. Regarded as the greatest of the Greek lyric poets.

Plato (*c.*428–*c.*348 BCE)
One of the founders of Western philosophy. Socrates was his teacher, Aristotle his student. Established the Academy in Athens, the first institution of higher learning in the West. He was the first to use dialogue and dialectic in his writing, notably on political philosophy in his *Republic* and *Laws*. Worked and taught most of his life in Athens, but also visited Sicily, where he tried to make the ruler of Syracuse a philosopher-king.

Plutarch (46–120 CE)
Known for his *Parallel Lives* (biographies of famous Greeks and Romans) still referred to by writers and historians. Author of biographies of Alexander the Great and Julius Caesar and other works which have not survived. Born in Greece, he became a Roman citizen; for the last 30 years of his life served as a priest at Delphi.

François Pouqueville (1770–1838)
French diplomat, writer, historian, archaeologist and physician. Kept hostage in Constantinople, appointed by Napoleon as ambassador to Ali Pasha of Ioannina. Travelled extensively throughout Turkish-occupied Greece. A passionate philhellene, he helped ensure that the French participated in the Battle of Navarino.

George Psychoundakis (1920–2006)
Cretan shepherd, poet and writer who joined the Greek resistance in 1941. Served as courier between British SOE groups concealed in the mountains of western Crete where he had been born and bred. His war diaries were translated by Patrick Leigh Fermor, his commanding officer, as *The Cretan Runner* (1955).

Mary Renault (1905–83)
English writer whose historical novels set in ancient Greece – *The Last of the Wine* (1956) and many others – made her famous. Travelled in Europe

but eventually settled in South Africa. One of the first novelists to write openly about homosexuality; she believed that people should not identify themselves primarily by sexual orientation.

Yiannis Ritsos (1909–90)

Major twentieth-century Greek poet, proposed for the Nobel Prize, had a childhood marred by family loss, illness and poverty. A Communist and left-wing activist, he spent several years in Greek prison camps. His poem 'Epitaphios' was banned by the Metaxas dictatorship in 1936 and burned in public under the Acropolis. In the 1950s the poem was set to music by Theodorakis and remains the anthem of the left.

Emmanuel Royidis (or Rhoides) (1836–1904)

Influential Greek writer, born on the island of Syros of a wealthy family from Chios. Educated mainly in Genoa and Berlin. In Athens he worked as publisher and journalist. His satirical novel *Pope Joan* (1866) led to his excommunication from the Greek Orthodox Church.

Sappho (*c.*630–*c.*570 ʙᴄᴇ)

Lyric poet of the island of Lesbos. Little of her work has survived, much from fragments of ancient parchment or pottery. The first woman to write passionately about her feelings, her poetry was admired by the ancients. Because many of her poems were to other women, the words 'sapphic' and 'lesbian', invented only in the last two centuries, refer to female homosexual love.

George Seferis (1900–71)

Poet and Nobel laureate (1963), born near Smyrna. Was studying law at the Sorbonne when in 1922 his family and all other Greeks were expelled from Anatolia. He joined the Greek Foreign Service; his last posting was as ambassador to the UK. His Nobel award, the first to a Greek writer, cited his 'eminent lyrical writing, inspired by a deep feeling for the Hellenic world of culture'.

Charles Seltman (1886–1957)

Classical scholar, Fellow of Queen's College, Cambridge, where he lectured in classics. Author of some 15 books, he at first specialised in ancient Greek art and coinage, and then in the 1950s wrote a series of paperbacks – among them *The Twelve Olympians* (1952) and *Wine in Antiquity* (1957) – that brought the classical past closer to the general public.

Anthony Sherley (or Shirley) (1565–1635)

Born in Sussex and educated at Oxford, diplomat, navigator and military adventurer, count of the Holy Roman Empire, Sherley is mainly known for his embassy to Shah Abbas the Great to promote trade between England and Persia.

Philip Sherrard (1922–95)

Educated at Cambridge with a degree in history. Visiting Athens in 1946 he became deeply attached to Greek culture and way of life, eventually making his home on the island of Evvia. His books on recent and living Greek poets and translations of their work brought them to the notice of the English-speaking world.

Angelos Sikelianos (1884–1951)

Poet and playwright, born on the island of Lefkas. Visited America, where he married; later travelled throughout Greece with his friend Nikos Kazantzakis. Remembered for his inspirational speech and poem at the funeral of Palamas, and for an appeal to the Nazis to save the lives of Greek Jews.

Simonides of Ceos (*c.*556–468 BCE)

The first major Greek poet who wrote poetry to be read rather than recited. Born on the island of Ceos (modern Kea), he lived mainly in Athens during the Persian Wars. Famous and highly paid for his epitaphs for fallen warriors and his victory odes for successful athletes. His last years were in Sicily, as the guest and friend of Hieron of Syracuse

Dionysios Solomos (1798–1857)

Poet born on the island of Zakinthos. Educated in Italy, his first poems were in Italian. In Greek he wrote in the demotic dialect of the people of his island. Though few of his poems were completed, and none published during his lifetime, he was a powerful influence on modern Greek literature. In 1865 his 'Hymn to Liberty' became the Greek national anthem.

Sophocles (497–406 BCE)

One of the three Greek tragedians – with Aeschylus and Euripides – whose plays have survived. Of the 120 he wrote only a few can be read today, the best-known being *Antigone, The Women of Trachis, Oedipus the King, Electra* and *Oedipus at Colonus*. Record prizewinner at the Athenian festivals of the Lenaea and Dionsysia and the most famous playwright of his times; his innovations significantly developed Greek drama.

William St Clair (1937–)
Historian, academic and author. Subjects of his many books include the history of books and reading, the Elgin Marbles and the Parthenon and the Greek war of independence. He also wrote biographies of Edward John Trelawny and of the Godwin and Shelley families.

Patricia Storace
American poet and novelist, born in Mobile, Alabama, and educated at Barnard College and Cambridge University. Winner of the Witter Bynner Poetry Prize in 1993. Author of a memoir of Greece, *Dinner with Persephone* (1996) and a novel *The Book of Heaven* (2014).

Strabo (64 BCE–24 CE)
Greek geographer and historian born in Amasia (modern Turkey), educated mainly in Rome, where he lived for most of his life. His *Geographica* describes the world and its peoples based on studies carried out during journeys that took him up the Nile to the edge of Ethiopia. Some of his observations on geology and volcanoes predate modern findings.

Judith Swaddling
Classical scholar and writer with special interest in Etruscan history. Curator of Etruscan and pre-Roman collections in the British Museum. Author of *The Ancient Olympic Games* (2008).

Alfred, Lord Tennyson (1809–92)
Poet laureate of Great Britain during much of Queen Victoria's reign and one of the most quoted of English poets. His best-known poems include 'The Lady of Shalott' (1832), 'Ulysses' (1832), 'In Memoriam A.A.H.' (1849) and 'The Charge of the Light Brigade' (1854).

William Makepeace Thackeray (1811–63)
Novelist and poet, born in Calcutta, British India, at five years old sent to school in England. Known today mainly as the author of the satirical novel *Vanity Fair;* in his lifetime his novels were extremely popular and as a writer he was ranked second to Dickens.

Thucydides (*c*.460–*c*.400 BCE)
Athenian historian, author of the *History of the Peloponnesian War*, covering the long and destructive conflict between Athens and Sparta. The first historian to explain events of the past based on evidence, known facts and on the realities of human nature rather than the intervention of the gods. His book is still recommended reading for politicians and the military.

John L. Tomkinson
Writer born in England. Author of many books about Greece, on the Orthodox Church, Greek festivals, Athens and Attica, besides editing the travel accounts of other writers, for example *Travellers' Greece: Memories of an Enchanted Land* (2002). Has lived in Greece since 1985, where he continues to write.

Edward John Trelawny (1792–1881)
Adventurer and last major figure of the Romantic age. Joined the navy as a teenager and fought with the Greeks in their fight for independence. Known today mainly for his friendship with Shelley and Byron in Italy.

C. A. Trypanis (1909–93)
Poet, born in Chios, educated abroad and in Athens. He spent several years in England and America and wrote much of his poetry in English, his second language.

Mark Twain (1835–1910)
The pen-name of Samuel Langhorne Clemens. Born in Hannibal, Missouri, he became a Mississippi riverboat pilot, then took up journalism and became a writer, author of *The Adventures of Tom Sawyer* and *The Adventures of Huckleberry Finn*. William Faulkner called him the 'father of American literature'.

Julia Ward Howe (1819–1910)
American poet and author famous for writing *The Battle Hymn of the Republic*, was from a wealthy New York banking family. She married the social reformer Samuel Gridley Howe, published verse and travelled. She was a strong supporter of women's suffrage and women's rights.

Evelyn Waugh (1903–66)
English novelist, considered the greatest of his generation. Famous as the author of *Decline and Fall* (1928), *A Handful of Dust* (1934) and *Brideshead Revisited* (1945), among many other novels and travelogues.

George Wheler (1651–1724)
Travel-writer, antiquarian and botanist, born in Holland of English parents exiled from England under Cromwellian rule. In 1673 he set out on a tour of Europe and two years later met Jacob Spon; together they travelled throughout Greece collecting antiquities and plants (*A Journey into Greece*, 1682).

C. M. Woodhouse (1917–2001)
Writer and politician. Educated at Winchester and New College, Oxford. An important figure in the Greek resistance in World War II and author of many books about modern Greek history, including biographies of leading Greek politicians.

CHRONOLOGY OF EVENTS

	Literary and Cultural Events	Political Events
BCE		
2000–1600	Minoan Crete.	
1600–1150	Late Bronze Age.	
c.1600	Volcanic eruption of Thera (Santorin).	
c.1400	Knossos destroyed.	
c.1350	Linear B (Greek) writing.	
c.1200		Mycenaean Greeks attack Troy?
1150–1100	Dorians invade Greece, establish new gods on Mount Olympus.	
776	First Olympic Games.	
750–700	First use of Greek alphabet. Homer: *Iliad* and *Odyssey*.	
645	Death of Archilochus of Paros.	
600	Sappho of Lesbos.	Development of coinage.
569		Pythagoras born in Samos.
546		Cyrus of Persia defeats Croesus of Lydia.
525	Aeschylus born in Athens.	
508		Cleisthenes introduces democracy in Athens.
500		Greek city-states control most of the Mediterranean and Black Sea coasts.
499		Start of the Persian Wars: coastal Ionian cities rebel against Darius.

	Literary and Cultural Events	*Political Events*
490		Battle of Marathon: Athenians defeat Persians.
486		Darius dies, Xerxes becomes Great King.
484	Herodotus born.	
480		Xerxes marches on Greece. Battles at Thermopylae and Artemision. Persians burn the Acropolis. Athenians and allies destroy Persian fleet at Salamis.
479		Spartans and allies defeat Persian army at Plataea.
472	Aeschylus: *Persians.*	
468	Death of Simonides of Ceos.	
460–429		Pericles leads Athens.
456	Death of Aeschylus.	
447	Parthenon building begins.	
445–426	Herodotus travelling and writing.	
*c.*443	Death of Pindar.	
442	Sophocles: *Antigone.*	
431		Outbreak of Peloponnesian War.
430–429		Plague at Athens. Death of Pericles.
425	Death of Herodotus.	
413		Athenian forces destroyed in Sicily.
411	Aristophanes: *Lysistrata.*	
406	Death of Euripides.	
407	Death of Sophocles.	
404	Thucydides: *History of the Peloponnesian War.*	Athens surrenders to Sparta.
*c.*400	Death of Thucydides.	
399		Trial and execution of Socrates.
396–347	Plato teaching and writing in Athens.	
380	Plato establishes Academy in Athens.	

	Literary and Cultural Events	*Political Events*
355	Aristotle founds the Lyceum in Athens.	
*c.*348	Death of Plato.	
343–342	Aristotle tutor of Alexander.	
337		Victory of Philip of Macedon over Greek states at Chaeronea.
334		Alexander invades Persian Empire.
326		Alexander reaches India.
323	Death of Diogenes the Cynic.	Death of Alexander the Great at Babylon.
322	Death of Aristotle.	
320		Rome emerges as major power.
218		Hannibal crosses the Alps.
202		Rome defeats Carthage.
146		Rome destroys Carthage. Rome extends its power over Greece, sacks Corinth.
49–30		Rome's civil wars, success of Octavian (who as Augustus will become the first Roman emperor).
33		Birth of Jesus of Nazareth.
31		Battle of Actium.
27		Southern Greece becomes Roman province of Achaia.
CE		
23	Death of geographer Strabo.	
49–52	St Paul in Greece.	
67		Nero in Greece, wins prizes in Olympic Games.
117–38		Hadrian emperor.
*c.*120	Death of Plutarch.	
*c.*150	Pausanias: *Guide to Greece*.	
306–37		Constantine the Great.
393	Olympic Games suppressed.	

	Literary and Cultural Events	*Political Events*
395	Roman Empire becomes Christian	Roman Empire divided in two: East (Byzantium) and West (Rome).
595	Schools of philosophy in Athens closed.	
600–800		Greece invaded by Gauls and Huns, and Slavs who stay and settle.
800–900		Byzantium restores rule over Greece.
1204		Fourth Crusade, destruction of Constantinople. Greece ruled by Venice or divided into 'Frankish' dukedoms.
1353		Ottoman Turks enter Europe.
1429		Turks capture Thessaloniki.
1453		Turks capture Constantinople, end of Byzantine Empire.
1453–1823		Greece under Turkish rule.
1571		Battle of Lepanto: first Turkish naval defeat.
1796		Napoleon sends envoys to Ali Pasha of Iannina.
1821–32		Greek War of Independence.
1824	Death of Lord Byron at Missolonghi.	
1826		Battle of Navarino: Turkish navy destroyed by British, French and Russian fleet.
1832		Otto of Bavaria installed as first king of Greece.
1857	Death of Dionysios Solomos.	
1864		Britain cedes Ionian Islands to Greece.
1881		Turkey cedes Thessaly to Greece.
1888	Death of Edward Lear.	
1911	Death of Alexandros Papadiamandis.	

	Literary and Cultural Events	*Political Events*
1912–13		Balkan Wars: Greece incorporates southern Macedonia, Epirus, Crete and east Aegean Islands.
1914		Britain annexes Cyprus from Turkey.
1915	Death of Rupert Brooke on Skyros	Dardanelles campaign.
1916–17		Greece enters World War I on side of Allies.
1919–22		Greece invades Turkish Asia Minor and is heavily defeated. Expulsion of Greeks from Smyrna (Izmir) and other coastal cities.
1922		Traumatic population exchange: 1.2 million Greeks leave Asia Minor and 300,000 Turks leave Greece for Turkey.
1931–40		General Metaxas dictator.
1933	Constantine Cavafy dies.	
1940		Mussolini invades Greece. Italian armies repulsed in Epirus. Germany invades.
1941		Germans capture Crete.
1941–4		Greece occupied. Starvation in Athens. Jews from Thessaloniki sent to Auschwitz. Resistance groups based in mountains.
1943	Death of Kostis Palamas.	
1944–9		Civil War. Royalist government, backed by Britain and USA, fight Communist rebels. Communists defeated.
1951	Death of Angleos Sikelianos.	
1957	Death of Kazantzakis.	
1963–4		Free elections, centrist government.
1963	George Seferis awarded Nobel Prize.	

	Literary and Cultural Events	*Political Events*
1966	Death of Odysseas Elytis.	
1967–74		Colonels' regime: junta of army officers take over government. King exiled.
1971	Death of George Seferis.	
1974		Monarchy abolished by referendum.
1981		Greece joins European Union.

SELECT BIBLIOGRAPHY

Abbott, G. F., *Songs of Modern Greece*, Cambridge, Cambridge University Press, 1900.

Aeschylus, *The Oresteian Trilogy*, trans. P. Vellacott, London, Penguin, 1954.

Apollonius of Rhodes, *The Voyage of Argo*, trans. E. V. Rieu, London, Penguin Classics, 1959.

Anderson, P., *Dolphin Days*, London, Victor Gollanz, 1963.

Andrews, K., *The Flight of Ikarus*, London, Weidenfeld & Nicolson, 1959.

Barnstone, W., *Greek Lyric Poetry*, New York, Bantam Classics, 1962.

Beard, M., *The Parthenon*, Cambridge, MA, Harvard University Press, 2002.

Beevor, A., *Crete: The Battle and the Resistance*, London, John Murray, 1991.

Borst, W. A., *Lord Byron's First Pilgrimage*, New Haven, CT, Yale University Press, 1948.

Botting, D., *Gerald Durrell*, London, HarperCollins, 1999.

Bowker, G., *Through the Dark Labyrinth: A Biography of Lawrence Durrell*, New York, St Martin's Press, 1997.

Brewer, D., *The Flame of Freedom: The Greek War of Independence*, London, John Murray, 2001.

Brooke, R., *Collected Poems*, London, Sidgwick and Jackson, 1924.

Byron, Lord, *Childe Harold's Pilgrimage*, London, John Murray, 1812–18.

Byron, R., *The Station: Athos, Treasures and Men*, London, Duckworth, 1928.

Carroll, M., *An Island in Greece*, London, Tauris Parke Paperbacks, 2009 (first published as *Gates of the Wind*, London, John Murray, 1965).

Cavafy, C., *The Poems of C. P. Cavafy*, trans. J. Mavrocordato, London, Hogarth Press, 1951.

Chadwick, J., *The Decipherment of Linear B*, Cambridge, Cambridge University Press, 1990.

Chandler, R., *Travels in Greece*, London, 1776.

Cockerell, C. R., *Travels in Southern Europe and the Levant*, 1810.

Collins, I., *John Craxton*, London, Lund Humphries, 2011.

Constantine, D., *In the Footsteps of the Gods*, London, Tauris Parke Paperbacks, 2011.

Cooper, A., *Patrick Leigh Fermor: An Adventure*, London, John Murray, 2012.

Curzon, R., *Visits to the Monasteries of the Levant*, London, 1849.

Dante Alighieri, *The Divine Comedy*, trans. J. D. Sinclair, Oxford, Bodley Head, 1939.

Dodwell, E., *Tour Through Greece*, London, 1819.

Durrell, G., *My Family and Other Animals*, London, Rupert Hart-Davis, 1956.

Durrell, L., *Prospero's Cell*, London, Faber and Faber, 1945.

—— *Reflections on a Marine Venus*, London, Faber and Faber, 1953.

Eisner, R., *Travellers to an Antique Land*, Ann Arbor, University of Michigan Press, 1991.

Elytis, O., *The Axion Esti*, trans. E. Keeley and G. Savidis, Pittsburgh, University of Pittsburgh Press, 1974.

Falconer, W., *The Shipwreck*, London, 1762.

Fielding, X., *The Stronghold*, London, John Murray, 1955.

Flecker, J. E., *Collected Poems*, New York, Martin Secker, 1935.

Fox, M., *The Riddle of the Labyrinth*, London, Profile, 2013.

Freely, J., *The Ionian Islands*, London, I.B.Tauris, 2008.

Herodotus, *The Histories*, trans. T. Holland, London, Penguin, 2013.

Homer, *The Iliad*, trans. E. V. Rieu, revised by P. Jones, London, Penguin, 2003.

—— *The Odyssey*, trans. R. Fagles, London, Penguin Classics, 1999.

Garrett, M., *A Literary Companion to Greece*, London, John Murray, 1994.

Graves, R., *The Golden Fleece*, London, Cassell, 1944.

Hodgkin, J., *Amateurs in Eden: A Bohemian Marriage, Nancy and Lawrence Durrell*, London, Virago, 2012.

Jones, N., *Rupert Brooke: Life, Death and Myth*, London, Richard Cohen, 1999.

Kazantzakis, N., *Zorba the Greek*, 1946.

Keeley, E., *Inventing Paradise*, Chicago, Northwestern University Press, 2002.

Knox, J., *Robert Byron*, London, John Murray, 2003.

Lancaster, O., *Classical Landscape with Figures*, London, John Murray, 1947.

—— *Sailing to Byzantium*, London, John Murray, 1969.

Lane Fox, R., *The Classical World*, London, Allen Lane, 2005.

Lattimore, R., *Greek Lyrics*, Chicago, University of Chicago Press, 1960.

Leake, W., *Travels in Northern Greece*, London, 1835.

Leigh Fermor, P., *Mani*, London, John Murray, 1958.

—— *Roumeli*, London, John Murray, 1966.

Leontis, Artemis (ed.), *Greece: A Traveler's Literary Companion*, San Francisco, Whereabouts Press, 1997

Levi, P., *The Hill of Kronos*, London, William Collins, 1981.

—— *Edward Lear: A Life*, London, Tauris Parke Paperbacks, 2013.

—— *A History of Greek Literature*, London, Viking, 1985.

Lithgow, W., *The Total Discourse of the Rare Adventures and Painefull Peregrinations of Long Nineteen Years Travayles From Scotland to the most Kingdoms of Europe, Asia and Africa*, London, 1632.

Llewellyn Smith, M., *Athens: A Cultural and Literary History*, Oxford, Signal, 2004.

Longford, E., *Byron's Greece*, London, Weidenfeld & Nicolson, 1975.

Lucas, F. L., *Greek Drama for Everyman*, London, Dent, 1954.

—— *From Olympus to the Styx*, London, Cassell, 1934.

MacCarthy, F., *Byron: Life and Legend*, London, John Murray, 2002.

Marchand, L., *Byron: A Portrait*, London, Cresset Library, 1971.

Marozzi, J., *The Man Who Invented History: Travels with Herodotus*, London, John Murray, 2008.

Mole, J., *The Sultan's Organ*, London, Fortune, 2012.

Moss, W. S., *Ill Met by Moonlight*, London, Harrap, 1950.

Mount, H., *Harry Mount's Odyssey: Ancient Greece in the Footsteps of Odysseus*, London, Bloomsbury, 2015.

Noakes, V., *Edward Lear: The Life of a Wanderer*, Stroud, Sutton, 2004.

Papadiamantis, A., *Tales from a Greek Island*, trans. E. Constantinides, Baltimore, MD, Johns Hopkins University Press, 1987.

Peachem, T., *The Compleat Gentleman*, London, 1634.

Plato, *Phaedo*, trans. H. Tredennick, London, Penguin, 1954.

Plutarch, *Lives of the Noble Greeks and Romans*, trans. R. Warner, London, Penguin, 1958.

Potts, J., *The Ionian Islands and Epirus*, Oxford, Signal, 2013.

Pouqueville, François, *Travels in Epirus, Albania, Macedonia and Thessaly*, London, Richard Philips, 1820.

Psychoundakis, G., *The Cretan Runner*, London, John Murray, 1955.

Richardson, J., *Lord Byron*, London, Folio Society, 1988.

St Clair, W., *Lord Elgin and the Marbles*, London, Oxford University Press, 1967.

Seferis, G., *Complete Poems*, trans. E. Keeley and P. Sherrard, London, Anvil Press Poetry, 1995.

Seltman, C., *The Twelve Olympians*, London, Penguin, 1953.

—— *Riot in Ephesus*, London, Penguin, 1958.

Shakespeare, N., *Bruce Chatwin*, London, Harvill, 1999.

Sherley [or Shirley], A., *His Persian Adventure*, London, 1601.

Sherrard, P., *The Marble Threshing Floor: Studies in Modern Greek Poetry*, Elstree, Valentine Mitchell, 1956.

Spencer, T., *Fair Greece, Sad Relic*, London, Weidenfeld & Nicolson, 1954.

Stoneman, R., *A Literary Companion to Travel in Greece*, Malibu, CA, J. Paul Getty Trust, 1994.

Storace, P., *Dinner with Persephone*, New York, Pantheon Books, 1996.

Strabo, *The Geography*, trans. H. L. Jones, London, William Heinemann, 1924.

Swaddling, J., *The Ancient Olympic Games*, London, British Museum Press, 2008.

Sweetman, D., *Mary Renault: A Biography*, London, Chatto & Windus, 1992.

Thackeray, W. M., *From Cornhill to Cairo*, London, Chapman & Hall, 1846.

Thucydides, *The Peloponnesian War*, trans. R. Warner, London, Penguin, 1954.

Tomkinson, John L., *Travellers' Greece: Memories of an Enchanted Land*, Athens, Anagnosis, 2006.

Traill, David A., *Schliemann of Troy: Treasure and Deceit*, London, John Murray, 1995.

Trelawny, E. J., *Recollections of the Last Days of Shelley and Byron*, London, Edward Moxon, 1858.

Trypanis, C. A., *The Pompeian Dog*, 1964.

Twain, M., *The Innocents Abroad*, Hartford, CT, American Publishing Co., 1869.

Ward Howe, J., *From the Oak to the Olive*, Boston, MA, Lee & Shepard, 1868.

Waugh, E., *Officers and Gentlemen*, London, Chapman & Hall, 1955.

Wheler, G., *A Journey into Greece*, 1682.

Wills, D., *The Mirror of Antiquity: 20th Century Travellers in Greece*, Cambridge, Cambridge Scholars, 2007.

Woodhouse, C. M., *The Philhellenes*, London, Hodder & Stoughton, 1971.

INDEX